PRESIDENTIAL CANDIDATE IMAGES

Communication, Media, and Politics

Series Editor
Robert E. Denton, Jr., Virginia Tech

This series features a broad range of work dealing with the role and function of communication in the realm of politics, broadly defined. Including general academic books, monographs, and texts for use in graduate and advanced undergraduate courses, the series will encompass humanistic, critical, historical, and empirical studies in political communication in the United States. Primary subject areas include campaigns and elections, media, and political institutions. *Communication, Media, and Politics* books will be of interest to students, teachers, and scholars of political communication from the disciplines of communication, rhetorical studies, political science, journalism, and political sociology.

Titles in the Series
The Millennium Election: Communication in the 2000 Campaign
    Edited by Lynda Lee Kaid, John C. Tedesco, Dianne G. Bystrom, and Mitchell McKinney
Strategic Political Communication: Rethinking Social Influence, Persuasion, and Propaganda
    Karen S. Johnson-Cartee and Gary A. Copeland
Campaign 2000: A Functional Analysis of Presidential Campaign Discourse
    William L. Benoit, John P. McHale, Glenn J. Hansen, P. M. Pier, and John P. McGuire
Inventing a Voice: The Rhetoric of American First Ladies of the Twentieth Century
    Edited by Molly Meijer Wertheimer
Communicating for Change: Strategies of Social and Political Advocates
    John P. McHale
Political Campaign Communication: Principles and Practices, Fifth Edition
    Judith S. Trent and Robert V. Friedenberg
The Rhetoric of Redemption: Kenneth Burke's Redemption Drama and Martin Luther King, Jr.'s "I Have a Dream" Speech
    David A. Bobbitt
Reelpolitik II: Political Ideologies in '50s and '60s Films
    Beverly Merrill Kelley
New Frontiers in International Communication Theory
    Edited by Mehdi Semati

Forthcoming
Entertaining Politics: New Political Television and Civic Culture
    Jeffrey P. Jones
Women's Political Discourse
    Molly A. Mayhead and Brenda DeVore Marshall
The 2004 Presidential Campaign
    Edited by Robert E. Denton, Jr.
Politeness and Political Debate
    Edward A. Hinck, Shelly S. Hinck, and William O. Dailey
Media and the Staging of American Politics
    Gary C. Woodward

PRESIDENTIAL CANDIDATE IMAGES

Edited by
Kenneth L. Hacker

ROWMAN & LITTLEFIELD PUBLISHERS, INC.
Lanham • Boulder • New York • Toronto • Oxford

ROWMAN & LITTLEFIELD PUBLISHERS, INC.

Published in the United States of America
by Rowman & Littlefield Publishers, Inc.
A wholly owned subsidiary of The Rowman & Littlefield Publishing Group, Inc.
4501 Forbes Boulevard, Suite 200, Lanham, MD 20706
www.rowmanlittlefield.com

P.O. Box 317, Oxford OX2 9RU, UK

Copyright © 2004 by Rowman & Littlefield Publishers, Inc.

All rights reserved. No part of this publication may be reproduced, stored in a retrieval system, or transmitted in any form or by any means, electronic, mechanical, photocopying, recording, or otherwise, without the prior permission of the publisher.

British Library Cataloguing in Publication Information Available

Library of Congress Cataloging-in-Publication Data

Presidential candidate images / edited by Kenneth L. Hacker.
  p. cm. — (Communication, media, and politics)
  Includes bibliographical references and index.
  ISBN 0-7425-3664-5 (cloth : alk. paper) — ISBN 0-7425-3665-3 (pbk. : alk. paper)
  1. Presidents—United States—Election. 2. Presidential candidates—United States—Public opinion. 3. Public opinion—United States. 4. Political campaigns—United States. 5. Communication in politics—United States. 6. Imagery (Psychology) 7. Political psychology.
I. Hacker, Kenneth L. II. Series.
  JK524.P664 2004
  324.7'3'0973—dc22
                                                                                    2004008428

Printed in the United States of America

™ The paper used in this publication meets the minimum requirements of American National Standard for Information Sciences—Permanence of Paper for Printed Library Materials, ANSI/NISO Z39.48-1992.

Contents

Introduction: The Continued Importance of the Candidate
              Image Construct   1
              Kenneth L. Hacker

1. Campaigns and Candidate Images in American
Presidential Elections   21
Susan A. Hellweg
2. Presidential Candidates' Personal Qualities: Computer
Content Analysis   49
William L. Benoit and John P. McHale
3. Candidate Images When Things Go Sour: Reaction to Scandal   65
Carolyn L. Funk
4. The "Authentic Candidate": Extending Candidate
Image Assessment   85
Allan Louden and Kristen McCauliff
5. A Dual-Processing Perspective of Candidate Image Formation   105
Kenneth L. Hacker
6. The Effects of Political Advertising on Candidate Images   133
Lynda Lee Kaid and Mike Chanslor
7. Presidential Debates and Candidate Image Formation:
1992, 1996, 2000   151
Walter R. Zakahi

8	Interpersonal Communication Styles of Political Candidates: Predicting Winning and Losing Candidates in Three U.S. Presidential Elections *Timothy Stephen, Teresa M. Harrison, William Husson, and David Albert*	177
9	Meta-Analysis of Presidential Candidate Images *Susan A. Hellweg and Brian H. Spitzberg*	197
10	Using Cognitive Measurement for Analysis of Candidate Images *Kenneth L. Hacker*	211
11	Measuring Candidate Images with Semantic Differentials *Lynda Lee Kaid*	231
Conclusion	Present and Future Directions for Presidential Candidate Image Research *Kenneth L. Hacker*	237
Index		245
About the Contributors		247

Introduction

The Continued Importance of the Candidate Image Construct

Kenneth L. Hacker

THE FIRST MAJOR BOOK ABOUT CANDIDATE IMAGES was *Candidates and Their Images*, written by Dan Nimmo and Robert Savage in 1976. In 1995, my edited volume for Praeger on candidate images, *Candidate Images in Presidential Elections,* was released. This book is a follow-up to the research and theory done in the 1995 candidate images book. However, it will become easily apparent to readers of the first book that this one brings in new theory, new data, some new authors, and some additional directions for future research. I have tried to combine the strengths of the 1995 book with new areas of focus that make this an even stronger resource for those interested in studying presidential candidate images and how they are formed during election campaigns.

While reviews of the first edition were generally positive, there were some pointed criticisms that have influenced the design of this edition. One criticism of the first volume was that it did not include a summary chapter by the editor. Consequently, there is a summation chapter in this book. Another critical note was that the first book did not sufficiently define candidate images as a construct. Therefore, I asked authors to attempt to be more precise in their definitions. A third criticism was that the book did not offer sufficient explanations of how images originate and change over time. Again, authors were asked to account for this. Fourth, there was some concern with there being too little empirical data in the chapters. As with the other issues, authors were asked to add more where possible. In addition to these concerns, chapter authors were also asked to address other common concerns about candidate images that can be found in the political communication literature.

This latter set of concerns included (1) Why are candidate images useful constructs as opposed to others such as candidate schemata, political attitudes, or simply candidate evaluations? (2) Why has there been so much discrepancy in the conceptual and operational definitions of candidate images? (3) What specific processes of communication during campaigns appear to be most related to the formation of candidate images? (4) As candidate images form, do they differ in structure and content? and (5) How do candidate images relate to other factors that influence voter decision making such as ideologies and partisanship?

The 1995 volume built on existing knowledge about candidate images that accumulated decades earlier. Most of the earliest research on candidate images treated the construct of image as source credibility (Hellweg, Dionisopoulos, & Kugler, 1989). The research at that time made very little effort to explain how images are different than attitudes and other constructs, and did little to relate image structures to processes of communication. Later image research examined candidate-specific image criteria for evaluation, changes in images during a campaign, and how campaigns can affect the agendas for image building (Hellweg, 1995). Still, despite the progress that will be read in this volume, there is a long way to go in order for there to be more theoretical development of the construct of presidential candidate image. We still need theories and models of image formation.

There were many important insights about candidate images in the 1995 volume. Previous candidate image research indicated that voters have limited amounts of cognitive resources to spend on candidate evaluation, and use a limited number of criteria to assess candidates and to form impressions of competence (Kendall & Paine, 1995). While voters do not appear to have detailed knowledge about candidate issue positions in general, researchers note that impressions of candidate competence are partially related to how voters perceive statements made about issues (Pfau, Diedrich, Larson, & van Winkle, 1993). There are indications that candidate images are very personal and that voters are likely to assess candidates in part by how they think the candidates will impact what is relevant in their lives (Savage, 1995).

Kathleen Kendall and Scott Paine noted that voting decisions are made within contexts of many other decisions and pressures for cognitive processing (Kendall & Paine, 1995). As campaigns present many messages, voters have methods to reduce the number of criteria they use to judge and contrast candidates. Once a voter has chosen his or her most important criteria for candidate evaluation, the voter can monitor campaign messages in a way that preserves cognitive energy and allows the campaign to be processed along with other everyday life problems and situations (Kendall & Paine, 1995).

In 1995, Hacker observed that voters rely on news media for candidate impressions, voters communicate with each other about what they perceive from the media news, information received affects political schemata, discussions among voters interact with stored schemata, and candidate selection is done on the basis of the candidate images (Hacker, 1995).

Lynda Kaid and Mike Chanslor (1995) noted that issue-attack ads are more effective than character-attack ads because the results are greater image discrimination and attitude polarization. They also pointed out that TV spots can build candidate images best by using issues as content. Exposure to advertising affects candidate images. Additionally, TV spots can generate negative images by generating impressions of boredom, fear, anxiety, and concern. Positive images are generated with messages of optimism, confidence, excitement, security, and patriotism.

In 1995, Dan Nimmo argued that the candidate image construct is closely related to symbolic interactionism. He argued that perception is an adaptive process in which the person picks out the stimuli for impulses that seek expression. Through an image, a person brings past experience to bear on current stimuli. Nimmo described candidate images as intervening structures that mediate between incoming and outgoing messages. Image formation is a series of message-image transactions. Images give meaning to messages, and messages give meaning to images. What candidates want voters to perceive (stimuli) and what voters see in the candidates (voter perception) are involved in the formation of candidate images. Nimmo also argued that candidate images have the following qualities: political role, partisan leadership, stylistic role, and personal qualities. The closer the fit of these to the same qualities of our ideal president image, the greater the likelihood of our vote. The information that voters process in their images is produced and shaped by their daily lives (Nimmo, 1995).

Robert Savage (1995) argued that knowledge regarding political socialization should inform us about candidate images in politics. According to Savage, what a person perceives about a candidate depends not only upon persuasive messages, but also upon existing schemata. Therefore a presidential candidate image is formed in the interactions between the past impressions and current messages. People tend to develop affective orientations before they develop more substantive cognitions. This is a crucial realization regarding candidate image formation. The affective orientation colors the impressions that follow. Sometimes a person becomes fixated at a lower level of cognitive development in relation to politics. This could be a scorn of all leaders or a childlike faith in them. Regression is moving back to such an early stage from a more mature one.

Children are likely to adopt positive images of leaders due to social acceptance in our culture, but can have negative images when there are problems with personal authority figures such as fathers (Savage, 1995). The initial attachment to party is affective. As with adult partisanship, studies indicate that there is a decline in party loyalty among youths. Partisanship, according to Savage (1995), has strong effects on candidate images. Party images incorporate impressions of issue positions of the parties. However, party identity becomes a social identity more than a political one. Party identity provides a perceptual screen with which the person filters messages and evaluates candidates. Because children grow up not perceiving the parties as necessarily involved in conflict, they do not grow up with partisan wars on their agendas and tend to view the two parties as more similar than they are (Savage, 1995).

With the declining importance of political parties for voter information and voting decisions, candidate images have become more important in American presidential elections. As parties have declined in significance, campaigns have become more candidate centered, or influenced by voter perceptions of the candidates above and beyond their party membership.

Where Are the Candidate Images?

While Kenneth Boulding (1956) defined *images* as general knowledge structures, Thomas Patterson (1980, p. 133) describes a candidate image as "the subjective impressions that voters have" of candidates. While this seems quite straightforward, there has been substantial confusion over terms like "image," "political image," "candidate image," and "imagery." This has resulted in large variation in the language used to describe voter perceptions. Regardless of this confusion, however, it is apparent that political communication scholars generally refer to candidate images as clusters of voter perceptions of candidates. In this book, the term *presidential candidate image* is used to add more precision to image term.

While psychological or cognitive factors like attitudes, values, and candidate images are all important to voting behavior and the relationships between campaign messages and voters' evaluation of candidates, it is important to remember that campaign contexts are dense environments of influence and that voter motivations vary by individuals and by elections. Stephen Wayne (1992) notes, for example, that voter interest level in a campaign, concerns about election outcomes, feeling about the duties of being a citizen, and political efficacy are important factors determining whether a person votes at all. Even more important than these, of course, is the factor of education (Wayne, 1992). Wayne notes that for those who will vote, partisanship is the strongest long-term determinant, while candidate images are important short-term vote determinants. According to Wayne, the personality components of candidate images include perceptions of leadership abilities, and the policy components entail impressions about candidates' positions on issues. Wayne argues that the persona-based components are more important because issues are not likely to be motivating unless they are salient to voters.

Wayne (1996) observes that two basic models of voting are prospective voting and retrospective voting. In prospective voting, voters evaluate candidates in relationship to their beliefs and policy preferences. In retrospective voting, they evaluate the presidential candidates in light of how they feel about the incumbent's president's record (Wayne, 1996). A key point here, however, is that retrospective voting also includes an assessment of the challenger as well as an assessment of the incumbent's record (Wayne, 1996). More importantly, Wayne (1996, p. 274) notes how presidential candidate images constitute one important determinant of voting choices and how they should be examined in relation to other determinants and in relation to changing circumstances:

> Candidates change, issues change, the public mood changes, and even the partisan identity of voters can shift. Thus, it is important to understand how the electorate evaluates these changes, how they feel about the candidates, how they perceive and evaluate them and their issue stands.

With the declining importance of political parties for voter information and voting decisions, candidate images have become more important in American presidential elections.[1] Candidate-centered presidential campaigns entail less potent roles for political parties and greater needs for candidates to appeal to voters with as many channels to voters as they can employ (Pfiffner, 1994).

There are three general presidential candidate image models in political communication research (Denton & Woodward, 2000). The first model is known as the candidate-driven image and is constituted mainly by the candidate's messages to the voters (Denton & Woodward, 2000). An example of this transmitted image is used by Waterman, Wright, and St. Clair (1999), who refer to presidential candidates as providing images to voters as with Ronald Reagan giving voters an image of optimism. The candidate-driven model of images is the oldest model and also the most challenged today. The second model of presidential candidate images is the voter-driven image. This model assumes that voters give attributes to the candidates and that these attributes constitute their images. The third model is the candidate-voter interactive view of images, which assumes the voters do indeed form their own images of candidates but that they do so in relation to messages and campaign events (Denton & Woodward, 2000).

Everything that candidates do and say contributes to the shaping of their images. This was very evident in the election of 2000, which was the closest presidential election in American history.[2] According to Federal Election Commission (FEC) statistics, Bush received 47.87 percent of the popular vote, while Gore received 48.38 percent of this vote.[3] In terms of electoral votes, the FEC reports that Bush received 271 Electoral College votes while Gore won 266 electoral votes. Since the electoral votes are the final tally, Bush won by five electoral votes and acquired only one vote above the 270 required to win the election. Uncertainty and court challenges regarding the Florida vote counts kept the election from being decided in terms of who received the Florida slate of electoral votes. A 5–4 U.S. Supreme Court decision ended the recounts taking place in Florida, and this action led to Bush receiving the Florida electoral votes and winning the election. William Flanigan and Nancy Zingale (2002) note that this was the first time since 1884 that the winner of the popular votes did not win the electoral votes.

While some observers may say that Bush won more by legal machinations than by persuasion, since Gore won more popular votes, it should be noted that the polls close to Election Day showed that Bush was gaining points on Gore. The campaign of 2000 offers fertile ground for exploring the development and management of presidential candidate images. Some studies found, for example, that a major shift in public opinion away from Gore concerned voters gaining impressions of the candidate having honesty problems.

There were misstatements, such as comments he made about hearing a union song as a child that was not actually written until after he was an adult. The misstatement impressions did damage to Gore's public image before the presidential debates. In those debates, Gore did well in the first one, slipped some in the second debate, and gained points in the third. However, the stories about dishonesty in his statements had done early damage to his image, and his opponents used them as proof that Gore could not be trusted. The lopsided election results may be partially related to the fact that Gore won the popular vote by gaining points in the debates but lost the electoral votes, at least allegedly, by losing early ground on negative personality impressions.

Polling data in the 2000 presidential campaign season indicate many interesting patterns. First, voters were drawn to the candidate who made them feel more secure. Bush began leading in poll numbers on personal characteristics while Gore was leading on certain issues. Still, Bush was also gaining on some issue positions. Bush was ahead on perceptions of aiding personal independence and being honest while Gore was ahead on caring for people. Gore began losing the latter advantage with swing voters, however. Bush gained strength with perceptions of having a vision and being ethical. However, he lost some points on being tied to special interests with the swing voters. The debates, in fact, appeared to have helped Bush more than Gore.

Most official predictions about the outcome of 2000 were wrong. The Bush campaign expected to win by about 8 percent in the popular vote and with about 320 electoral votes. Some forecasters predicted Gore gaining as high as 60 percent of the popular vote (Mann, 2001).

Falsified explanations of the 2000 election outcomes included a "Clinton fatigue" narrative—a story holding little water in light of the observation that 77 percent of polled Americans said Clinton's presidency was a success while only 35 percent liked him as a person. Perhaps 2 percent of the national vote was attributable to it (Gallup, 1999). Some pundits thought that voters did not perceive the economy as doing well, when in fact they did. Another possible and false explanation was that Gore was perceived by voters as being too liberal. In fact, Gore was viewed as a moderate and led moderates over Bush by 8 percent (Mann, 2001). It was also falsely surmised that voters did not attribute good economic times to Clinton, when polls indicated that 66 percent did (Pomper, 2001).

Plausible explanatory factors for Bush doing so well and Gore having problems include the following observations. Less than 50 percent of those polled in 1999 had a favorable image of Gore in 1999 (Gallup, 1999). More people in the year before the election thought that Bush's policies would take the United States in the right direction (Gallup, 1999). More people also thought that Bush would continue the economic good times attributable to President Clinton (Gallup, 1999). Voters began to use honesty as a more salient criterion as the election progressed. Forty percent indicated that honesty is more important than caring about people like themselves, having strong leadership, and having a vision (*USA Today*/Gallup Poll, 2000). While many Americans perceived the Clinton economy quite favorably, only 20 percent of voters saw the good economy as a major reason for their voting decision (Mann, 2001). By 52 percent to 45 percent, more Republicans viewed the election as more important than previous ones (*USA Today*/Gallup, 2000).

Shortly before Election Day, voters had doubts about Gore's trustworthiness. Sixty-six percent said Gore would say anything to get elected, while only 43 percent said that about Bush (CNN/*Time*, 2000). Polls indicated that one-fifth of voters approved of Clinton as president but not as a person, and Gore won only 63 percent of their votes in contrast to 85 percent of those who favored Clinton both as president and person (Mann, 2001). The Bush campaign succeeded with portraying Bush as a moderate rather than a right-wing conservative and blurred issue differences while defining Gore as dishonest. While Gore led on issues 52–34, voters cared more about other criteria (Penn, 2001). Gore took 60 percent of the right-track voters (Penn, 2001).

Gore failed to make the election about retrospective evaluation, and this allowed Bush to talk about the good economy and then make the election about two unknown new directions (Pomper, 2001). More Democrats than Republicans defected because Gore did not use partisanship and ideology appeals strongly enough (Pomper, 2001). With less perceived differences between candidates, there is less voter turnout.

A *USA Today*/Gallup poll conducted July 3, 2000, indicated that honesty was an important attribute for voters in 2000. At this early point in 2000, Bush and Gore were nearly even in perceived honesty. This contrasts with the 1992 election when voters also valued honesty most and then leadership abilities and candidate issue positions. An ABC–*Washington Post* poll (2000) indicated that 46 percent of Americans reported trusting Bush with the economy more than Gore (41 percent). Public reservations about Gore extended to his leadership skills. Most respondents perceived Bush as being a strong leader. Poll respondents ranked Bush and Gore about evenly on the issue of Social Security.

Another issue area, Bush's proposal for Social Security recipients investing part of their payments in stocks, was favored. Gore was favored as the candidate more likely to understand the problems of average Americans. Poll data during the campaign indicated that while 75 percent of respondents considered the economy in good shape, they were not transferring their approval of the economy into approval of Gore. This makes sense in light of current research on candidate images. Since voters care about policies, issues, and character simultaneously, they can make judgments together or separately about each area.

A CNN/*Time* poll in early 2000 indicated that Gore was seen by more voters as having the knowledge necessary for being president (March 8, 2000). Yet more voters saw Bush as being strong and decisive. Gore was viewed by more voters as having the necessary experience and ability to be president. A *Newsweek* poll (March 9–10, 2000) showed that former McCain supporters preferred Gore over Bush.

We have to be careful about the claims that voters are not focusing on issues or are only thinking about personalities. Political science research has found that voters may be unaware of specific candidate issue positions but also that they assume that the candidates they prefer agree with them on key issues. This suggests that they may project candidate issues positions onto their preferred candidate (Flanigan & Zingale, 1994). Issue positions and voting choice are significantly related. Issue positions increase in salience for voters as voters become more informed about them and as candidates differentiate themselves on various issues, and voters can compare candidate issue positions to their own issue positions (Flanigan & Zingale, 1994).

The Gallup poll of January 22, 2000, indicated that most people were happy with the direction of the nation in 2000 and with the state of the economy. Satisfaction with the nation was at 69 percent, which was the highest number in decades. Data indicated that 83 percent of Americans were as satisfied with the state of the economy. Gallup data indicated that most voters were more concerned with leadership and vision than with particular issue positions. Voters who were Republicans indicated that they considered leadership and vision as most important, followed by issue positions. So did independents. Democrats were nearly equal on issues and leadership.

Despite the general tendency for voters to reward an incumbent executive party when economic conditions are good, there is some instability in the economy-vote relationship that has not been adequately explained. Some researchers have proposed responsibility for economic conditions as a moderating variable that affects the economy-vote relationship in presidential elections (Rudolph & Grant, 2002). This challenges older assumptions about incumbent presidency automatically being assigned credit or blame for the state of the economy. Obviously, this model is a bit mechanistic since little thought beyond a broad assessment of the economy is required on the part of voters. Research shows that economic conditions have more effect on presidential voting choices when those conditions are attributed to the incumbent candidate (Rudolph & Grant, 2002).

Candidates joust over credit or blame in the context of influencing how voters attribute responsibility for economic conditions. In 2000, Gore tried to take some credit for good economic times and Bush tried to keep him from getting that credit. In 2004, John Kerry attributes job losses and stock market losses to Bush, while Bush tries to assign blame to other factors such as the war on terrorism. If campaigns were not important, as some scholars venture to claim, voters would have automatically assigned blame or credit to Gore, but instead, we see that there was a struggle over how to frame the Clinton years of prosperity. Bush offered a frame of the hard work of ordinary Americans, not Clinton and Gore, being the source of credit. A study done on the electorate in 2000 by Thomas Rudolph and J. Tobin Grant (2002) found that voting choice for president was affected by evaluation of the economy but that the effect increases with attribution of responsibility to the incumbent. Also, when the economy was attributed to the incumbent, effects of other issue positions were outweighed by the economy perceptions (Rudolph & Grant, 2002).

Flanigan and Zingale (2002) note the following about the presidential candidate images of Bush and Gore in 2000. First, they note that overall evaluations of Bush were nearly balanced on positive and negative impressions of both personal qualities and issue positions. Positive Bush issue components were impressions about his positions on taxes, abortion, and gun control (Flanigan & Zingale, 2002). Gore was more positive than negative on issues but the reverse on the personality side of his presidential candidate image (Flanigan & Zingale, 2002). Flanigan and Zingale (2002) argue that Bush could not do much to change the perceptions that he had little foreign policy knowledge but he could hope that foreign policy issues did not become important in the campaign. This view neglects the fact that campaigns do not hope for such things as much as they work to make them happen.

There is wide variety in how the candidate image construct is defined and operationalized, but there is convergence on a general conceptualization of candidate image as cognitive representations made in the process of voter perception of candidate messages (Hacker, 1995). The construct is vital to the study of campaign communication because voters make decisions in relation to two bases of influences: long-term forces and short-term forces (Flanigan & Zingale, 1994).

Long-term forces include partisanship and socialization. Short-term forces include candidate images and political party images. Thus, candidate images can be seen as one important determinant of candidate selection (Flanigan & Zingale, 1994). In the absence of evaluating the candidates on personalities or issues, voters will tend to follow partisanship motivations (Flanigan & Zingale, 2002). When candidate images become salient to how voters are evaluating presidential candidates, partisanship declines in significance (Flanigan & Zingale, 2002). Flanigan and Zingale (2002) argue that a vote for president can be seen as the product of the strength of partisanship and the effect of short-term factors like candidate images.

Flanigan and Zingale (1994) note that aggregate candidate images, those candidate images typical of the entire electorate (like "public opinion"), are variable in content and include impressions about both personalities and issues. Flanigan and Zingale (1994) cite evidence to support their claim that there are numerous determinants of voting choice, with candidate images being among the set of causes. Party identification is one of the most important. The retrospective evaluation of an incumbent president is also important. Ideology also influences voting decisions. Issue impact is present, but in a lesser role compared to the other factors. Flanigan and Zingale (2002) argue that the two most important determinants in the 1992 presidential election were party identification and retrospective evaluation. These researchers argue that in the absence of any information about the candidates, issues, or short-term forces, voters will vote on the basis on their partisanship. When, however, they are affected by short-term forces like candidate images, they may be deflected away from party loyalty. Thus, the higher the degree of short-term force influence on their vote, the less the impact of party preference on their vote. Flanigan and Zingale (1994, p. 171) observe that "an individual's vote in an election can be viewed as the product of the strength of partisanship and the impact of the short-term forces on the individual."

Numerous political scientists have argued that issues appear to be of minor significance to voter decisions about candidates because researchers ask few questions about issues or ask questions that are more researcher-derived than voter-derived; in other words, voters are evaluating issues that may be of more importance to the researchers than to the voters themselves. To impact voting, voters must have knowledge and concern regarding the issues, candidates must have differentiated stands on those issues, and voters must be able to compare the candidate issue positions to their own positions (Flanigan & Zingale, 1994). While many voters do not have positions on issues, those that do display consistency between their positions on issues and their voting choices (Flanigan & Zingale, 1994).

It has been argued that candidate images are the intersection of campaign messages and voter perceptions. Voters are informed by many sources, but eventually they define candidates and campaigns for themselves (Trent & Friedenberg, 1991). One key factor affecting images is historical circumstances. In 1932 the Great Depression assured FDR's appeals for change, the Vietnam War helped Richard Nixon in 1968, Watergate helped Carter in 1976, and good economic conditions helped Clinton in 1996. The Persian Gulf War did not substantially help George Bush in 1992.

Some research indicates that we compare our images of opponents or contenders with ideal president images. Researchers have described what they believe are the traits that most American voters would like to have in a president. For many decades, it was thought that candidates are compared cognitively along a standard set of criteria such as source credibility items. New studies, however, appear to have refuted this assumption, which is known as unitary decision making (Flanigan & Zingale, 1994; Hellweg, 1995).

Why Candidate Images and Campaigns Still Matter

Americans pay closer attention to presidential elections than other elections in our nation (Flanigan & Zingale, 2002). While voters are not likely to know much about candidates, this is also true about their knowledge concerning issues, economics, and foreign policy. Voting studies seek to identify the main determinants of presidential candidate evaluation and selection.

Widely known and respected political campaign consultant Richard Wirthlin (2002), in a recent speech, drew attention to how much message strategies can affect the dynamics of election campaigns and how important visions and themes are to producing changes in perceptions of the candidates. Wirthlin (2002) argues that studies show that presidential candidates must clearly and frequently articulate their vision for what they wish our nation to become. He also argues that winning presidential candidates find the weaknesses in their public images and use persuasive messages to change those perceptions. The most central Wirthlin strategy is to persuade by reasoning and motivating by linking his candidates (such as Ronald Reagan) to emotions and values.

There are frequent references to how little campaigns matter since most partisans vote for their party's candidate and there is only a small percentage of voters who are not likely to follow aggregate patterns in voting such as voting consistently with party, ideological leaning, and voting in favor of an incumbent who has done well with economics and foreign policy. This line of reasoning can neglect the simple fact that campaigns matter most for what they can do for the undecided voters and swing voters who ultimately tilt the election in one candidate's favor. Bill Clinton recently noted in an interview (Tomasky, 2003) that the 2004 election can be won by either party since both have a large base but there is a determining percentage of independent voters who will move toward one candidate more than the other for reasons of campaign persuasion. Voting research confirms Clinton's assumptions. Markus (1993) reports that the small percentage of votes that cannot be attributed to long-term factors can decide a presidential election and that voters who are not converted by campaigns may be made aware of the long-term factors by the campaigns. Additionally, we know that campaigns serve to educate voters (see Zakahi on debates, this volume), generate issue agendas, and motivate people to register and vote. While noting that campaigns cannot provide the kind of makeovers that Al Gore sought in 2002, Flanigan and Zingale (2002) argue that in 1988, George Bush Sr. sunk Michael Dukakis with vicious attack messages. They note that images of well-known candidates cannot be changed nearly as easily as those of unknown candidates.

Thomas Holbrook (1994, p. 973) says that election forecasting models provide "extremely accurate explanations" of presidential elections. Such models depend mainly on presidential popularity and the state of the economy (Holbrook, 1994). In fact, they are more likely to be somewhat correct and somewhat explanatory. Holbrook asks the question if presidential campaigns matter, while political communication scholars are likely to wonder how they cannot matter. Still, Holbrook draws attention to the important fact that much of what presidential candidates have to work with in their communication during the campaign is beyond their control. This does not mean that campaigning has no effects or importance, but rather that the effects can have less relative importance than retrospective voting where voters make choices based on the record of the incumbent. Partisanship continues to have a major influence on voting decisions along with the state of presidential popularity and the economy (Holbrook, 1994). Holbrook (1994) shows how campaign events like conventions and debates have significant effects on public images of candidates at the same time that campaign events have more predictable effects on election outcomes.

Possible Candidate Image Formation

Obviously, the candidate image is more of an image of the candidate rather than a representation of factors or things related to the candidate. This means that mental representations of presidential candidates are necessarily personalized and can change as they are filled in with perceptions about issues. One purported scenario is that candidates generate positions on issues in order to generate persona perceptions, and voters then select their preferred persona for president. The problem with this view is that studies continue to show that candidate issue positions and candidate persona perceptions are heavily associated (Hacker, Zakahi, Giles, & McQuitty, 2000), and that voters support candidates who are consistent with their ideologies and issues preferences (Flanigan & Zingale, 1998).

A second scenario is that voters incorporate issue and personality perceptions into unified cognitive models. A third scenario is that candidate images are simply short-term persona impressions that play a minor role in voting decision making. This view is expressed in the Funk chapter (this volume). There are many issues that have to be addressed in the discussions about candidate images today that were less important than in 1995 and 1976. Carol Funk (1996) argues that there is nothing less rational about voting for a president on the basis of personal traits than on the basis of candidate issue positions. This is because trait judgments might include judgments regarding the abilities to conduct the duties of a president (Funk, 1996).

One of the most important characteristics of candidate images is that they are changeable. If they were not, there would be little need for political consultants, participation in debates, and expenditures on advertising. Candidates can present their views on issues in varying ways to increase their levels of support on issue positions. Flanigan and Zingale (2002) correctly note that candidates cannot change their job experience or religion. While this is true, it is by no means proof that candidates cannot change perceptions of their personal qualities.

There is disagreement among scholars about the importance of issues in candidate images. Yet in most presidential elections, there is a clear positive relationship between issue orientations and candidate support. For example, in 2000, those favoring increasing governmental services overwhelmingly voted for Gore, and those favoring decreasing governmental services overwhelmingly voted for Bush (Flanigan & Zingale, 2002). Increased spending on defense, less spending to help African Americans, and opposition to abortion would predict voting for Bush over Gore in 2000 (Flanigan & Zingale, 2002).

There remains a need for conceptual clarity even if there is no standardization of conceptual definitions. More convergence in conceptual definitions should occur over time as old ideas may be falsified and new ones subjected to empirical testing. Candidate images are important not only because they form the basis for evaluating and contrasting candidates, but also because they serve as filters for new messages about the candidates (Patterson, 1980).

There are many bright spots in all of the social sciences concerning perception and cognitive processes. More integration of what we know about perception, cognition, and communication should be brought into discussions about candidate images, which despite the wide divergence in conceptual and operational definitions have always signified mental pictures or cognitive representations.

There is a need to account for the fact that voters are often poorly informed about candidates and issues and that the agenda-setting effects of news media tend to create an agenda for campaign perception. Perhaps more importantly, the framing and priming effects that were discovered in the agenda-setting studies indicate that the news media also serve to present sets of candidate attributes that are used by voters to evaluate presidential candidates.

While political communication scholars study candidate images as mental representations that change over time, it is important to keep in mind that these images must be related to communication processes for them to shed light not only on political perception but also on communication.

What's in the Book

In the first chapter of this book, Susan Hellweg reviews the literature and directions for candidate image research, adding observations to those she made in the 1995 book. The chapter examines the history of candidate image research for the past forty years. This includes an assessment of key conceptual and operational definitions of the candidate image construct as well as discrepancies in how the construct is defined and used. The points of convergence in candidate image research and theory are also noted.

Presidential candidates' personal qualities are analyzed and discussed in the second chapter by William L. Benoit and John P. McHale. Their chapter employs a typology of presidential candidates' personal qualities (e.g., honesty, compassion, and strength) and uses computer content analysis to examine presidential TV spots from 1952 to 2000. Candidates are contrasted on the basis of the frequency of their discussion of particular character traits including partisanship, incumbency or challenger status, and who is winning and losing. This chapter provides an empirical basis for researchers who seek to build a theory of candidate images that focuses on the personal qualities in presidential television spot messages.

In chapter 3, Carolyn Funk assesses the scandal of Bill Clinton and how it affected his images. The observations and analysis can apply to candidates other than Clinton. It is common for presidential candidates to encounter problems with their images related to reports of alleged scandalous behavior. This chapter explains how candidate images change in response to news of political scandals. Funk reviews how candidates and the public both respond to scandals. The chapter also examines the impact of scandal for candidates who were previously well known as public figures as compared to those who are new to the public eye. Finally, we consider how candidate images in the aftermath of scandal vary depending on the eye of the beholder. Partisans, for example, are more willing to give a candidate the benefit of the doubt when it comes to believing reports of scandal (as occurred for Gary Hart in 1988 and Bill Clinton in the 1990s) and tend to downplay the importance of the scandal for other political judgments.

In chapter 4, Allan Louden and Kristen McCauliff make an argument about some of the anomalies found in candidate image research. They address how character or persona perceptions work in relationship to candidate issue perceptions. Specifically, they reiterate an argument made by researchers and consultants alike, namely, that issue statements by candidates are used to form perceptions of their character.

Kenneth Hacker discusses a theoretical connection between persuasion research and research on presidential candidate images in chapter 5. This produces a dual processing approach to candidate image formation. Candidate image research and theory have been cited in both political science and political communication research as comprising an area of short-term change, but there has been a paucity of theoretical precision in conceptualizing what actually constitutes candidate images. This chapter presents a linkage from persuasion theory and research to the candidate image construct and shows how cognitive processing of persuasive messages, including campaign messages, involve two basic routes of mental processing—one that is argument- or policy-based and the other that is imagery- or cue-based.

In chapter 6, Lynda Kaid and Mike Chanslor discuss the ways that political advertising affects presidential candidate images and voter decision making This chapter analyzes data from four presidential elections (1988, 1992, 1996, and 2000) to determine the ways in which exposure to televised political spots affects voter evaluations of candidates. Data are presented that indicate that exposure to ads does affect how voters see candidate images, sometimes negatively and sometimes positively. Image characteristics of candidates also seem to be related to the emotional content of television spots and to voting for the candidates. The analyses also suggest differences for some candidates in evaluations according to the gender of the voter.

Walter Zakahi, in chapter 7, explains how presidential debates make a unique contribution to presidential candidate image formation. This chapter is especially important because of the fact that some political scientists have attempted to minimize the role of debates in voter decision making, and most political communication researchers have not been able to pinpoint the specific contributions to image formation that are made in the debates as opposed to other sources of messages such as advertising and news. The chapter focuses on the debates during the 1992 Clinton, George Bush, and Perot campaign; the 1996 Clinton and Dole campaign; and the 2000 George W. Bush and Gore campaign. Zakahi examines and explains how presidential candidate images are affected by the debates, strategies employed by candidates leading up to the debates (e.g., the curious strategy of lowering expectations for a candidate), specific strategies employed by the candidates during the debates (e.g., in 2000 the Gore team seemed to have a different strategy for each of the three presidential debates), and finally the importance or value of defining moments in the debates.

In chapter 8, Tim Stephen, Teresa Harrison, William Husson, and David Albert discuss their research concerning how presidential candidate communication behaviors become part of presidential candidate images. The chapter fills in some gaps in the candidate image literature concerning how candidate evaluations are affected by the communication behaviors of the presidential candidates. Winners are contrasted to losers in terms of their communication behaviors. The authors argue that the effects of these behaviors are much greater than the effects of candidate issue positions on voter evaluations. There is an interesting connection here between this importance of behaviors and the increasing use of television in campaigns.

In chapter 9, there is a concern with a meta-analytic approach to studying presidential candidate images. Susan Hellweg and Brian Spitzberg describe and analyze the use of statistical procedures for meta-analysis in deriving key findings about candidate images across sets of multiple studies.

Kenneth Hacker, in chapter 10, describes cognitive measures that may be employed in the study of presidential candidate images. This chapter describes a variety of methods that can be used to identify cognitive impressions of presidential candidates, including cognitive response methods and voter discourse analysis.

In chapter 11, Lynda Kaid revisits the use of semantic differential measurement for the study of candidate images. Since 1957, this methodology has been used to measure constructs that people use to evaluate objects of perception. It continues to be a useful and straightforward method for comparing images of competing candidates as well as for measuring message effects on images.

While it is common to link communication presentations done through various media to changes in candidate images, it is difficult to sort out the media effects from the content effects. As with contrasting one medium from another, such sorting involves attempting to see which media attribute is responsible for observed differences among various media (O'Keefe, 2002).

Despite the persistence and perceptual utility of partisanship, voters may vote against party when issues become more salient in terms of preferred policy positions. Flanigan and Zingale (1991, p. 94) note, "Neither social circumstance nor political parties seem to provide such clear-cut, persuasive cues for most individuals that their own values and perceptions cannot operate independently."

By the time the reader reaches the end of this book, she or he will have encountered many insights about presidential candidate images and voting behavior. I urge the reader to leave with not only knowledge about images but also some considerations about ethics. Richard Waterman et al. (1999, p. 2) describe an "expectations gap thesis" that says that there are substantial gaps between what Americans believe presidents are capable of doing and what they are actually able to do in office. They note that this thesis has been present in the literature on the American presidency for at least thirty years. Perhaps by learning more precisely how presidential candidate images are formed, how they affect voting choices, and what kinds of ethics issues are involved in their manipulation, we can help to encourage more rationality and deeper thinking in how we all evaluate our candidates for president.

Notes

1. Political parties continue to be very important for voting, but parties have declined in terms of both voter loyalty and the increase in the number of Americans who identify themselves as independents (Wayne, 1996).
2. One might wonder if the 1876 presidential election was not closer since the winner had only one more electoral vote than the loser. However, one must look at the percentages of both popular and electoral votes to see the difference between 1876 and 2000.
3. The FEC statistics are available online at www.fec.gov.

References

Boulding, Kenneth. 1956. *The Image.* Ann Arbor: University of Michigan Press.
Denton, Robert, and Gary Woodward. 2000. *Political Communication in America.* Westport, Conn.: Praeger.

Flanigan, William, and Nancy Zingale. 1991. *Political Behavior of the American Electorate*. Washington, D.C.: Congressional Quarterly Press.
———. 1994. *Political Behavior of the American Electorate*. Washington, D.C.: Congressional Quarterly Press.
———. 1998. *Political Behavior of the American Electorate*, 9th ed. Washington, D.C.: Congressional Quarterly Press.
———. 2002. *Political Behavior of the American Electorate*, 10th ed. Washington, D.C.: Congressional Quarterly Press.
Funk, Carol. 1996. "Understanding Trait Inferences in Candidate Images." *Research in Micropolitics* 5: 97–123.
Hacker, Kenneth L. 1995. "Interpersonal Communication and the Construction of Candidate Images." In *Candidate Images in Presidential Elections*, edited by Kenneth Hacker, 65–82. Westport, Conn.: Praeger.
Hacker, Kenneth L., Walter R. Zakahi, Maury J. Giles, and Shaun McQuitty. 2000. "Components of Candidate Images: Statistical Analysis of the Issue-Persona Dichotomy in the Presidential Campaign of 1996." *Communication Monographs* 67: 227–238.
Hellweg, Susan. 1995. "Campaign and Candidate Images in American Presidential Elections." In *Candidate Images in Presidential Elections*, edited by Kenneth Hacker, 1–17. Westport, Conn.: Praeger.
Hellweg, S. A., G. N. Dionisopoulos, and D. B. Kugler. 1989. "Political Candidate Image: A State of the Art Review." In *Progress in Communication Sciences*, vol. 9, edited by Brenda Dervin and Melvin Voigt, 43–78. Norwood, N.J.: Ablex.
Holbrook, Thomas M. 1994. "Campaigns, National Conditions, and U.S. Presidential Elections." *American Journal of Political Science* 38: 973–998.
Kaid, Lynda, and Mike Chanslor. 1995. "Changing Candidate Images: The Effects of Political Advertising. In *Candidate Images in Presidential Elections*, edited by Kenneth Hacker, 83–97. Westport, Conn.: Praeger.
Kendall, Kathleen, and Scott Paine. 1995. "Political Images and Voting Decisions." In *Candidate Images in Presidential Elections*, edited by Kenneth Hacker, 19–35. Westport, Conn.: Praeger.
Mann, Thomas. 2001. "A Considered Opinion: Why a Presidential Dead Heat in 2000?" *Brookings Review* 19: 1–2.
Markus, Gregory. 1993. "The Impact of Personal and National Economic Conditions on the Presidential Vote: A Pooled Cross-Sectional Analysis." In *Controversies in Voting Behavior*, edited by Richard Niemi and Herbert Weisberg, 152–166. Washington, D.C.: Congressional Quarterly Press.
Nimmo, Dan. 1995. "The Formation of Candidate Images during Presidential Campaigns." In *Candidate Images in Presidential Elections*, edited by Kenneth Hacker, 51–63. Westport, Conn.: Praeger.
Nimmo, Dan, and Robert L. Savage. 1976. *Candidates and Their Images: Concepts, Methods, and Findings*. Pacific Palisades, Calif.: Goodyear.
O'Keefe, Daniel. 2002. *Persuasion Theory and Practice*, 2nd ed. Thousand Oaks, Calif.: Sage.

Patterson, Thomas. 1980. *The Mass Media Election: How Americans Choose Their President.* Westport, Conn.: Praeger.

Penn, Mark. 2001. "Turning a Win into a Draw." New Democrats Online. www.ndol.org/ndol_ci.cfm?kaid=127&subid=179&contentid=2922

Pfau, M., T. Diedrich, K. M. Larson, and K. M. van Winkle. 1993. "Relational and Competence Perceptions of Presidential Candidates during the Primary Election Campaigns." Paper presented at the International Communication Association Convention, Washington, D.C., May.

Pfiffner, James, P. 1994. *The Modern Presidency.* New York: St. Martin's Press.

Pomper, Gerald. 2001. "The 2000 Presidential Election: Why Gore Lost." *Political Science Quarterly* 116: 201–223.

Rudolph, Thomas J., and J. Tobin Grant. 2002. "An Attributional Model of Economic Voting: Evidence from the 2000 Presidential Election." *Political Research Quarterly* 55: 805–823.

Savage, Robert. 1995. "Creating the Eye of the Beholder: Candidate Images and Political Socialization." In *Candidate Images in Presidential Elections*, edited by Kenneth Hacker, 37–49. Westport, Conn.: Praeger.

Tomasky, Michael. 2003. "The Clinton Formula." *American Prospect.* http://www.prospect.org/print/V14/10/tomasky-m.html.

Trent, Judith, and Robert Friedenberg. 1991. *Political Campaign Communication.* New York: Praeger.

Waterman, Richard, Robert Wright, and Gilbert St. Clair. 1999. *The Image-Is-Everything Presidency: Dilemmas in American Leadership.* Boulder, Colo.: Westview Press.

Wayne, Stephen W. 1992. *The Road to the White House.* New York: St. Martin's Press.

———. 1996. *The Road to the White House.* New York: St. Martin's Press.

Wirthlin, Richard. 2002. "Polls, Politics, Public Policy, and Presidential Leadership." Myles Martel Lecture in Leadership and Public Opinion, University of Connecticut, April 26.

1

Campaigns and Candidate Images in American Presidential Elections

Susan A. Hellweg

THE STUDY OF IMAGES HAS COMMANDED scholarly attention from various disciplines within the social sciences, one of the most concentrated efforts being in the political context. Although the concept of political image has been examined by scholars in political science, sociology, and communication, little agreement has been reached concerning the concept. Arthur Miller, Martin Wattenberg, and Oksana Malanchuk (1985), in fact, argued that image is "one of the most important but least understood facets of American politics" (p. 183).

The purpose of this chapter is to discuss candidate image research in the context of American presidential elections. More specifically, it examines how candidate image has been defined and studied in this context, as well as patterns revealed in these studies; the relationship between candidate image and voting behavior, in terms of unitary and nonunitary models of decision making; the role of candidate and voter demographics in the perception of candidate image; the relationship between candidate image and campaign issues; the nature of candidate image components and the temporality associated with these components; how candidate image is conceptualized by voters across presidential campaigns; mediated portrayals of candidate image; and directions for future research within the areas discussed. This chapter reviews both empirical research and conceptual analyses from the political science, sociology, and communication literature.

How Candidate Images Have Been Defined and Studied

Candidate image has been variously defined in the literature as being "stimulus determined," that is, specifically projected by a politician, or as being "perceiver determined," that is, composed of attributes given to a politician by the electorate (Nimmo, 1976; Nimmo, Mansfield, & Savage, 1974a; Nimmo & Savage, 1971, 1975; Siegel, 1964). A second conceptual variant in the literature defining candidate image focuses on whether image represents a static entity or exists in an evolutionary sense. Finally, the literature is inconsistent in describing candidate image as belonging to a single referent in isolation from others or in comparison to others (Hellweg, Dionisopoulos, & Kugler, 1989).

Candidate image has been examined by social scientists for forty years. The majority of the studies evident in the political science, communication, and sociology literature on candidate image have been centered on the 1972 and 1980 presidential campaigns, with the exception of studies examining image within the political debates context, where the 1976 presidential campaign predominates (Hellweg et al., 1989). Political candidate image studies have primarily employed a source valence conceptualization of image, source credibility instrumentation often being the vehicle for measuring candidate perception. This research has largely utilized semantic differential scales to measure candidate image as well as factor analytic techniques to assess its dimensions. Some few studies have relied upon *Q-methodology*. Researchers have favored perceiver-determined conceptualizations of candidate image over stimulus-determined ones. In the vast majority of studies on candidate image, college students have served as subjects. A minority of studies have utilized telephone interviewing techniques with the general public to ascertain candidate assessments.

Research on candidate image has been directed at delineating the dimensions, functions, and election-specific conceptualizations of political images. Investigators have examined how images are formulated and cognitively processed, how they evolve over time, whether or not they affect voting behavior, how they fit into the voter decision-making process, the effects of candidate and voter demographic variables upon image perception, the relative positioning of campaign issues and candidate images in electoral processes, the influence of interpersonal communication among voters in candidate image conceptualizations, and mediated portrayals of candidate image, primarily in the context of campaign advertising and debates. Ideal conceptualizations of candidates and presidential incumbents and challengers have been the focus of this research; the majority of studies have analyzed campaigns in isolation from one another.

Candidate Image Perceptions and Voting Behavior

Justifications for investigating candidate image are often grounded in the assumption that perceptions of candidates are related to decision-making behaviors of voters. Ernest Rose and Douglas Fuchs (1968) cautioned against speculating about the existence of such a causal relationship. Other researchers have been less reticent to claim such a relationship.

Richard Fagen (1966) argued that projection of a positive image is of more importance to a candidate than information that could be conveyed. Peter Natchez and Irwin Bupp (1968) and Dan Nimmo and Robert Savage (1976) concluded that candidate image offers the single best predictor of voting behavior. Richard Boyd (1969) concluded that 38.6 percent of the variance in voting defection can be accounted for by perceptions of candidate image. Keith Stamm, Alice Burgess, Michael Jordan, and Susan Lim (1985) asserted that issues have "nothing to do with an election's outcome" (p. 4); projected candidate image is the important element. William Brooks (1967) observed that candidate image is "a primary factor in persuasion" (p. 273). On the basis of their review of the literature, David Rarick, Mary Duncan, David Lee, and Laurinda Porter (1977) concluded that "voters' perceptions of candidates can significantly influence their voting behavior" (p. 260).

At the presidential election level, researchers have determined that candidate image is at least a factor in determining electoral outcomes (Brooks, 1967; Brummett, 1981; Campbell, 1979; DeLancey & Swanson, 1981; Kennamer & Chaffee, 1981; Maddox, 1980; Nimmo, Mansfield, & Savage, 1974b; Pike, 1985; Rarick, Duncan, Lee, & Porter, 1977; Zandpour, 1985) and a strategic concern in campaign development (e.g., Newman, 2001; Rudd, 1986).

In a study conducted by Peter Andersen and Robert Kibler (1978), eight dimensions of source valence (competence, extroversion, sociability, composure, social attraction, physical attraction, attitude homophily, and background homophily) were tested to determine their effects on voter preference in connection with a Democratic primary campaign in Florida. On the basis of the data collected, the researchers concluded that attitude homophily is "an excellent predictor of voter preference" (p. 11), such that voters tend to favor candidates with attitudes similar to theirs.

In a study of presidential primaries, James Campbell (1983) attempted to examine causal relationships between candidate image and voter intentions, concluding that both "image voting and image rationalization are significant phenomena," with image voting probably being slightly more pronounced (p. 302).

Unitary versus Nonunitary Voter Decision Making

For the most part, studies examining candidate image have conceptualized the voting process as involving a unitary decision by the voter, where an individual casts a preference for one electoral contender over another (Nimmo & Savage, 1971, 1976). This view has been further emphasized in studies of ideal candidate conceptualizations, arguing that the voter conceives an ideal criterion by which to evaluate candidates involved in a campaign (e.g., Trent, Mongeau, Trent, Kendall, & Cushing, 1993).

A series of three studies has questioned the unitary assumption of voter decision-making processes. In the first study, Susan Hellweg and Stephen King (1983) identified standard discriminating coefficients for Jimmy Carter and Ronald Reagan during the 1980 general election campaign. These indicated a different order of criteria for the two contenders, each carrying unique discriminating strengths, and an opposite valence for the criteria associated with each. Their findings suggested that dissimilar standards are incorporated in the evaluation of political opponents.

Utilizing perceptual data across election levels in the 1984 general election balloting (presidential, vice presidential, mayoral, judicial), Hellweg, King, and Steve Williams (1988) found that incumbent positioning does make a difference in the selection of criteria by which to evaluate candidates (with the incumbent potentially setting the perceptual agenda for the challenger) and that these criteria are idiosyncratic to the particular candidates involved and the election context. In addition, their research suggested that once these idiosyncratic criteria are isolated, voting behavior can be accurately predicted.

In the context of the 1988 general election campaign, Hellweg, William Walker, King, and Brian Spitzberg (1990) examined comparative candidate evaluation and the potential for image agenda setting. Among their findings, it was determined that a candidate can set the image agenda for an opponent at specific points in time, but not progressively over time.

Issue-image Positioning in Voter Decision Making

The question of the relative weight of image versus issue criteria in voter evaluations of candidates has been the subject of a number of research studies in the political science and communication literature. Michael Leff and Gerald Mohrmann (1974) asserted that campaign oratory is aimed at ingratiation as a means to gain the favor of potential voters. Robert Anderson (1973) contended that such oratory centers around characterization, or "the public and usually verbal expression of self-concept or political evaluation made by a political actor in the public drama" (p. 77). Two competing paradigms described by Thomas Clark (1979) reflect differing positions on this controversy: the rational campaign model, focusing on the effects of issue-oriented messages; and the image campaign model, placing the primary emphasis on candidate images and the secondary emphasis on the issues discussed in the campaign.

The rational campaign model argues that the public must be kept abreast of salient campaign issues and that given this information, voters are capable of making an informed and logical decision in the voting booth. According to Clark (1979), from the perspective of this model, the campaign can be described as "something of a public referendum to determine which candidate best articulates the common concerns of the electorate and best proposes answers to those concerns" (p. 122). It could be argued that this model allows for congruence with the tenets of basic democratic principles. Thomas Marshall (1983) contended that campaign issues link elected officials to the public in an important way. Charles E. Wahl (1959) asserted that in no other arena, except for the context of religious convictions, "is the average person more convinced of the logical defensible, and wholly rational nature of his decisions" than in the voting booth (p. 263). Several studies have attempted to document the argument for voter rationality in the electoral process. For example, John Jackson and Roy Miller (1973) determined in a study of issue, image, and partisan influence in the context of 1972 campaigns at various levels that while the second and third areas of concern produced some effect, considerations of issues acted as primary voter factors.

Herbert Weisberg and Jerrold Rusk (1970) and Rusk and Weisberg (1972) noted a direct relationship between the issue positions conveyed by campaign contenders and the perceptual differences registered by voters in evaluating the candidates. In a study of political campaign advertisements, Gina Garramone (1983) concluded that respondents exposed to issue messages feel more informed than when they are provided image messages. In an examination of twenty-six presidential primary campaigns, David Gopoian (1980) determined that issue information was the primary focus of the campaigns.

Other researchers have argued for the primacy of image stimulus information in candidate evaluation. David Sears (1969) contended that the electorate prefers to personalize politics, that image data are easier to process, and, in fact, that voters discard the informational bases of their decision making (e.g., issue position data). Clark (1979) asserted that

> since gaining as many votes as possible is the goal of almost all political candidates, candidates face the dilemma of having to appear to conduct their campaigns according to the rational model while in reality conducting them according to the image model. (p. 123)

Clark contended that candidates engage in strategic ambiguity in the campaign process, arguing that "if candidates speak out clearly and completely on politically volatile issues, they risk dividing and losing important segments of their political support, and in consequence, risk losing the election" (p. 122). Michael McGee (1978) argued that asking the electorate to vote on the basis of issues instead of images may be an impossibility, suggesting in addition that, "since we try to make 'popular sovereignty' at least an ideological reality, it is also impossible for leaders who wish to honor and speak for 'the people' to adhere to 'issue' criteria" (p. 153).

Lance Bennett (1977) furthered this view in an exhaustive taxonomy of the subsumption of issues by the image model, stating the following about the way in which issues are conveyed by political contenders:

> They are seldom defined to the degree necessary to debate clear policies or programs that might derive from them, (b) they are generally linked to familiar characterizations of the candidates or the parties rather than to conditions or causes that fall beyond the scope of the election, (c) they may be defined by the candidates in different terms for different audiences, (d) they are seldom defined in terms that will arouse controversy or that will risk damage to the candidate's public image, (e) they are often linked to claims of the personal qualities of the opponent or to propositions about leadership, and (f) they are usually restricted to a fairly small range of substantive concerns. (pp. 220–221)

Based on an analysis of voting patterns in presidential elections from 1952 to 1964, Natchez and Bupp (1968) found that images are more easily accepted by voters because of their cognitive simplicity, asserting that issues require supportive information and have a tendency to become "highly fractionated, idiosyncratic and inconsistent" (p. 437).

In a study of images and issues in the 1976 presidential campaign, Churchill Roberts (1981) asserted that the electorate first examines the likeability of a political contender before adopting issue positions. Likewise, Marshall (1983), in an examination of preconvention candidate messages, argued for the primacy of image information during the early phases of a campaign.

Congruence between the rational campaign model and the image campaign model has been documented in some empirical research. For example, Kathleen Kendall and June Yum (1984) tested the power of homophily, issues, and images as predictors of blue-collar voting behavior in the context of the 1980 presidential election. On the basis of their findings, the researchers determined that homophily plays the largest role, with images and issues following. The researchers argued that all three elements are linked together in electoral behavior. However, they also asserted in connection with any emphasis on issue-based decision making that "certainly a well educated electorate and careful choices are highly desirable. But there is a hidden elitism in the view that intelligent voting decisions must be based on specific issues, an assumption that any other way of doing it is inadequate and inappropriate" (p. 719).

On the issue-image controversy, Dwight Davis (1981) argued that issues and image meld together in the voter decision-making process, stating that "images result from the interaction of candidate messages received by voters and voters' subjective processing of the messages" (p. 473). This suggested that images are formulated in the minds of voters even when the candidate message appears to be issue oriented.

In the context of political debates, where the comparison of arguments would seem to be the central focus, some research has demonstrated the importance of image information. In studies by Sidney Kraus and Raymond Smith (1977) and by Jack Dennis, Steven Chaffee, and Sun Yuel Choe (1979), candidate perception was found to be significantly influenced by image information. In addition, David Vancil and Sue Pendell (1984) concluded that among the viewers they surveyed of the 1980 presidential debate between Carter and Reagan, 56 percent focused on issue information, 25 percent cited personality and leadership information as primary to their perceptions of the candidates, and 19 percent reported that issue and personality-leadership information were of equal importance.

In a more recent study of the issue-image controversy, Kenneth Hacker and Walter Zakahi (1994) found that personality variables were a greater predictor of support for George Bush in the context of the 1992 presidential campaign than were issue variables, although the latter were also determined to be significantly related to support levels. On the basis of their findings, the researchers concluded that issues should not be treated as being isolated from candidate personality evaluations in the assessment of voter support for candidates. Craig Hullett (1998) found support for an integrative judgment pattern for issue and image considerations in response to congressional debates. Allan Louden (1994) has contended that the "issue/image dichotomy is artificial and misleading in that both the messages projected by candidates and perceived by voters are, in fact, a complex blend of issue and image information" (p. 171), describing issue data as verifiable/consequential and image data as intuitive/ephemeral. He argues that it has become difficult to discuss accounts of political candidate campaigning outside of the issue/image framework. Further, he suggests that voters undergo an inferential process in absorbing campaign messages, such that "issue information informs image evaluation" (p. 180). Hacker, Zakahi, Maury Giles, and Shaun McQuitty (2000) demonstrated in the context of the 1996 presidential race that issues and candidate persona were significantly correlated.

Demographic Considerations in Voter Decision Making

Some research has been conducted to ascertain the effects of candidate ethnicity, physical attractiveness, voter party affiliation, and voter and candidate gender on perceptions of candidate image and voting behavior. In addition to scholarly interest in focusing on these variables, the presidential candidacies of Jesse Jackson, Douglas Wilder, Elizabeth Dole, and Al Sharpton, and the vice presidential candidacy of Geraldine Ferraro, among others, encourage attention in this regard.

Noting a significant decline in partisan effects on voting, James Carlson (1984) argued that ethnicity should be considered in the measurement of image formation and effect. On the basis of a study of candidate physical attractiveness and voting behavior, Ann Bowman (1980) concluded that (1) attractive female politicians are at a significant perceptual disadvantage with the electorate, (2) unattractive female politicians seem to experience greater political success, and (3) attractive male politicians have the greatest chance for political success. While Virginia Sapiro (1981–1982) isolated a definite stereotyping of female candidates in her study, Donald Nobles and Dennis Gunderson (1976) and Ronald Hedlund, Patricia Freeman, Keith Hamm, and Robert Stein (1979) found no such effect, if other factors remain equal. A study by Karrin Vasby Anderson (2002) found evidence that while gender was an overriding consideration for Hillary Rodham Clinton's actions as first lady, it turned into a "tacit subtext" for her New York senatorial race. The author notes that "the failed presidential bid of Elizabeth Dole and the political resilience of Hillary Rodham Clinton suggest that gender remains a significant but complicated variable in U.S. politics" (p. 106). In a study designed to test the androgynous quality of masculinity in the context of political victory or defeat, Carlson and Mary Kay Boring (1981) demonstrated that both male and female candidates are evaluated as more masculine when victorious, the opposite in defeat.

Goldie Shabad and Kristi Andersen (1979) found that female members of the electorate are not more personality oriented in their voting behavior, as had been hypothesized.

Li-Ning Huang (2000) demonstrated the importance of information-processing goals of the electorate (i.e., the extent of effortful versus effortless information processing, the extent of impression-driven versus non-impression-driven information processing) in the acquisition of candidate information, as well as political sophistication. In a study conducted by Jerry Allen, Joan O'Mara, and Ben Judd (1985), it was discovered that voter sex contributed significantly to the evaluation of Geraldine Ferraro's competence, character, social attraction, and background homophily, with female voters favoring her in these areas. David Houston and Kelly Doan (1999) discovered that the assessment of a shared ideology candidate is significantly damaged when specific evidence for opponent character assertions is not provided in campaign advertisements, while no such effect is the case for an opposing ideology candidate. Teresa Harrison, Timothy Stephen, William Husson, and B. J. Fehr (1991) found that (1) while both image data based on interpersonal behaviors of candidates and respondent political positions contribute significantly to predictions of voter preference, the former are more important in doing so than the latter; and (2) for male respondents, their political positions are more important in predicting voter preferences than are the interpersonal behavioral data on the candidates.

In terms of voter political party affiliation, Roberta Siegel (1964) found no effect in the conceptualization of the ideal president, nor did Hellweg (1978) for the ideal political candidate. Judith Trent, Paul Mongeau, Jimmie Trent, Kendall, and Ronald Cushing (1993) tested voter perceptions of presidential selection criteria on the basis of political party affiliation of the respondents. Their findings suggested that for the 1988 presidential primary campaign, when the major candidates represented the same generation, members of neither party felt that age was a particular concern, but that for the 1992 presidential primary campaign, when the Democratic frontrunners were notably younger than the incumbent president, those respondents identifying themselves as Democrats indicated that age was an important issue. Finally, in both campaigns, when marital infidelity allegations were directed toward the leading Democratic contender, respondents identifying themselves as Republicans considered this factor to be significantly more a concern than did their Democratic counterparts. In a study of the 1996 first presidential campaign debate, William Benoit, David Webber, and Julie Berman (1998) found that candidate evaluations varied as a function of respondent liberal-moderate-conservative leanings and voting intentions, with 69 percent indicating that the reasons for their voting intentions had to do with candidate policy, while 31 percent reported that character reasons were involved.

Political Candidate Image Components

A number of studies are available in the literature that have been designed to ascertain the components of political candidate image. Some of these studies have been aimed at specific electoral levels (e.g., presidential, gubernatorial, senatorial), often in the context of actual candidates; a few have examined conceptualizations of the ideal political candidate. Research in this area has generally involved the administration of scales to respondents and the use of factor analytic techniques to determine the composition of the construct. Often candidate image has been examined through source valence conceptualizations.

Dimensions of public-figure credibility have been examined in several studies. James McCroskey (1966) identified character and trustworthiness as its components. David Berlo, James Lemert, and Robert Mertz (1969–1970) isolated three dimensions of public-figure credibility: safety, qualification, and dynamism. McCroskey, Thomas Jensen, and Cynthia Todd (1972) found five factors for public-figure credibility: competence, character, composure, extroversion, and sociability.

In a similar vein, Andersen and William Todd (1975) isolated three dimensions of public-figure homophily: attitude-belief homophily, background homophily, and personality homophily. In a subsequent augmentation to this research, Andersen and William Todd de Mancillas (1978) identified two dimensions of public-figure homophily: attitude homophily and background homophily.

In another study examining fifteen public-figure evaluations, Jacob Wakshlag and Nadyne Edison (1979) found that competence, sociability, character, composure, extroversion, similarity, and physical attraction were incorporated in the comparisons the respondents were asked to make, while task and social attraction were not. On the basis of their findings, the researchers concluded that attraction, credibility, and perceived similarity are incorporated in a latent structure, becoming relevant when the public figures are communicating, but not in the general evaluation of these sources.

In a somewhat similar vein, Husson, Stephen, Harrison, and Fehr (1988), using 1984 presidential candidates Ronald Reagan and Walter Mondale as a basis for analysis, determined that communication behavior ratings of the two candidates significantly predicted candidate preferences. It is perhaps important to note that the researchers utilized a 100-item inventory of verbal and nonverbal behavior typically incorporated in studies of interpersonal settings, arguing that typical candidate image research is aimed at an assessment of static traits.

Several studies have analyzed presidential images specifically in determining components of the construct. William Kjeldahl, Carl Carmichael, and Robert Mertz (1971) found that respondents utilized two dimensions, genuineness and leadership, in evaluating contenders in the 1968 Oregon primary. Lynda Kaid and Robert Hirsch (1973) isolated two dimensions that were incorporated in evaluations of Edmund Muskie when he was running for president: trustworthiness and demeanor. For presidential candidates Edward Kennedy and George McGovern, Thomas McCain and Paul Rowand (1973) discovered that three credibility factors were employed in their evaluation: leadership, extroversion, and composure.

In a study examining the perceived credibility and charisma of John Kennedy, George McGovern, Richard Nixon, and "The Presidency of the U.S.," Leslie Baxter, Thomas Young, and John Bittner (1973) found five-factor solutions for each, with at least six charisma items associated with the individual target sources. A distinct charisma factor was isolated for "The Presidency" conceptualization.

A few studies in the candidate image literature have found that image perception can be conceived in dichotomous ways. Siegel (1964) found that image can be divided into job-crucial attributes (e.g., honesty, intelligence, and independence) and personal attributes (e.g., speaking ability and friendliness). Nimmo and Savage (1976) found it useful to distinguish between political role attributes (those associated with their acts and qualifications as public officials) and stylistic role attributes (those not directly political, such as the way in which they communicate their capabilities to members of the electorate, and personal qualities). Fred Greenstein (1965) offered a similar dichotomy in the conceptualization of a president. Baxter, Young, and Bittner (1973) found that political figures are evaluated in terms of two orientations, personal attraction considerations and/or power-strength considerations. Nimmo (1974) suggested that "popular images of political leaders are an amalgam of both role and style considerations, and in attempting to 'build' his image no politician can run simply as a governmental 'technician' or as a popular 'celebrity'" (p. 127).

Ideal candidate image has been a focus of several studies. Asking her subjects to indicate three criteria among ten that would fit a president, Siegel (1966) found honesty was ranked as number one, intelligence was the second factor, and the third consideration was independence. From these findings, the researcher concluded that job-crucial attributes are more important to identifying an ideal president than are personal ones. Nimmo, Michael Mansfield, and Savage (1974a) examined the image of the ideal president in the context of the 1972 general election, finding that this conceptualization emphasizes public official experience and personal qualities and plays down politician and dramatic qualities.

In a study conducted by Percy Tannenbaum, Bradley Greenberg, and Fred Silverman (1977), respondents were requested to report their conceptualizations of the ideal president against two presidential candidates, Richard Nixon and John Kennedy. Using seven-point semantic differential scales for instrumentation purposes (a seven being the highest evaluative interval), the researchers found that the ideal president is positioned (1) between six and seven for seven items (wise, fair, experienced, strong, active, deep, and calm), (2) between five and six on two items (virile and colorful), and (3) between four and five for three items (liberal, young, and warm).

In another study designed to measure perceptions of idealness utilizing seven-point semantic differential scales, Hellweg (1979) found that the ideal political candidate was conceptualized by respondents as being (1) "extremely" believable, reliable, good, energetic, just, honest, responsible, competent, and intelligent; (2) "quite" experienced, bold, poised, sociable, admirable, nice, relaxed, cheerful, intellectual, kind, good-natured, trained, and expert; and (3) "slightly" attractive, adventurous, verbal, calm, talkative, extroverted, and aggressive. When asked to conceptualize the ideal political candidate in relationship to themselves, the respondents suggested that the ideal candidate would be (1) "quite" similar in beliefs; (2) "slightly" similar in goals for the country, political party, political attitudes, cultural background, politician preferences, and political beliefs; and (3) "neutral," in terms of similarity in personality, social class, educational background, and goals in life.

Nimmo and Mansfield (1985) demonstrated that the ideal president is conceptualized in terms of the following attributes: honesty, integrity, intelligence, careful analysis in decision making, reasoned statesmanship and leadership, firm issue stands, and a willingness to consult with others.

Temporality of Candidate Image

In order to determine the stability of candidate image, several studies have examined perceptual data on actual candidates over an election campaign. A few additional studies have analyzed the candidate image of particular politicians across election campaigns.

In the Kaid and Hirsch (1973) study described earlier, which identified trustworthiness and demeanor as dimensions of Edmund Muskie's presidential candidate image, the researchers noted a favorable image shift as a function of respondent exposure to a Muskie rally. Measurements of image perception were taken prior to the rally, immediately after the event, and two to three weeks later.

Scott Baudhuin (1974) analyzed image data collected in reference to Richard Nixon at two significant points in time: the first when he was initiating his 1972 presidential campaign against George McGovern, the second just before his August 15, 1973, Watergate address. Through the administration of credibility scales to students and community members, Baudhuin found that Nixon's evaluation changed with time and that similar factor patterns were incorporated in the evaluations. Image perceptions of Nixon, McGovern, and the ideal president were assessed before and after the 1972 general election in a study by Nimmo, Mansfield, and Savage (1974a) through the use of Q-methodology. While the three target images stayed basically stable over the two administrations, Nixon's image became somewhat more negative. More specifically, those respondents identifying themselves as moderate to strong Democrats and liberal McGovern supporters changed their evaluations of Nixon, as the electoral victor, from a positive to a negative one.

Four 1972 presidential candidates (Nixon, McGovern, Muskie, and George Wallace) were evaluated on fourteen bipolar scales in terms of political, leadership, and personal rating categories in a study conducted by Samuel Mudd and Alan Pohlman (1976). The researchers performed a twelve-month follow-up measure of image evaluation for all four candidates, but after eighteen months only Nixon was assessed. Evaluations of Muskie and Wallace did not change over the twelve-month period. Significant differences were found for both Nixon and McGovern, the eventual contenders for the presidency. During the November 1972–November 1973 period, Nixon came to be seen as less influential, credible, logical, and cautious, but more liberal on foreign policy. In contrast, his opponent was perceived as being more cautious, less flexible, and more conservative on foreign policy and domestic issues. After the eighteen-month assessment in May 1974, Nixon was viewed differently by the respondents, being found less influential, credible, powerful, logical, cautious, and articulate, but more homely and liberal on foreign policy.

John Carter (1981) procured image assessments of Carter, Reagan, and John Anderson, as well as the ideal president, before and after the 1980 general election, finding that (1) evaluations of an ideal president stabilized over time; (2) at the second measurement interval, the images of Carter and Reagan generally depolarized, except among strong Carter supporters whose image of Reagan failed to change; (3) evaluations of Carter's leadership ability gained ground with depolarization, particularly among those who opposed him; and (4) greater image stability was noted for experienced voters.

David Switzer and Jo Keller (1981), in another study of the 1980 presidential election campaign, demonstrated that evaluations of Carter by his supporters grew more negative from May through October of the election year. At the same time, Anderson supporters remained stable in the assessments of the types of traits desired and the positive nature of their evaluations within this period.

Hellweg et al. (1990) examined image perceptions of George Bush and Michael Dukakis over four points in time during the 1988 general election campaign, finding that (1) voter conceptualizations of candidate image do not become substantially more factorially complex as the campaign moves closer to election day; and (2) while a candidate may establish an image agenda for an opponent, this occurs at specific points in time and not progressively over time. Using the 1976, 1980, and 1984 presidential debates for analysis, Nimmo and Mansfield (1985) demonstrated that while images of contenders would change either after particular debates or across elections, perceptions of the ideal presidential candidate were more stable.

Utilizing the same semantic differential credibility scales, Hellweg and King (1983) and Hellweg et al. (1988) found interesting comparisons in the image criteria for Reagan between the 1980 and 1984 presidential campaigns as he moved from challenger to incumbent status. As noted in Hellweg et al. (1988), while in the earlier study, reflecting the 1980 campaign, Reagan's factor structure consisted of competence and character, in the second study, reflecting the 1984 campaign, his factor structure was composed of competence, extroversion, and sociability. It is also interesting to note that in the Hellweg et al. (1988, 1990) studies, using the same credibility instrument, Bush's primary image criterion was character, measured at one point in time in the first study and measured at four points in time in the second study.

Finally, Trent et al. (1993), looking at data from 236 journalists and 444 voters who attended presidential political rallies in New Hampshire in 1988 and 1992, found that presidential selection criteria are relatively stable across election campaigns, except that attributes associated with candidates and circumstances surrounding them may cause the importance attached to particular criteria to vary in the minds of the electorate.

Media Studies of Candidate Image

The vast majority of studies centered on mediated portrayals of candidate image have been conducted in the context of candidate advertising and campaign debates. This section examines studies that pertain to general and comparative media concerns.

McCain and Rowand (1973) assessed camera treatment effects in the coverage by the three major networks of speeches presented by 1972 presidential candidates Edward Kennedy and McGovern, specifically in terms of their perceived credibility. While the audio portion of the broadcasts remained the same, the video coverage varied by network. The researchers examined four camera treatment variables: length of shot, image size, camera angle, and severity of camera angle; only the length of the camera shots did not differ significantly among the network broadcasts. On the basis of their data analysis, the researchers noted a significant relationship between the particular broadcast watched and the perceived extroversion level of Edward Kennedy, with no such relationship found for perceptions of leadership or composure.

In another study focusing on the 1972 presidential campaign, Erwin Atwood, Adrian Combs, and Jo Anne Young (1973) measured credibility perceptions of McGovern and Nixon before and after exposure to a half-hour, nationally televised biography created as a news-oriented program. The researchers found that the credibility factor structures reversed for the candidates in the pretest and post-test assessments, with the McGovern factor structure consisting of qualification, dynamism, and safety and the Nixon factor structure being safety, dynamism, and qualification. As a result of exposure to the program, respondents evaluated McGovern more favorably than they did Nixon on the safety and dynamism dimensions; for the qualification dimensions, some differences between the candidates became more apparent, while others disappeared.

Helena Czepiec (1976), using the 1972 presidential campaign as a basis of analysis, demonstrated that political party identification has a greater impact upon image adoption than does news exposure, creating a reinforced identification, particularly among those who are weak party affiliators, who are politically uninvolved, and who have more reasons to view the news than not to. In fact, the researcher found that for both McGovern and Nixon, more positive evaluations resulted from the news exposure, with partisan viewers more favorably disposed toward the candidate of their own party.

Richard Hofstetter, Cliff Zukin, and Terry Buss (1978) found that television exposure to the 1972 presidential campaign resulted in an increased interest in campaign issues and in the personalities of the candidates. The researchers concluded that network news functions to reinforce or intensify preexisting image perceptions of candidates and issue positions. In the context of the 2000 presidential campaign, Benoit, McKinney, and Michael Stephenson (2002) demonstrated that primary debate viewing featuring contenders from either major party can influence voter perceptions of candidate character and policy, as well as change voter intentions or increase their confidence in the choices they make. In a related study, Benoit, McKinney, and Lance Holbert (2001) found that Bush created more favorable perceptions of his character (not his policy stances), while Gore did just the opposite in the first 2000 presidential debate.

Using the 1980 presidential campaign as a basis of analysis, Gary Pike (1984) discovered that low to moderate television-dependency levels were associated with more positive evaluations of Carter and Reagan, while moderate to high levels produced less positive evaluations of the two contenders. Doris Graber (1985) examined media portrayals during the 1984 presidential campaign, concluding that policy skills and negative traits or skills are covered in broadcasts, but without pictorial components, while most messages about candidate character attributes and campaigning skills and most positive messages are projected on television with pictorial components. In another study of the 1984 presidential campaign, Wenmouth Williams, Mitchell Shapiro, Lemuel Scofield, and Craig Cutbirth (1985) demonstrated that while the three major television networks played a fairly important role in setting the campaign issue agenda, they accomplished little in the way of image-setting effects.

Michael Pfau, Tracy Diedrich, Karla Larson, and Kim Van Winkle (1993) examined relational and competence perceptions of candidates during the 1992 presidential primary campaign in relationship to the television coverage provided. Their findings suggest that during the New Hampshire primary coverage, voters across the country are introduced to candidates through television and in the process formulate relational perceptions about the contenders. According to the researchers, as time progresses in the campaign, these perceptions are overworked by ones pertaining to candidate competence, taking on a decisive role *for* the formulation of voter attitudes and candidate preferences.

In a study of the 1988 and 1992 election campaign activities surrounding the New Hampshire primary, Trent et al. (1993) discovered that while there were significant differences between journalists and voters in constructing criteria for selecting a president, these differences were centered on the degree of convictions held about the relative importance of various criteria, rather than on whether or not the particular attributes were desirable or not. King (1995) conducted a content analysis of the campaign news stories and op/ed items during the 1992 general election campaign in the *New York Times*, the *Washington Post*, and the *Los Angeles Times*, noting that (1) in the *New York Times*, 50.3 percent of the news articles and 53.6 percent of the op/ed pieces made a statement about candidate character (8.1 and 41.8 percent explicitly, respectively); (2) in the *Washington Post*, 51.1 percent of the news articles and 50.7 percent of the op/ed pieces discussed candidate character (5.2 and 38.3 percent explicitly, respectively), and (c) in the *Los Angeles Times* 55.1 percent of the news articles and 40.3 percent of the op/ed pieces made mention of candidate character (7.3 and 26.4 percent explicitly, respectively).

Shawn Parry-Giles (2000) builds a case for the media's reliance on stereotypical image constructions through an examination of news recycling and repetition, camera shot positioning, spectator positioning, and the creation of reductionist process as functions of economic incentives and product promotion, specifically in the case of Hillary Rodham Clinton. Terry Robertson, Kristin Froemling, Scott Wells, and Shannon McCraw (1999) argue that women tend to be fragmented toward "male issues" in politics, and since the media focuses on these issues, female representation is adversely affected. Mary Douglass Vavrus (2000) describes the way in which there has been a dramatic shift in news discourse in recent years in conceptualizing the role of women in politics, from the role of "political power wielders" to "soccer moms," as a group of swing voters defined generally by their role as mothers. Trevor Parry-Giles and Shawn Parry-Giles (1996) discuss the increasing intimacy and intrusion in politics through the use of televisual images, featuring self-disclosure and personal revelation (e.g., by appearances of candidates on talk shows). They argue that these appearances may challenge the typical interpersonal distancing between candidate and voter associated with looking "presidential," perhaps dispelling the heroic and mythic personas created by past campaigns, making campaigns more candidate centered than policy centered. The researchers conducted an analysis of three presidential candidates' campaign films to draw their conclusions about how contemporary political contenders engage in personal displays to achieve their political ends. Louden (1994) contends that the 1992 presidential election opened up candidate opportunities for engagement with media audiences otherwise not reached before, through daily talk shows, appearances on programs aimed specifically at young voter audiences, coverage of participatory-oriented town hall meetings, and the like, allowing for candidates to locate "culturally relevant means to preempt the imperious control of news clips and sound bites" (p. 175) associated with traditional news coverage of political campaigns.

A few studies have comparatively analyzed the influence of various media forms in communicating image information about candidates. Larry Kokkeler (1974) tested the relationship between media selection (television, newspapers) and voter perceptions of candidate image. He found that (1) the channel through which the electorate receives campaign information, the type of message received, and candidate image perception are related; (2) while this interaction affects the perceived image of a challenger, it does not do so for the incumbent; (3) the type of message received, rather than the amount of information received, affects candidate image perceptions; and (4) issue information is related to image perceptions only through television, while data regarding personal candidate attributes are related to candidate image perceptions only through newspapers.

Hofstetter et al. (1978), using data from the 1972 presidential campaign, concluded that newspaper reading provided the strongest correlation with imagery; spot advertising and longer paid programming were found to have only a little correlation with imagery. Jack McLeod, Carroll Glynn, and Daniel McDonald (1983) demonstrated, in the context of the 1980 presidential campaign, that television-reliant voters utilized candidate image data more in making decisions about Carter and Reagan than did newspaper-reliant voters. This effect was not found for Anderson.

Future Directions for Candidate Image Research

This chapter has reviewed candidate image research, emanating from the political science, communication, and sociology literature, in connection with American presidential campaigns. In this analysis, the ways in which candidate image has been defined and studied were examined, as were patterns emerging from these studies; the image-voter behavior relationship was explored, particularly in terms of unitary versus nonunitary decision-making models, demographic effects connected with candidates and voters, and the image-issues controversy prevalent in the literature; image components and their stability across single and multiple campaigns were discussed; and mediated portrayals of candidate image were described.

A number of concerns relating to the study of candidate image remain unresolved. In addition, recent studies in particular areas suggest new ways of looking at the construct and advancing research. While the early source valence studies of candidate image pointed to specific dimensions of credibility, homophily, and attraction associated with specific candidates or even ideal candidates, more recent research has indicated a possibility that the construct needs to be viewed more behaviorally (e.g., Husson et al., 1988) and in less static terms. Other research has suggested that such studies need to conceptualize candidate image contextually in terms of what is occurring during the campaign that might affect the determination of what perceptual criteria are important in evaluating a particular candidate (Trent et al., 1993).

The majority of candidate image studies assume a unitary view of the voter decision-making process, whether this involves a comparison between candidates or a comparison to an ideal conceptualization. Research by Hellweg and King (1983) and by Hellweg et al. (1988, 1990) indicates that this process may be more complex, involving the use of candidate-specific criteria.

The increasing prevalence of female and minority candidates and officeholders provides an important area for research. The candidacies of Geraldine Ferraro, Jesse Jackson, Douglas Wilder, Hillary Rodham Clinton, Elizabeth Dole, and Al Sharpton, among others, have offered opportunities in this regard. Research by Shawn Parry-Giles (2000), Robertson et al. (1999), and Vavrus (2000) suggests a myriad of possibilities for gender effects research on candidate image in the political context.

Another unresolved area in candidate-image research remains in the image-issue controversy. Hacker and Zakahi (1994) suggest not viewing issues as being isolated from candidate personality assessments. A review of the study by Trent et al. (1993) would seem to support this position. Roger Aden (1988) furthers the view that issue and image are not separate entities, but rather issue is part of image. Likewise, Hullett (1998) describes them as integrally related. Louden (1994) argues that issue information informs image evaluation. Future research needs to determine exactly how the two work together in the determination of candidate preferences by voters.

It could be argued that for some elections, image has become "the issue" of the campaign. Examples would include campaigns where controversy or uncertainty about a particular candidate has been a primary focus—in particular, where concerns have arisen over an incumbent's or challenger's character (e.g., Edward Kennedy), trustworthiness (e.g., Richard Nixon), competence (e.g., Jimmy Carter), age (e.g., Ronald Reagan), or personal affairs (e.g., Nelson Rockefeller, Thomas Eagleton, Gary Hart, and Bill Clinton). In contrast, other campaigns have seemed single-issue focused, such as the 1968 presidential campaign when the primary questions in the minds of the electorate were how to resolve the Vietnam conflict and which candidate could effect such a resolution. This and the evidence presented in the Trent et al. (1993) study suggest that candidate image is campaign specific.

Only a few studies have examined candidate image across campaigns—in particular, in terms of candidates who have run for president more than once (e.g., George McGovern, Richard Nixon, Jimmy Carter, Ronald Reagan, George Bush, Jesse Jackson, Robert Dole, Hubert Humphrey, Gary Hart, and Jerry Brown). The progression from challenger to incumbent status in terms of perceived images could be an integral part of this research.

Pfau et al. (1993) suggest the importance of looking at candidate image based on initial perceptions created at the time of the New Hampshire primary campaign and measuring the shift in image criteria as the campaign progresses. Similarly, Savage (1986) and Trent (1986) point to the importance of understanding the surfacing period and how the American public formulates initial images of politicians announcing their candidacy. While some research has been conducted to test the temporal effects of candidate image perception, longitudinal studies examining image perceptions across candidates over entire campaigns to see how they more fully develop as the contenders become increasingly well known across the country and as the field narrows down to the general election campaign would seem worthy of pursuit.

Hellweg et al. (1990) found some evidence for candidate-image agenda setting by George Bush in the 1988 presidential election. One could intuitively make the argument that as the candidates engage in dialogue during the campaign through their independent speeches, their campaign advertisements, and their debates, each attempts to focus the public on discrediting elements of the opponent, while attempting to gain support for his or her candidacy. The effects that an opponent has on the formulation and maintenance of a candidate-generated image are worthy of study, as is the potential ceiling effect that the media may reach in covering an image-related story on a political contender (e.g., whether or not the public was overly saturated with stories of Bill Clinton's draft status, the Gennifer Flowers story in the 1992 presidential campaign, and so on). Marya Doerfel and Pamela Marsh's (2003) study of the 1992 presidential debates invites studies of the third-party factor in the way that assessments of candidates are played against one another differently when there are three parties involved in a debate.

Comparable media studies on image perception have examined television and newspapers as vehicles of campaign information. As the 1992 presidential election campaign illustrated, there are a growing number of ways to reach voters beyond the nightly newscast sound bites, campaign advertisements, and candidate debates. New candidate venues such as talk-show interviews have encouraged the increase of candidate-controlled messages, allowing for a likely increase in intimate, self-disclosure (Parry-Giles & Parry-Giles, 1996), perhaps changing the way images are developed with the public. Such appearances may "humanize" candidates to the public in various ways, the use of radio talk shows having positively correlated with images of Robert Dole and negatively correlated (along with use of the Internet) for Bill Clinton in the context of the 1996 presidential election (Johnson, Braima, & Sothirajah, 1999). This bears further investigation. Another area of interest is the increasing role of the journalist as adversary of the politician as opposed to objective commentator (Valentino, Buhr, & Beckmann, 2001) in campaign coverage and image interpretation.

Note

Editor's Note: This is a revision of the 1995 chapter by this author, "Campaign and Candidate Images in American Presidential Elections," in *Candidate Images in Presidential Elections*, edited by K. Hacker, 1–17 (Westport, Conn.: Praeger, 1995).

References

Aden, Roger C. 1988. "The 'Irrational' Voter: Toward a Realistic Model of Political Communication." Paper presented at the International Communication Association convention, New Orleans, Louisiana, May.

Allen, Jerry L., Joan O'Mara, and Ben Judd. 1985. "Changes in the Evaluation of Female Candidates from Ella Grasso to Geraldine Ferraro." Paper presented at the International Communication Association convention, Honolulu, Hawaii, May.

Andersen, Peter A., and Robert J. Kibler. 1978. "Candidate Valence as a Predictor of Voter Preferences." *Human Communication Research* 5: 4–14.

Andersen, Peter A., and William R. Todd. 1975. "Scales for the Measurement of Homophily with Public Figures." Paper presented at the International Communication Association convention, Chicago, April.

Andersen, Peter A., and William R. Todd de Mancillas. 1978. "Scales for the Measurement of Homophily with Public Figures." *Southern Speech Communication Journal* 43: 169–179.

Anderson, Karrin Vasby. 2002. "From Spouses to Candidates: Hillary Rodham Clinton, Elizabeth Dole and the Gendered Office of U.S. President." *Rhetoric & Public Affairs* 5: 105–132.

Anderson, Robert. 1973. "The Characterization Model for Rhetorical Criticism of Political Image Campaigns." *Western Journal of Speech Communication* 37: 75–86.

Atwood, L. Erwin, Adrian Combs, and Jo Anne Young. 1973. "Multiple Facets of Candidate Image Structure: Effects of the McGovern Television Biography." Paper presented at the Association for Education on Journalism convention, Fort Collins, Colorado, August.

Baudhuin, E. Scott. 1974. "From Campaign to Watergate: Nixon's Communication Image." *Western Speech* 38: 182–189.

Baxter, Leslie A., Thomas J. Young, and John R. Bittner. 1973. "Identifying the Charisma Factor in Political Communication." Paper presented at the International Communication Association Convention, Montreal, Quebec, April.

Bennett, W. Lance. 1977. "The Ritualistic and Pragmatic Basis of Political Campaign Discourse." *Quarterly Journal of Speech* 63: 219–238.

Benoit, William L., Mitchell S. McKinney, and R. Lance Holbert. 2001. "Beyond Learning and Persona: Extending the Scope of Presidential Debate Effects." *Communication Monographs* 68: 259–273.

Benoit, William L., Mitchell S. McKinney, and Michael T. Stephenson. 2002. "Effects of Watching Primary Debates in the 2000 U.S. Presidential Campaign." *Journal of Communication* 52: 316–331.

Benoit, William L., David J. Webber, and Julie Berman. 1998. "Effects of Presidential Debate Watching and Ideology on Attitudes and Knowledge." *Argumentation and Advocacy* 34: 162–172.

Berlo, David K., James B. Lemert, and Robert J. Mertz. 1969–1970. "Dimensions for Evaluating the Acceptability of Message Sources." *Public Opinion Quarterly* 33: 563–576.

Bowman, Ann. 1980. "Physical Attractiveness and Electability: Looks and Votes." Paper presented at the Midwest Political Science Association convention, Chicago, April.

Boyd, Richard W. 1969. "Presidential Elections: An Explanation of Voting Defection." *American Political Science Review* 63: 488–514.

Brooks, William D. 1967. "A Field Study of the Johnson and Goldwater Campaign Speeches in Pittsburgh." *Southern Speech Journal* 32: 273–281.

Brummett, Barry. 1981. "Gastronomic References, Synecdoche, and Political Images." *Quarterly Journal of Speech* 67: 138–145.

Campbell, James. 1983. "Candidate Image Evaluations: Influence and Rationalization in Presidential Primaries." *American Politics Quarterly* 11: 293–313.

Campbell, James E. 1979. "Jimmy Carter and the Rhetoric of Charisma." *Central States Speech Journal* 30: 174–186.

Carlson, James M. 1984. "The Impact of Ethnicity on Candidate Image." *Polity* 16: 667–672.

Carlson, James M., and Mary Kay Boring. 1981. "Androgyny and Politics: The Effects of Winning and Losing on Candidate Image." *International Political Science Review* 2: 481–491.

Carter, John J. 1981. "Voter Images in the 1980 Election: A Panel Study Using Q Technique." Ph.D. diss., University of Missouri, Columbia.

Clark, Thomas D. 1979. "An Exploration of Generic Aspects of Contemporary American Campaign Organizations." *Central States Speech Journal* 30: 122–133.

Czepiec, Helena. 1976. "The Impact of Television News and Party Identification on Candidate Image Adoption." Ph.D. diss., Ohio State University, Columbus.

Davis, Dwight K. 1981. "Issues Information and Connotation in Candidate Imagery: Evidence from a Laboratory Experiment." *International Political Science Review* 2: 461–479.

DeLancey, Charles A., and David L. Swanson. 1981. "The Development of Impressions of Candidates in the 1980 Presidential Campaign: A Constructivist Perspective." Paper presented at the Speech Communication Association convention, Anaheim, California, November.

Dennis, Jack, Steven H. Chaffee, and Sun Y. Choe. 1979. "Impact on Partisan, Image, and Issue Voting." In *The Great Debates: Carter vs. Ford 1976*, edited by Sidney Kraus, 314–330. Bloomington: Indiana University Press.

Doerfel, Marya L., and Pamela S. Marsh. 2003. "Candidate-Issue Positioning in the Context of Presidential Debates." *Journal of Applied Communication Research* 31: 212–237.

Fagen, Richard R. 1966. *Politics and Communication*. Boston: Little, Brown.

Garramone, Gina M. 1983. "Issue versus Image Orientation and Effects of Political Advertising." *Communication Research* 10: 59–76.

Gopoian, David. 1980. "The Determinants of Issue-Voting in Presidential Primaries." Paper presented at the Midwest Science Association convention, Chicago, April.

Graber, Doris A. 1985. "Television Coverage of the 1984 Campaign." Paper presented at the Speech Communication Association convention, Denver, Colorado, November.

Greenstein, Fred I. 1965. "Popular Images of the President." *American Journal of Psychiatry* 122: 523–529.

Hacker, Kenneth, and Walter Zakahi. 1994. "Reconsidering the Issue-Image Dichotomy: A Statistical Test of Key Candidate Image Construct Assumptions." Paper presented at the Western States Communication Association Convention, San Jose, California, February.

Hacker, Kenneth L., Walter R. Zakahi, Maury J. Giles, and Shaun McQuitty. 2000. "Components of Candidate Images: Statistical Analysis of the Issue-Persona Dichotomy in the Presidential Campaign of 1996." *Communication Monographs* 67: 227–238.

Harrison, Teresa M., Timothy D. Stephen, William Husson, and B. J. Fehr. 1991. "Image versus Issues in the 1984 Presidential Election: Differences between Men and Women." *Human Communication Research* 18: 209–227.

Hedlund, Ronald D., Patricia K. Freeman, Keith E. Hamm, and Robert M. Stein. 1979. "The Electability of Women Candidates: The Effects of Sex Stereotype." *Journal of Politics* 41: 513–524.

Hellweg, Susan A. 1978. "The Measurement of Gerald Ford against the Ideal Political Candidate as a Function of Respondent Political Party Affiliation in the Context of the 1976 General Election." Paper presented at the International Communication Association convention, Chicago, April.

———. 1979. "An Examination of Voter Conceptualizations of the Ideal Political Candidate." *Southern Speech Communication Journal* 44: 375–385.

———. 1995. "Campaign and Candidate Images in American Presidential Elections." In *Candidate Images in Presidential Elections*, edited by K. Hacker, 1–17. Westport, Conn.: Praeger.

Hellweg, S. A., G. N. Dionisopoulos, and D. B. Kugler. 1989. "Political Candidate Image: A State-of-the-Art Review." In *Progress in Communication Sciences*, vol. 9, edited by B. Dervin and M. J. Voight, 43–78. Norwood, N.J.: Ablex.

Hellweg, Susan A., and Stephen W. King. 1983. "Comparative Evaluation of Political Candidates: Implications for the Voter Decision Making Process." *Central States Speech Journal* 34: 134–138.

Hellweg, S. A., S. W. King, and S. E. Williams. 1988. "Comparative Candidate Evaluation as a Function of Election Level and Candidate Incumbency." *Communication Reports* 1: 76–85.

Hellweg, Susan A., William A. Walker, Stephen W. King, and Brian H. Spitzberg. 1990. "Comparative Candidate Evaluation: Voter Intention as a Function of the Grounding of Image Criteria and Image Agenda Setting by Candidates." Paper presented at the International Communication Association convention, Dublin, Ireland, June.

Hofstetter, C. Richard, Cliff Zukin, and Terry R. Buss. 1978. "Political Imagery and Information in an Age of Television." *Journalism Quarterly* 55: 562–569.

Houston, David A., and Kelly Doan. 1999. "Can You Back That Up? Evidence (or Lack Thereof) for the Effects of Negative and Positive Political Communication." *Media Psychology* 1: 191–206.

Huang, Li-Ning. 2000. "Examining Candidate Information Search Processes: The Impact of Processing Goals and Sophistication." *Journal of Communication* 50: 93–114.

Hullett, Craig R. 1998. "Audience Recall of Issues and Image in Congressional Debates." *Argumentation and Advocacy* 34: 189–203.

Husson, William, Timothy Stephen, Teresa M. Harrison, and B. J. Fehr. 1988. "An Interpersonal Communication Perspective on Images of Political Candidates." *Human Communication Research* 14: 397–421.

Jackson, John S., and Roy E. Miller. 1973. "Campaign Issues, Candidate Images, and Party Identification at Multiple Electoral Levels." Paper presented at the Midwest Political Science Association convention, Chicago, May.

Johnson, Thomas J., Mahmoud A. Braima, and Jayanthi Sothirajah. 1999. "Doing the Traditional Media Sidestep: Comparing the Effects of the Internet and Other Nontraditional Media with Traditional Media in the 1996 Presidential Campaign. *Journalism and Mass Communication Quarterly* 76: 99–123.

Kaid, Lynda L., and Robert O. Hirsch. 1973. "Selective Exposure and Candidate Image: A Field Study over Time." *Central States Speech Journal* 24: 48–51.

Kendall, Kathleen E., and June O. Yum. 1984. "Persuading the Blue-Collar Voters: Issues, Images and Homophily." In *Communication Yearbook 8*, edited by Robert N. Bostrom, 707–722. Beverly Hills, Calif.: Sage.

Kennamer, David J., and Stephen H. Chaffee. 1981. "Communication of Political Information during Early Presidential Primaries: Cognition, Affect, and Uncertainty." Paper presented at the International Communication Association convention, Minneapolis, Minnesota, May.

King, Elliot G. 1995. "The Flawed Characters in the Campaign: Prestige Newspaper Assessments of the 1992 Presidential Candidates' Integrity and Competence." *Journalism and Mass Communication Quarterly* 72: 84–97.

Kjeldahl, William O., Carl Carmichael, and Robert J. Mertz. 1971. "Factors in a Presidential Candidate's Image." *Speech Monographs* 38: 129–131.

Kokkeler, Larry. 1974. "Source, Message, Channel and Candidate Image: An Exploration Study." Paper presented at the International Communication Association convention, New Orleans, Louisiana, April.

Kraus, Sidney, and Raymond G. Smith. 1977. "Issues and Images." In *The Great Debates: Kennedy vs. Nixon 1960*, edited by Sidney Kraus, 289–312. Bloomington: Indiana University Press.

Leff, Michael, and Gerald P. Mohrmann. 1974. "Lincoln at Cooper Union: A Rhetorical Analysis of the Text." *Quarterly Journal of Speech* 60: 346–358.

Louden, Allan. 1994. "Voter Rationality and Media Excess: Image in the 1992 Presidential Campaign." In *The 1992 Presidential Campaign: A Communication Perspective*, edited by R. Denton, 169–187. Westport, Conn.: Praeger.

Maddox, William S. 1980. "Candidate Images among Voters and Nonvoters in 1976." *American Politics Quarterly* 8: 209–220.

Marshall, Thomas R. 1983. "Evaluating Presidential Nominees: Opinion Polls, Issues, and Personalities." *Western Political Quarterly* 3: 61–83.

McCain, Thomas A., and Paul Rowand. 1973. "The Effect of Camera Treatment on Political Speakers' Credibility: Network Television Coverage of the Speeches of Ted Kennedy and George McGovern to the 1972 Democratic National Convention." Paper presented to the International Communication Association convention, Montreal, April.

McCroskey, James C. 1966. "Scales for the Measurement of Ethos." *Speech Monographs* 33: 65–72.

McCroskey, James C., Thomas Jensen, and Cynthia Todd. 1972. "The Generalizability of Source Credibility Scales for Public Figures." Paper presented at the Speech Communication Association convention, Chicago, December.

McGee, Michael C. 1978. "Not Men but Measures: The Origins and Support of an Ideological Principle." *Quarterly Journal of Speech* 64: 141–156.

McLeod, Jack M., Carroll J. Glynn, and Daniel G. McDonald. 1983. "Issues and Images: The Influence of Media Reliance in Voting Decisions." *Communication Research* 10: 37–58.

Miller, Arthur H., Martin P. Wattenberg, and Oksana Malanchuk. 1985. "Cognitive Representations of Candidate Assessments." In *Political Communication Yearbook 1984*, edited by Keith R. Sanders, Lynda Lee Kaid, and Dan Nimmo, 183–210. Carbondale: Southern Illinois University Press.

Mudd, Samuel, and Alan Pohlman. 1976. "Sensitivity of Image Profile and Image Clarity Measures to Change: Nixon through Watergate." *Journal of Applied Psychology* 61: 223–228.

Natchez, Peter B., and Irwin C. Bupp. 1968. "Candidates, Issues, and Voters." *Public Policy* 17: 409–437.

Newman, Bruce I. 2001. "Image-Manufacturing in the USA: Recent U.S. Presidential Elections and Beyond." *European Journal of Marketing* 35: 966–970.

Nimmo, Dan. 1974. *Popular images of politics: A taxonomy*. Englewood Cliffs, N.J.: Prentice-Hall.
———. 1976. "Political Image Makers and the Mass Media." *Annals of the American Academy of Political and Social Science* 427: 33–44.
Nimmo, Dan, and Michael W. Mansfield. 1985. "Change and Persistence in Candidate Images: Presidential Debates across 1976, 1980, and 1984." Paper presented at the Speech Communication Association convention, Denver, Colorado, November.
Nimmo, Dan, Michael Mansfield, and Robert L. Savage. 1974a. "Effects of Victory or Defeat upon the Images of Political Candidates." *Experimental Study of Politics* 3: 1–30.
———. 1974b. "Partisanship, Communications, and the Images of Presidential Candidates, 1952–1972." Paper presented at the International Communication Association convention, New Orleans, Louisiana, April.
Nimmo, Dan, and Robert L. Savage. 1971. "Political Images and Political Perceptions." *Experimental Study of Politics* 1: 1–36.
———. 1975. "Image Topologies in a Senatorial Campaign: A Comparison of Forced vs. Free Distribution Data." *Political Methodology* 2: 293–318.
———. 1976. *Candidates and Their Images: Concepts, Methods, and Findings*. Pacific Palisades, Calif.: Goodyear.
Nobles, Donald G., and Dennis F. Gunderson. 1976. "Relationships among Sex of Candidate, Sex of Voter, and Candidate Acceptability." Paper presented at the International Communication Association convention, Portland, Oregon, April.
Parry-Giles, Shawn J. 2000. "Mediating Hillary Rodham Clinton: Television News Practices and Image-Making in the Postmodern Age." *Critical Studies in Media Communication* 17: 205–226.
Parry-Giles, Trevor, and Shawn J. Parry-Giles. 1996. "Political Scopophilia, Presidential Campaigning, and the Intimacy of American Politics." *Communication Studies* 47: 191–205.
Pfau, Michael, Tracy Diedrich, Karla M. Larson, and Kim M. Van Winkle. 1993. "Relational and Competence Perceptions of Presidential Candidates during the Primary Election Campaigns." Paper presented at the International Communication Association convention, Washington, D.C., May.
Pike, Gary R. 1984. "Television Dependency, Candidate Images, and Voting Behavior in the 1980 Election." Paper presented at the International Communication Association convention, San Francisco, May.
———. 1985. "Toward a Transactional Model of Political Images: Collective Images of the Candidate in the 1984 Election." Paper presented at the International Communication Association convention, Honolulu, Hawaii, May.
Rarick, David L., Mary B. Duncan, David G. Lee, and Laurinda W. Porter. 1977. "The Carter Persona: An Empirical Analysis of the Rhetorical Visions of Campaign '76." *Quarterly Journal of Speech* 63: 258–273.
Roberts, Churchill. 1981. "From Primary to the Presidency: A Panel Study of Images and Issues in the 1976 Election." *Western Journal of Speech Communication* 45: 60–70.
Robertson, Terry, Kristen Froemling, Scott Wells, and Shannon McCraw. 1999. "Political Advertising, Women, Sexes, Candidates, Political Campaigns." *Communication Quarterly* 47: 333–342.

Rose, Ernest D., and Douglas Fuchs. 1968. "Reagan vs. Brown: A TV Image Playback." *Journal of Broadcasting* 12: 247–260.

Rudd, Robert. 1986. "Issues as Image in Political Campaign Commercials." *Western Journal of Speech Communication* 50: 102–118.

Rusk, Jerrold G., and Herbert F. Weisberg. 1972. "Perceptions of Presidential Candidates: Implications for Electoral Change." *Midwest Journal of Political Science* 16: 388–410.

Sapiro, Virginia. 1981–1982. "If U.S. Senator Baker Were a Woman: An Experimental Study of Candidate Images." *Political Psychology* 3: 61–83.

Savage, Robert L. 1986. "Statesmanship, Surfacing and Sometimes Stumbling: Constructing Candidate Images during the Early Campaign." *Political Communication Review* 2: 43–57.

Sears, David O. 1969. "Political Behavior." In *The Handbook of Social Psychology*, vol. 5, edited by Gardner Lindzey and Elliot Aronson, 315–458. Reading, Mass.: Addison-Wesley.

Shabad, Goldie, and Kristi Andersen. 1979. "Candidate Evaluations by Men and Women." *Public Opinion Quarterly* 43: 18–35.

Siegel, Roberta S. 1964. "Effect of Partisanship on the Perception of Political Candidates." *Public Opinion Quarterly* 2: 483–496.

———. 1966. "Image of the American Presidency: Part II of an Exploration into Popular Views of Presidential Power." *Midwest Journal of Political Science* 10: 123–137.

Stamm, Keith, Alice Burgess, Michael Jordan, and Susan Lim. 1985. "Voter's Characterizations of Presidential Candidates: A Constructivist's Approach to Political Communication." Paper presented at the International Communication Association convention, Honolulu, Hawaii, May.

Switzer, David E., and Jo E. Keller. 1981. "The Formation and Modification of Voter's Impressions of the 1980 Presidential Candidates." Paper presented at the International Communication Association convention, Minneapolis, Minnesota, May.

Tannenbaum, Percy H., Bradley S. Greenberg, and Fred R. Silverman. 1977. "Candidate Images." In *The Great Debates: Kennedy vs. Nixon 1960*, edited by Sidney Kraus, 271–288. Bloomington: Indiana University Press.

Trent, Judith S. 1986. "They Keep Running and the Rules Keep Changing: An Overview of the Early Campaign from 1972 to 1988." *Political Communication Review* 2: 7–17.

Trent, Judith S., Paul A. Mongeau, Jimmie D. Trent, K. E. Kendall, and Ronald B. Cushing. 1993. "The Ideal Candidate: A Study of the Desired Attributes of the Public and the Media across Two Presidential Campaigns." *American Behavioral Scientist* 37: 225–239.

Valentino, Nicholas A., Thomas A. Buhr, and Matthew N. Beckmann. 2001. "When the Frame Is the Game: Revisiting the Impact of 'Strategic' Campaign Coverage on Citizens' Information Retention." *Journalism and Mass Communication Quarterly* 78: 93–112.

Vancil, David L., and Sue D. Pendell. 1984. "Winning Presidential Debates: An Analysis of Criteria Influencing Audience Responses." *Western Journal of Speech Communication* 48: 62–74.

Vavrus, Mary Douglass. 2000. "From Women of the Year to 'Soccer Moms': The Case of the Incredible Shrinking Women." *Political Communication* 17: 192–213.

Wahl, Charles E. 1959. "The Relationship between Primary and Secondary Identification: Psychiatry and the Group Sciences." In *American Voting Behavior*, edited by Eugene Burdick and Arthur J. Brodbeck, 262–280. Glencoe, Ill.: Free Press.

Wakshlag, Jacob J., and Nadyne G. Edison. 1979. "Attraction, Credibility, Perceived Similarity, and the Image of Public Figures." *Communication Quarterly* 27: 27–34.

Weisberg, Herbert F., and Jerrold G. Rusk. 1970. "Dimensions of Candidate Evaluation." *American Political Science Review* 64: 1167–1185.

Williams, Wenmouth, Jr., Mitchell Shapiro, Lemuel Scofield, and Craig Cutbirth. 1985. "Agenda Setting Research in the 1984 Presidential Campaign: The Effects of the Media on Issues and Images." Paper presented at the Speech Communication Association convention, Denver, Colorado, November.

Zandpour, Frank. 1985. "1984 Presidential Candidates, Voters' Cognitive Styles and Preferences." Paper presented at the International Communication Association convention, Honolulu, Hawaii, May.

2
Presidential Candidates' Personal Qualities: Computer Content Analysis

William L. Benoit and John P. McHale

IMAGE IN POLITICAL COMMUNICATION can refer to the impression of a candidate for office held by voters. These impressions are formed out of a myriad of messages—messages from the candidate, from opposing candidates, from the news media, and from friends and acquaintances. This chapter focuses on the part of a candidate's image that pertains to his or her character (personal qualities).

Political candidates' personal qualities are a basic building block in the public's construction of candidate images, consistent with the overall theme of this book. Impressions of the candidates' images are based on voters' perceptions of the personal qualities that candidates display—or boast about in their campaign messages. We suggest that candidate image constructs are based more on perceptions of personal qualities as aspects of candidate character than on the candidates' policy stands. Walter Zakahi's chapter (this volume) identifies the role that image plays in debates. In order to supplement that work, we focus on television spots as a vital venue for presentation of candidate image. An important caveat to our work is acknowledgment that the term *image* is derived from the Latin *imago*, an imitation or copy: The candidate image is a construct developed by voters, based on messages from the candidates and other sources, and a candidate's image is not necessarily an accurate reflection of the candidate's "true" personality.

The literature in the realm of political communication typically distinguishes between the two concepts of issue and image (see, e.g., Hacker, Zakahi, Giles, & McQuitty, 2000; Hinck, 1993; Leff & Mohrmann, 1974; Rudd, 1986; Stuckey & Antczak, 1995). The functional theory of political campaign discourse (Benoit,

1999, 2000, 2001; Benoit, Blaney, & Pier, 1998, 2000; Benoit & Brazeal, 2002; Benoit & Harthcock, 1999; Benoit et al., 2002; Benoit, Wells, Pier, & Blaney, 1999; Brazeal & Benoit, 2001) posits that political campaign messages can address two topics: policy (issue) and character (image). William Benoit and Allison Harthcock (1999) distinguish between policy and character in this fashion:

> Themes that concern governmental action (past, current, or future) and problems amenable to governmental action were considered *policy* utterances.
>
> Themes that address characteristics, traits, abilities, or attributes of the candidates (or parties) were considered *character* utterances. (p. 346, emphasis in original)

This theory further subdivides each topic into finer subdivisions of policy (*past deeds*—accomplishments or failures; *future plans*—campaign promises or means; and *general goals*—objectives or ends) and character (*personal qualities*—like courage, compassion, or honesty; *leadership ability*—including experience in elective office; and *ideals*—principles or values). We focus on character generally and on personal qualities specifically in this chapter (for a review of research on candidate image, see Hellweg, 1995).

The topic of presidential candidates' personal qualities merits our consideration for several reasons. First, a substantial number of voters indicate that the most important determinant of their presidential vote is personal character. Richard Boyd (1969), analyzing data from the National Election Studies surveys from 1956 through 1964, concluded that "attitudes toward the candidate [as opposed to attitudes toward the party or toward policy] are the major statistical explanation of voting defection" (p. 63). In other words, when partisans break ranks to support the candidate of the other party, character is the primary reason. During the 1996 presidential campaign, between 24 and 27 percent of respondents reported that character was more important than positions on the issues when they choose a president (NBC/*Wall Street Journal*, 1996). Thus, a candidate's personal character is a significant factor in presidential vote choice for many voters.

Character may be even more important in presidential primary campaigns. Thomas Marshall (1984), for example, indicated that "personal qualities are stronger predictors of voter choices during presidential primaries than issues or ideology" (p. 756). Daniel Williams, Stephen Weber, Fordon Haaland, Donald Mueller, and Robert Craig (1976), studying the 1972 New Hampshire primary, found that most respondents indicated that the candidates' personal attributes were more important to their vote decision than issue positions. After the investigation and impeachment of President Clinton, character may have become even more important in the 2000 primary: "A year after Clinton's trial, a *Los Angeles Times* poll revealed that nearly three-quarters of Iowa caucus-goers say they were supporting their candidate because of a personal trait rather than his stance on the issues" ("Character," 2000, p. 7A). Of course, given that the two major political parties tend to have different policy emphases (Petrocik, 1996), one would expect fewer policy differences to arise in a contest between candidates of the same party (in the primary campaign) than between candidates of different parties (in the general campaign). Thus, presidential candidates may stress character in the primary season even more than in the general election campaign.

However, even those voters who are more concerned with policy or issues have strong reasons to carefully consider the candidates' personal character. Candidates are well known for making campaign promises. Those promises mean nothing if we cannot trust the candidates who are elected to work to fulfill their campaign promises. One Iowa citizen in 2000 provided this anecdotal evidence to support this claim: "Honesty and integrity are it for me.... Health care and all that is important, but nothing they promise means much if they're lying about it" ("Character," 2000, p. 7A). Furthermore, it seems likely that unexpected situations will arise during a president's four years in the White House. Because such events are unexpected, the presidential candidates probably will not have taken positions (or made campaign promises) on what to do in such unforeseen situations. When the unexpected occurs, like the spike in gasoline prices in 2001 or the terrible tragedy of 9/11, voters must be able to *trust* the president to enact an appropriate policy response.

Finally, studies reveal that presidential candidates devote a substantial portion of their campaign discourse to discussing their—and their opponent's—personal qualities. For example, Benoit et al. (1999) found that 44 percent of the utterances in presidential nomination acceptance addresses from 1960 to 1996 pertained to character rather than policy. Benoit (1999) revealed that four in every ten comments in presidential television spots from 1952 to 1996 concern character. William Benoit et al. (2002) found that 37 percent of utterances in presidential primary debates from 1948 to 2000 concerned character. Clearly, presidential candidates believe that character matters. However, precisely *what* they talk about when they discuss personal qualities is not yet well understood.

Literature Review

Several studies have taken up the challenge of investigating particular qualities or traits of candidates. Marshall (1984) identified four categories that are relevant to personal qualities: trust, leadership, age, and class. Of these categories, two are demographic variables (age and class) and one is leadership, which we conceptualize as distinctive from a candidate's personal qualities.

Roberta Sigel (1966) indicated that six important qualities for a president were honesty, intelligence, independence, careful spending, problem-solving ideas, and sympathy for the common man. Thrift (being a "careful spender") and problem solving pertain more to policy or leadership rather than personal qualities (for a discussion of leadership, see Smith & Smith, 1994); however, honesty, intelligence, independence, and sympathy are personal qualities. Arthur Miller, Martin Wattenberg, and Oksana Malanchuk (1986) developed five general categories of candidate personality evaluation: competence, integrity, reliability, charisma, and a personal dimension (personal background and appearance).

Judith Trent, Cady Short-Thompson, Paul Mongeau, Andrew Nusz, and Jimmie Trent (2001; see also Trent, Mongeau, Trent, Kendall, & Cushing, 1993; Trent, Trent, Mongeau, & Short-Thompson, 1997) have studied the qualities of the "ideal candidate." They advanced the eleven categories of having experience in office, being an energetic and aggressive leader, being faithful to one's spouse, being a forceful public speaker, having moral character, talking about the nation's problems, being honest, being younger than 65, being male, remaining calm and cautious, and having solutions to problems. One trait (younger than 65) is a demographic variable, and talking about the nation's problems concerns policy or issues rather than a character trait of the candidates.

This review of the literature on perceptions of candidate personal qualities supports two claims. First, there is scant agreement in the literature concerning the nature of personal qualities in this literature. To integrate the lists of candidate character traits reviewed earlier, we first bracketed those traits that concern the candidates' *leadership ability* (leadership, competence, experience, problem-solving ideas) rather than their *personal qualities*, *demographics* (age, class, personal background, and appearance), and *policy* (talks about the nation's problems, has solutions to problems, is a careful spender). This procedure leaves honesty, intelligence, independence, and sympathy (Sigel, 1966); trust (Marshall, 1984); integrity and compassion (Kinder, 1986); integrity, reliability, and charisma (Miller et al., 1986); and being faithful to one's spouse, a forceful speaker, moral, honest, calm, and cautious (Trent et al., 1997). Obviously, there is little overlap in these lists: No trait appears in all of the lists of personal qualities, and only integrity and honesty appear in as many as three of the six lists. Therefore, by no means has the literature developed a consensus on the nature of presidential candidates' personal qualities. Second, research has not focused on what the *candidates' discourse* says about their personal qualities.

We used grounded theory (the method of constant comparison) to develop a typology of personal qualities appearing in their sample of general presidential television spots from 1952 to 1996 (Benoit & McHale, 2003). Television spots were used because ads permit candidates to emphasize the topics they choose (unlike debates, which are largely structured by questions) and because they tend to be developed for a more general audience (than acceptance addresses). We (2003) identified four general dimensions (each with specific subdivisions): morality, empathy, sincerity, and drive. Then we employed computer content analysis to determine the frequency with which these traits were discussed in presidential primary and general television spots. We found a positive correlation between the frequency with which personal qualities appear in primary and general spots. However, empathy was discussed more in the primary and morality more in the general campaign. We also contrasted spots from Republicans and Democrats. Republicans used more sincerity than Democrats, whereas Democrats discussed empathy more than their counterparts. Finally, winners (those who won their party's nomination in the primary; those who won the general election) discussed drive more than losers, whereas losers discussed empathy and morality more than winners.

However, our initial study, exploratory in nature, leaves several questions unanswered. First, it is limited to television spot texts: We have no idea how these personal qualities are discussed in other message forms. Second, it fails to contrast incumbents and challengers (in general campaign messages). Third, it is limited to presidential campaign messages. Finally, it is exclusively concerned with what candidates discuss in their campaign messages, ignoring voter preferences. This study will extend our 2003 study (Benoit & McHale, 2003) by investigating these questions.

Research Questions

RQ1. How are the four dimensions of presidential candidates' personal qualities (sincerity, empathy, morality, and drive) used in presidential campaign message forms?

RQ2. Do incumbents and challengers differ in their discussion of personal qualities?

RQ3. Are there longitudinal trends in the discussion of character by presidential candidates?

RQ4. Do presidential and congressional candidates differ in their discussion of personal qualities in television spots?

RQ5. What personal qualities are most important to voters?

The first three research questions will be answered in study 1, the fourth research question will be the subject of study 2, and the final question will be addressed in study 3.

Study 1

Sample

Table 2.1 displays the sample of campaign messages analyzed: 910 primary and 918 general television spots from 1952 to 2000, 31 presidential primary and 18 general debates (1960, 1976–2000), and 26 acceptance addresses (1952–2000). This provides an extensive and longitudinal set of key presidential campaign messages. The sample of congressional television spots available for analysis is smaller, consisting of 80 spots from 1984 to 2000.

Method

This study performed computer content analyses on these political campaign texts. We (Benoit & McHale, 2003) developed a list of synonyms and related terms that we used as a search term list for computer content analysis. We replicate their procedures here with our sample of texts.

One concern in content analysis is the quality of the categories (the word list in computer content analysis). The procedures employed to develop these categories attest to the quality of our categories. Use of utterances from candidates about their personal qualities to develop categories means that these word lists are *relevant* to our question. Using every unique utterance to develop categories means that the word lists are *exhaustive* (at least for presidential TV spots). The method of constant comparison (and particularly the rule that excerpts classified in one category are to be distinct from the excerpts placed in other categories) means that our categories are *mutually exclusive* as well (the three hallmarks of content analysis; Budd, Thorp, & Donohue, 1967).

However, a limitation of computer content analysis is the fact that words have multiple meanings. This means, of course, that some of the words we employed in our content analysis could have been used in these texts in other

TABLE 2.1
Sample of Campaign Messages

	Years	Number
Primary Spots	1952–2000	910
Primary Debates	1984–2000	31
Acceptances	1952–2000	26
General Spots	1952–2000	918
General Debates	1960, 1976–2000	18
Congressional Spots	1984–2000	80

senses besides personal qualities. We employed the computer program Concordance (2002) for our analysis, and one of its features is that it displays the context for each "hit" from the text. For example, one of the terms we used to find references to decency was "good." We retained uses like "I think he's an honest, *good* man" but not usages like "*Good* evening" or "Nearly a year ago they closed the plant for *good*." Thus, we deleted ambiguous terms from the search term list.

Results

Table 2.2 provides the data for the first research question. It reveals that morality is by far the most frequently discussed dimension of personal quality: It occurs almost 60 percent more often than the second most frequently discussed dimension, drive. Not surprisingly, morality was the most frequently discussed aspect of personal qualities in four of five of the message forms investigated here. Drive was the second most frequently discussed dimension of personal quality across message form (and second in three of the five message forms). Empathy was the third most frequently discussed dimension, and sincerity was the least most commonly discussed aspect of personal quality. The emphasis on morality may reflect the idea that the presidency is the highest office in the land and the most powerful elected official in the land. Such awesome power may require high moral purpose for the individual who would wield that power.

Table 2.2 also provides support for the claim that these dimensions of personal qualities may transcend particular message forms. Morality is ranked first in all but one message form, where it is second. Drive is the second most common dimension in three forms and third in another. Sincerity is the third most frequent dimension in three forms and fourth in the remaining two media. Only empathy varies widely. In the general campaign, empathy is the least frequent dimension of personal qualities, but this aspect of character is most frequent in acceptance addresses and is either second or third most fre-

TABLE 2.2
Frequency of Personal Qualities in General Presidential Television Spots

	Primary TV Spots	Primary Debates	Acceptances	General TV Spots	General Debates	Total
Morality	639 (1)*	2495 (1)	721 (2)	934 (1)	1526 (1)	6315 (1)
Empathy	528 (3)	1476 (2)	774 (1)	477 (4)	611 (4)	3866 (3)
Sincerity	446 (4)	1049 (3)	465 (4)	583 (3)	856 (3)	3399 (4)
Drive	602 (2)	1021 (4)	652 (3)	718 (2)	1010 (2)	4003 (2)

* Rank.

quent in the primary campaign (this is the only quality to receive every rank from first to fourth). Given that the acceptance addresses are presented at the party convention and that primary campaign messages are aimed at party members, empathy may be easier to establish than with the more heterogeneous audience for general television spots and general debates. Nevertheless, the consistency of emphasis suggests that candidates are presenting a fairly consistent character message across media.

The second research question concerned the proclivities of incumbents and challengers. We excluded primary messages from this analysis. In every election year, the party that does not occupy the White House (e.g., the Republicans in 2000) has neither an incumbent candidate nor a single challenger. Furthermore, in many campaigns (e.g., 1956, 1964, 1972, 1984, and 1996) the incumbent party candidate does not face a challenge in the primary (so there is an incumbent but no challenger in those primary races).

Table 2.3 reports the data from acceptances, general television spots, and general debates. *Chi-square* analyses reveal that in every message form, there was a significant difference in the emphasis of the four dimensions of personal qualities. However, inspection of the table reveals that the only consistent difference across these three message forms is morality: Incumbents consistently discuss morality more than challengers in their campaign messages. This may mean that incumbents are particularly likely to take the moral high ground whereas challengers are more likely to dwell on specifics.

Research question 3 investigated whether longitudinal trends can be discerned in the use of the four dimensions of personal qualities over time. We employed general television spot data to answer this question (debates and primary spots are sporadic, and acceptance addresses may be focused to a partisan audience). These data are displayed in figure 2.1.

TABLE 2.3
Personal Qualities Discussed by Incumbent-Party and Challenger-Party Candidates

	Sincerity	Empathy	Morality	Drive	X^2 (df = 3)
Acceptances					
Incumbents	**239**	**221**	**399**	**307**	10.1 p .025
Challengers	234	167	278	277	
General TV Spots					
Incumbents	281	193	**472**	**373**	17.2 $p < .001$
Challengers	**302**	**284**	462	346	
General Debates					
Incumbents	400	241	**307**	471	36.2 $p < .001$
Challengers	**456**	**370**	713	**539**	

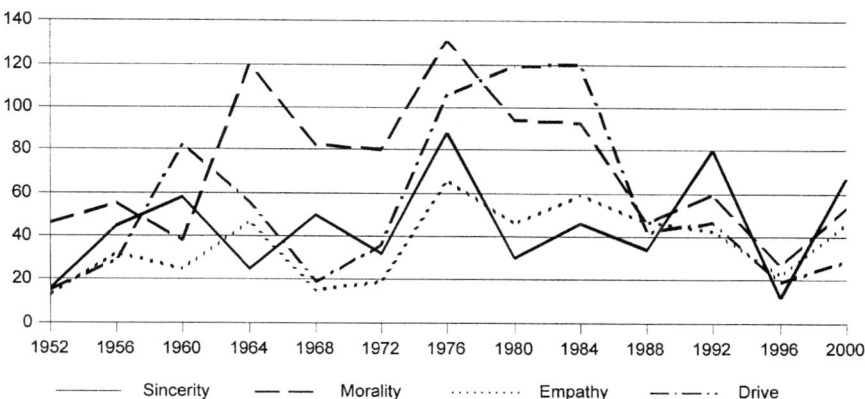

FIGURE 2.1
Personal Qualities in Presidential Television Spots

Several features of these data are interesting. First, the discussion of morality increased sharply in 1964. Republican nominee Barry Goldwater, arguably a conservative ideologue, said this in a 1964 television spot: "The national morality, by example and by persuasion, should begin at the White House, and have the good influence to reach out to every corner of the land." Morality remained high in the late 1960s and 1970s, possibly due to concerns over the Vietnam War.

Discussion of sincerity peaked in 1976, after the Watergate break-in and cover-up and President Richard Nixon's resignation and pardon by President Gerald Ford. A spot for President Ford featured a citizen explaining that "the reason I like him [Ford] is his honesty." Ford's ads repeatedly insisted that he was honest. On the other hand, a commercial for challenger Jimmy Carter declared that "I really believe he [Carter] can restore that honesty, integrity, openness and competence in government that we so sorely need in our country today." Both candidates discussed this dimension of presidential personal qualities. Sincerity was frequently discussed again in 1992, after George Bush's 1988 acceptance address pledge—"Read my lips: No new taxes"—was broken in his first term of office. Video footage of this pledge appeared in several of challenger Bill Clinton's ads; this spot quotes newspaper commentary: "The *Observer* says new information about Mr. Bush's role in the Iran arms for hostages deal and the breaking of his 'Read my lips no tax pledge' raise doubts about his trustworthiness." Emphasis on the dimension of sincerity varied from election to election.

The economy was troubled in 1976, and candidates discussed their drive (willingness to work hard) to improve the economy in their television ads. After lamenting the economic situation, Jimmy Carter proclaimed his readiness to work to improve the country: "It's a long tough job; it's time we got started." The situation continued to deteriorate, and in 1980, drive became the most frequently discussed dimension of personal qualities. For example, in 1980 Republican challenger Ronald Reagan asked,

> Do we want to go on as we have, with more of the same? More runaway government, more runaway spending? If you say no, if you feel as I do, with your support and working together, we'll do the things that have to be done. We can do it; I pledge to you we will do it.

Again, there are fluctuations in the dimension of drive that may, in part, be driven by the nature of events in the world (economic situation).

Study 2

The fourth research question compared presidential and congressional television spot texts. The sample of computer texts of congressional spots available for analysis was limited to 1984–2000 (Brazeal & Benoit, 2001). Because the longitudinal analysis just discussed suggests that there could be fluctuations in the dimensions of personal qualities over time, we restricted the sample of presidential television spot texts employed for this analysis to the same years (although comparison of tables 2.2 and 2.4 reveals that the ranking of the four dimensions was identical in the entire sample and in the recent subsample of presidential advertisements).

A *chi-square* test found that the distribution of these dimensions of personal quality is different in presidential and congressional television spots. Inspection of table 2.4 reveals that the most striking difference is in the use of empathy. Empathy is the least frequent dimension in presidential spots but the most common component of congressional spots. The audience for presidential television spots (national) is, of course, more heterogeneous than the audience for congressional spots. This should mean that it is easier for congressional candidates to demonstrate empathy for voters.

TABLE 2.4
Personal Qualities in Presidential and Congressional TV Spots, 1984–2000

	Presidential Spots, 1984–2000	*Congressional Spots, 1984–2000*
Morality	279 (1)*	76 (2)
Empathy	217 (4)	102 (1)
Sincerity	239 (3)	66 (4)
Drive	257 (2)	68 (3)

* Rank.

Study 3

The third study reported here, answering research question 5, is a preliminary attempt to extend our understanding of political candidates' personal qualities by moving beyond the texts of candidate campaign messages. Specifically, we surveyed voters to ascertain which personal qualities they believed were most important for presidential candidates to possess.

Sample

Because we lacked the resources to survey a random national sample of voters, we approached this as exploratory research, employing a convenience sample for our data. One hundred and three students in undergraduate communication courses (64 females and 39 males, ages ranging from 18 to 21) completed a survey asking them to list the five most important personal qualities for a presidential candidate. Another twenty-seven nonstudents completed the same survey (14 females and 13 males; ages ranged from 23 to 61). Thus, our total sample was 130 voters. The nature of our sample, of course, means that these results must be considered tentative but possess heuristic value.

Procedures

We asked each respondent to list the five most important qualities for a presidential candidate to possess. We deleted responses that concerned policy, demographic characteristics, or leadership (as we did when reviewing the literature on character above). The remaining responses were grouped into the categories developed by us in 2003 (Benoit & McHale, 2003). Voters in our sample also listed three dimensions that were not found in the analysis of personal qualities in presidential television spots (Benoit & McHale, 2003). These data are reported in table 2.5, along with totals from the presidential candidates' messages.

TABLE 2.5
Most Important Presidential Personal Qualities for Voters

Category	Voters	Campaign Messages
Morality	87 (3)*	6391 (1)
Empathy	77 (5)	3968 (3)
Sincerity	149 (1)	3465 (4)
Drive	86 (4)	4071 (2)

* Rank.

Results

Although the nature of our sample (convenience) must be clearly kept in mind as a limitation, the results of our survey of voters provide interesting food for thought. The single most important personal quality identified by voters is sincerity; however, sincerity is the dimension least frequently addressed by presidential candidates in their campaign messages. The voter emphasis may reflect a distrust of politicians (fueled at times by situations like the "credibility gap" of Vietnam, the Watergate cover-up, President George Bush's broken "Read my lips: No new taxes" promise, and President Bill Clinton's deception concerning his relationship with Monica Lewinsky). Perhaps politicians should address this concern more frequently in their campaign messages than they do currently.

Therefore, although there is some congruence between voter perception of the relative importance of presidential candidate personal qualities and emphasis in presidential campaign messages, there are differences as well. It seems clear that further work in this area with a random, national sample of voters is justified.

Implications

We now have a clearer picture of the nature of personal qualities in political campaign messages. There are four principal dimensions: morality, empathy, sincerity, and drive. Morality is discussed more often in presidential campaign messages than any other dimension. Drive (the second most frequently discussed dimension) and empathy (third) are discussed more frequently than sincerity. Furthermore, with the exception of empathy (which occurs most often in acceptance addresses and least often in general campaign messages), the relative frequency with which these dimensions are discussed is fairly consistent across campaign message form.

Incumbents, who might be expected to adopt the moral high ground, discuss morality more than challengers in every message form. No other consistent distinction emerged in the personal qualities discussed in incumbents' and challengers' messages.

Examination of these dimensions over time reveals, as one might expect, that the relative frequency of these dimensions varies over time. We speculate that events (e.g., Vietnam, Watergate, and the economy) and candidates (e.g., Goldwater, Bush, and Clinton) could have played a role in these fluctuations.

We also learned that there is a fair degree of consistency between the dimensions of personal qualities discussed in presidential and congressional television advertising. However, we also found that empathy is discussed most frequently in congressional spots but least often in presidential spots. This is likely due to the more heterogeneous nature of the audience for presidential spots than for congressional ones.

Finally, our exploratory study of voters suggests that they value sincerity, a dimension of personal quality mentioned less frequently than other dimensions by candidates in their messages. This may reflect a distrust of politicians, who may need to do more to attempt to counteract this attitude in their messages. However, we again stress that the results must be tempered because of the nature of the sample.

There are obviously opportunities for further research. First, we have examined three message forms: television spots (primary and general), debates (primary and general), and acceptance addresses. Analysis of other message forms (e.g., radio ads, television talk-show appearances, websites, and direct mail) could supplement this work. Second, the sample of nonpresidential messages is limited to eighty television spots. Analysis of more spots and other message forms would be a useful addition to the literature. Third, more work should be conducted using voters. Replication of the third study with a national random sample of voters would be useful. It would also be possible to conduct experimental studies of the effects of messages that stress different dimensions of personal qualities on voters. Clearly, the personal qualities of presidential candidates are important. We now have a better understanding of this aspect of their image.

References

Benoit, W. L. 1999. *Seeing Spots: A Functional Analysis of Presidential Television Advertisements from 1952 to 1996.* New York: Praeger.
Benoit, W. L. 2000. "A Functional Analysis of Political Advertising across Media, 1998." *Communication Studies* 51: 274–295.
Benoit, W. L. 2001. "The Functional Approach to Presidential Television Spots: Attacking, Defending 1952–2000." *Communication Studies* 52: 109–126.
Benoit, W. L., J. R. Blaney, and P. M. Pier. 1998. *Campaign '96: A Functional Analysis of Acclaiming, Attacking, and Defending.* New York: Praeger.
———. 2000. "Acclaiming, Attacking, and Defending: A Functional Analysis of U.S. Nominating Convention Keynote Speeches." *Political Communication* 17: 61–84.
Benoit, W. L., and L. M. Brazeal. 2002. "A Functional Analysis of the 1988 Bush-Dukakis Presidential Debates." *Argumentation and Advocacy* 38: 219–233.
Benoit, W. L., and A. Harthcock. 1999. "Functions of the Great Debates: Acclaims, Attacks, and Defense in the 1960 Presidential Debates." *Communication Monographs* 66: 341–357.

Benoit, W. L., and J. P. McHale. 2003. "Presidential Candidates' Television Spots and Personal Qualities." *Southern Communication Journal* 68: 319–334.

Benoit, W. L., P. M. Pier, L. M. Brazeal, J. P. McHale, A. Klyukovksi, and D. Airne. 2002. *The Primary Decision: A Functional Analysis of Debates in Presidential Primaries.* Westport, Conn.: Praeger.

Benoit, W. L., W. T. Wells, P. M. Pier, and J. R. Blaney. 1999. "Acclaiming, Attacking, and Defending in Nomination Convention Acceptance Addresses." *Quarterly Journal of Speech* 85: 247–267.

Boyd, R. W. 1969. "Presidential Elections: An Explanation of Voting Defection." *American Political Science Review* 63: 498–514.

Brazeal, L. M., and W. L. Benoit. 2001. "A Functional Analysis of Congressional Television Spots, 1986–2000." *Communication Quarterly* 49: 436–454.

Budd, R. W., R. K. Thorp, and L. Donohue. 1967. *Content Analysis of Communication.* New York: Macmillan.

"Character, Not the Economy, Drives Voter Choices in 2000." 2000. *Columbia Daily Tribune,* January 23, 7A.

Concordance. Version 3.0. 2002. www.rjcw.freeserve.co.uk.

Hacker, K. L., W. R. Zakahi, M. J. Giles, and S. McQuitty. 2000. "Components of Candidate Images: Statistical Analysis of the Issue-Persona Dichotomy in the Presidential Campaign of 1996." *Communication Monographs* 67: 227–238.

Hellweg, S. A. 1995. "Campaigns and Candidate Image in American Presidential Elections." In *Candidate Images in Presidential Elections,* edited by K. L. Hacker, 1–17. Westport, Conn.: Praeger.

Hinck, E. A. 1993. *Enacting the Presidency: Political Argument, Presidential Debates, and Presidential Character.* Westport, Conn.: Praeger.

Kinder, D. R. 1986. "Presidential Character Revisited." In *Political Cognition: The Nineteenth Annual Carnegie Symposium on Cognition,* edited by R. Lau and D. O. Sears, 233–255. Hillsdale, N.J.: Erlbaum.

Leff, M. C., and G. P. Mohrmann. 1974. "Lincoln at Cooper-Union: A Rhetorical Analysis of the Text." *Quarterly Journal of Speech* 60: 346–358.

Marshall, T. 1984. "Issues, Personalities, and Presidential Primary Voters." *Social Science Quarterly* 65: 750–760.

Miller, A. H., M. P. Wattenberg, and O. Malanchuk. 1986. "Schematic Assessment of Presidential Candidates." *American Political Science Review* 80: 521–540.

NBC/*Wall Street Journal.* 1996. *Roper Center at the University of Connecticut: Public Opinion Online.* Storrs: Roper Center at the University of Connecticut, March 1–5, May 10–14, June 20–25, August 2–6, September 12–17, and October 19–22. www.lexis-nexis.com.

Petrocik, J. R. 1996. "Issue Ownership in Presidential Elections, with a 1980 Case Study." *American Journal of Political Science* 40: 825–850.

Rudd, R. 1986. "Issues as Image in Political Campaign Commercials." *Western Journal of Speech Communication* 50: 102–118.

Sigel, R. S. 1966. "Image of the American Presidency—Part II of an Exploration into Popular Views of Presidential Power. *Midwest Journal of Political Science* 10: 123–137.

Smith, C. A., and K. B. Smith. 1994. *The White House Speaks: Presidential Leadership as Persuasion*. Westport, Conn.: Praeger.

Stuckey, M. E., and F. J. Antczak. 1995. "The Battle of Issues and Images: Establishing Interpretive Dominance." In *Presidential Campaign Discourse: Strategic Communication Problems*, edited by K. E. Kendall, 117–134. Albany: State University of New York Press.

Trent, J. S., P. Mongeau, J. D. Trent, K. Kendall, and R. Cushing. 1993. "The Ideal Candidate: A Study of the Desired Attributes of the Public and the Media across Two Presidential Campaigns." *American Behavioral Scientist* 37: 225–239.

Trent, J. S., C. Short-Thompson, P. A. Mongeau, A. K. Nusz, and J. D. Trent. 2001. "Image Media Bias, and Voter Characteristics: The Ideal Candidate from 1988–2000." *American Behavioral Scientist* 44: 2102–2124.

Trent, J. S., J. D. Trent, P. Mongeau, and C. Short-Thompson. 1997. "The Ideal Candidate Revisited: A Study of the Desired Attributes of the Public and the Media across Three Presidential Campaigns." *American Behavioral Scientist* 40: 1001–1019.

Williams, D. C., S. J. Weber, G. A. Haaland, R. H. Mueller, and R. E. Craig. 1976. "Voter Decision Making in a Primary Election: An Evaluation of Three Models of Choice." *American Journal of Political Science* 20: 37–49.

3

Candidate Images When Things Go Sour: Reaction to Scandal

Carolyn L. Funk

CANDIDATE IMAGES AREN'T ALWAYS GUSHING with admiration. More and more frequently, presidential candidates face image trouble from reports of their scandalous behavior. This chapter looks at how candidate images change in response to political scandal. First, I identify what is meant by scandal. Then, I look in detail at the varying public reactions to scandal and the conditions that lead to those varying reactions. Scandal situations highlight the complex mix of factors that underlie candidate images. For example, I consider how candidate images in the aftermath of scandal vary depending on the eye of the beholder. Partisans are more willing to give a candidate the benefit of the doubt when it comes to believing reports of scandal (as occurred for Gary Hart in 1988 and Bill Clinton in the 1990s) and tend to downplay the importance of the scandal for other political judgments. Further, how candidates and other political figures respond to the scandal influences the nature of public reaction to the scandal and, ultimately, the candidate's electoral fortunes.

How Candidate Images Change in Response to Political Scandal

Why Focus on Reaction to Scandal?

No consideration of candidate images would be complete without some attention to the more negative aspects of candidate images. While all candidates would rather have a public image filled with superlatives, quite often candidates face image troubles, especially when they are connected to "scandal." The great puzzle of political scandals stems from the fact that not all politicians are equally harmed by their connection with scandal. For many, connection with a scandal can effectively put an end to a public career; for others, however, association with a scandal does not end their political viability. Candidate images are damaged to varying degrees in response to scandal. This variation in reaction to scandal provides a useful context in which to examine candidate images and lends a better understanding of the factors that influence candidate images.

What Is Meant by Scandal?

These days, it seems like any news that suggests improper behavior by someone in government gets labeled a scandal. While the term *scandal* is often used loosely in colloquial language and contemporary politics, there is an important distinction between political scandal and corruption. Corruption typically refers to illegal or otherwise improper behaviors directly related to holding public office. *Graft*, for example, is often used to denote improper financial gain due to one's position such as by accepting bribes in exchange for votes on legislation or other acts. The term *scandal*, on the other hand, is used here to denote behaviors of a more personal nature by a politician.[1] The relevance of the wrongdoing to official duties is by definition more ambiguous in the case of scandal than it is for corruption. Fittingly, public response is more uniformly negative in response to corruption (Peters & Welch, 1978) and more variable in response to scandal.

Marital infidelity or a variety of other sexual acts are often considered scandalous. Tax evasion, knowingly hiring illegal aliens, illegal drug use, or driving while under the influence of alcohol would be considered scandals as well. These are scandalous behaviors because they are in conflict with society's moral standards, not because they represent direct misuses of one's position as an elected official. This definition allows for the fact that one society's moral standards do not always match that of another society. Sexual escapades are often considered more scandalous by the U.S. public than in some other societies. French citizens, for example, seemed to accept the existence of former President François Mitterand's longtime mistress and illegitimate child in a way that is hard to imagine occurring in the United States. Further, moral standards sometimes change over time, as we have seen with sexual mores in the United States over the last several decades.

Private behaviors by a politician are not scandalous, of course, until they become publicized. Information about these behaviors is disseminated through the mass media—across many outlets and continuing anywhere from a few days to many months of coverage. A number of influences may be at work behind the scenes to determine which politicians become involved in scandals (i.e., publicized behaviors that are in conflict with society's moral standards) and which politicians may engage in these same behaviors without being subject to public attention.[2] Reporters don't often stumble on this information by pure chance. Often, one or more persons must be willing to publicize scandalous information out of either personal distaste or professional competition with the politician involved.

Similarly, once known, a number of factors may be involved in determining the nature, tone, and extent of media coverage for scandalous behaviors (see Sabato, Stencel, & Lichter, 2000; Thompson, 2000). In the 2000 presidential election, some news and entertainment media noted Al Gore's "exaggerations" when Gore implied that he had a personal hand in inventing the Internet, for example. This incident was not treated as immoral behavior but as a character tendency to inflate his contributions. Had the same incident been treated as a lie, it would have been more likely to be seen as a scandal with the accompanying potential for more serious negative effects. Even the same scandalous behavior can be covered in different ways. Many U.S. congresspersons were involved in the check-kiting scandal of the 1990s. The tone of local media coverage for congresspersons varied, however; not surprisingly, where the tone was more positive, incumbents were more likely to win reelection (Shea, 1999). The extent of coverage also has an important influence on the salience of the scandal to the public eye, and salience, in turn, has important implications for the impact of the scandal on judgments about the candidate (Iyengar & Kinder, 1987). Clearly, the nature, tone, and extent of media coverage can have an important influence on public reaction to scandalous behaviors. While these issues are important, the factors that determine when and how scandalous behavior is covered by the media are outside the scope of the present chapter.

The Puzzle of Teflon Politicians

In general, being connected with a scandal is bad for business—that is, the business of getting reelected. A number of studies have found a significant negative impact of scandal on electoral margins (Abramowitz, 1988, 1991; Peters & Welch, 1980; Rundquist, Strom, & Peters 1977; also see Stoker, 1993; Fackler & Lin, 1995). In essence, news of a scandal constitutes negative information about the public officeholder. There is considerable evidence that negative information has a stronger effect on judgments than does equivalent positive information. This "negativity effect" is well established in research on person perception (e.g., Fiske, 1980; Kanouse & Hanson, 1972; Skowronski & Carlston, 1989) and holds for evaluations of politicians as well (Holbrook et al., 2001). Perceived trait weaknesses of a presidential candidate are better predictors of overall evaluations than are perceived strengths (Klein 1991, 1996; Lau 1982, 1985). Scandal information, then, by virtue of its negativity, is likely to be given considerable attention and weight in evaluating officeholders.

While most politicians involved in scandal find their reputation at least bruised by the scandal, some manage to retain their political viability, as did presidential candidate Bill Clinton in 1992 after allegations of an extramarital affair with Gennifer Flowers. Ronald Reagan was dubbed the "Teflon president" in the early 1980s because, like the product, it appeared that nothing (bad) sticks to him. In more recent times, the great puzzle of public opinion toward President Clinton centers on why public support for Clinton was so high despite his sexual involvement with former White House intern, Monica Lewinsky. In the final days of the campaign, news that George W. Bush had been arrested on a drunk driving charge more than twenty years prior appeared to have little impact on voters. This made the big scandal story of 2000 seem like a nonscandal story. As these cases clearly remind us, public response to scandal is more variable than initially assumed. This variability comes from two main sources, namely, contextual information about the candidate and contextual information about the scandal. These two broad influences on public reaction will be addressed in more detail below.

Candidate Image Formation

Candidate image is a broadly conceived and loosely defined concept (see Hacker, 1995; Hellweg, 1995, and this volume). Candidate images are typically distinguished from party affiliations of the candidate and issues positions of candidates in models of voting behavior. As a result, candidate images are sometimes defined de facto as a composite of characteristics of the candidate other than party and issue position.

A core component of candidate images consists of the candidate's perceived trait qualities. Actually, traits are a core component of our images for all sorts of other persons whether a family member, acquaintance, or public figure. There are many terms in the English language used to describe specific traits—intelligent, warm, cunning, smarmy, and belligerent, to name a few out of more than 18,000! Judgments about the trait qualities of a politician are, in essence, generalizing from bits and pieces of known information into personality dispositions, or at least tendencies for behavior. Observations of a candidate based on a thirty-second advertisement or an hour-long debate may lead to inferences that he or she is adept at handling questions, is warm and caring about others, is mean-spirited in attacking an opponent, or is afraid to take a controversial stand. These trait impressions are based on a wide range of micro behaviors, both verbal and nonverbal. Other known characteristics—such as having grown up on a farm, being from the South, graduating from Yale, or liking to golf—also can be a basis for trait inferences.

Judgments about candidate traits tend to be made spontaneously as information is encountered (Carlston, 1980; Gilbert, Pelham, & Krull, 1988; Newman & Uleman, 1990; Uleman & Moskowitz, 1994). Snippets of behavior—such as Richard Nixon's rapid eye movements from side to side, or his apparent five o'clock shadow during the 1960 presidential debates—can lead to trait impressions such as being shifty or unreliable without any explicit prompting.

The distinction between candidate trait images as separate from issue positions is a false dichotomy. Issue positions themselves can foster trait impressions, and candidates intend for them to do so. John F. Kennedy is reputed to have purposefully taken positions on foreign policy issues during the campaign not only for the sake of making his position public but also to help create an image of himself as a knowledgeable statesman (Jacobs & Shapiro, 1994). Nixon, similarly, chose how much to talk about foreign policy issues with an eye to influencing voter perceptions of his competence and strength as a leader (Jacobs, Druckman, & Ostermeier, 2001). "Candidates use issues not just to appeal to voters who agree with them on policy but to convey messages about their personal qualities" (Salmore & Salmore, 1989, p. 113). Candidates talk about policy areas "as a means for projecting their personal attributes" (Jacobs et al., 2001). Issue and character appeals are, then, closely intertwined (see Kaid & Chanslor, 1995; Kern, 1989; Jacobs & Shapiro, 1994; Jacobs et al., 2001; Just et al., 1996; Nimmo & Savage, 1976; Moore, 1995).

Candidate images tap the distinctive characteristics of individual candidates. That said, trait judgments help to simplify the multitude of information we encounter about a given political figure. While there are thousands of different trait terms, candidates' trait images tend to fit into one of three dimensions: trustworthiness, warmth, and competence or leadership traits (Funk, 1999, 1996a). These three dimensions were found to explain, or provide a "good fit" with, the pattern of trait judgments made about presidential candidates. So while the content of candidate images varies to match the different characteristics and personalities of the candidates, the structure of candidate trait images appears to be the same across candidates.

Importantly, the influence of candidate trait images on global or overall candidate evaluations varies across candidates and electoral contexts. For some candidates, such as Bill Clinton in 1992 and 1996, overall evaluations were influenced by trait images on all three dimensions of competence, integrity, and warmth. For other candidates, such as Michael Dukakis in 1988 or

Walter Mondale in 1984, only competence judgments had a strong influence on overall evaluations. This pattern of results fits with the notion that the distinctive aspects of candidate images in a specific electoral context influence how overall evaluations are formed. This view contrasts with many past models of vote choice that assumed that the same criteria were used in forming candidate evaluations regardless of the candidate or electoral context. These distinctive aspects of candidate images tend to be highlighted by campaign messages that work to focus voters on particular aspects of candidate images and thereby "prime" different bases for candidate evaluations (Mendelsohn, 1996).

Cognitive Factors Influencing Changes in Candidate Images

The campaign is the chief source of information from which candidate images are formed. The campaign provides exposure to a wide variety of information relevant to the presidential candidates and sets that information in a context that influences how it is interpreted. In today's age of impersonal politics, most contact with campaigns comes through mass media channels. News media traditionally provide the bulk of this information, but more and more, entertainment media also provide information about the candidates either through late-night humor routines, talk shows, or other venues (Arterton, 1993). And, of course, paid advertising also provides information about the candidate—sometimes the only information that citizens encounter. This mix of sources, coupled with informal discussion, works to highlight candidate traits, stereotype faults and sometimes strengths, and generally help to create memorable, unified impressions into a gestalt for each candidate.

Campaigns as communicated through mass media provide the information that fuels the formation of candidate images in our mind's eye. This process is thought to be essentially the same whether it involves political figures or other persons. Once initial impressions have been formed, however, they are resistant to change. A number of cognitive processes come into play such as a primacy effect giving more weight to the first information encountered about a person compared to later information, and a memory advantage for information consistent rather than inconsistent with prior impressions. These processes are behind the adage that "first impressions count"; once a candidate image is established, it may be quite difficult to change (see e.g., Anderson, 1965; Fiske & Neuberg, 1990; Hendrick & Constantini, 1970; Higgins & Bargh, 1987; Holbrook et al., 2001). Coupled with a tendency to pay more attention to negative than positive information, it follows that it is harder to change an initial negative impression than an initial positive impression. Thus, the danger was greatest for Bill Clinton during the 1992 presidential campaign when he was a relatively unknown figure nationwide and news of his alleged affair with Gennifer Flowers surfaced.

Established candidate images are not just positive and negative. They have particular components—some candidates are seen as bumbling while others are poised, some are inarticulate and others eloquent, some are self-aggrandizing and others self-effacing, some are evasive and others forthright. A memory advantage for information that is consistent with established candidate schema means that some scandals will fit particularly well with established images while others will be inconsistent. Scandals that mesh well with established candidate images will tend to reinforce an existing stereotype or judgment about the candidate. This should make it harder to change a candidate image in this regard and may make it easier to believe allegations of scandal. Richard Nixon was widely known as "Tricky Dick" well before the time of the Watergate scandal. This may have made allegations about his behavior in the Watergate scandal easier to accept in the public mind because they were consistent with an established schema about Nixon. Similarly, allegations that "Slick Willie" Bill Clinton had an affair with Monica Lewinsky were consistent with prior images of him as a womanizer and one who would shade the truth.

When the scandal information is inconsistent with an established image, it may be easier to elude the negative effects of scandal information. So, for example, allegations that Robert Dole was involved in an extramarital affair during his first marriage fit less well with established impressions of him and were never a particularly thorny issue in his 1996 presidential bid. Similarly, Chuck Robb, who served as governor of Virginia and later U.S. senator, may have been helped by his earlier public image as a "milk-drinking marine" when later allegations were made about his presence at some parties where others were using illegal drugs and his "massages" with a beauty pageant winner.

Complexities in How Scandals Influence Public Judgments

The relationship between new scandal information and prior images of a candidate points to the complexities in how scandals can influence judgment. There are four main kinds of judgments potentially affected by the scandal.

1. *Overall Evaluations.* Most attention has been focused on the effect of the scandal on global or overall evaluations of the candidate. These are closely related to vote choice and as such are the closest predictors of an effect on the electoral fortunes of a candidate.

2. *Perceptions as Honest and Trustworthy.* A second key effect is focused more directly on changes in candidate images, especially in terms of candidate honesty and trustworthiness.
3. *Judgments about the Scandal.* A third kind of effect concerns a wide variety of judgments and affective reactions to the scandal. These judgments include things such as beliefs about the guilt of the candidate, the deservingness of the candidate to experience troubles, and the motivations of other figures connected to the scandal. This broad class of judgments plays an important mediating role in the effect of the scandal on overall evaluations of the candidate.
4. *Scandal, Politicians, and the Political System.* Lastly, there may be a broader effect on judgments related to the political system such as the prevalence of scandal in politics. These too could have a mediating effect on judgments in specific cases of scandal.

In a literal sense, the notion that Teflon politicians are unaffected by a scandal is false. That notion stems from thinking only about whether overall evaluations are negatively affected by scandal. While there are many variations in the type and nature of scandalous behavior, all typically raise questions about the honesty, trustworthiness, or integrity of the politician. In most cases, the scandalous behavior is initially hidden from public view and hence involves some degree of misrepresentation by the politician to the public. Often, there is other misrepresentation such as that to a spouse in cases of marital infidelity or to government agencies as in cases of tax evasion. Almost by definition, then, scandals are expected to have a negative impact on a candidate's image of trustworthiness or integrity. When people marvel that someone like President Clinton seemed to be unaffected by the scandal emanating from his involvement with Monica Lewinsky, they are really referring to the lack of impact on overall candidate evaluations or overall job performance evaluations. Even politicians, like Clinton, whose overall evaluations remain high after a scandal becomes known are likely to see impressions of their integrity, honesty, or trustworthiness hurt (Funk, 1996b; Kagay, 1999).

In addition, a number of judgments are typically formed in response to the scandal itself. One judgment, for example, concerns belief in the scandal allegations. The veracity of scandalous accusations is almost always in doubt for some period of time. Later effects on overall candidate evaluations are mediated by belief in the truth of the charges. Other mediating judgments include beliefs about the seriousness of the moral lapse and the relevance of the scandal to official duties of the officeholder. It was through these mediating judgments that Clinton appeared to fare best, particularly in terms of the relevance of his behavior for his performance as president. Similarly, when news of

George W. Bush's past arrest for drunk driving surfaced in the final days of the 2000 election, mediating judgments about the limited relevance of this information appeared to help buffer any negative impact from this potentially scandalous information. Other judgments about the cause and deservingness of the candidate to experience troubles can also influence the extent to which the public is sympathetic to the candidate in times of scandal (Feather, 1993, 1994).

Broader influences on judgment are possible but difficult to prove with certainty. For example, it may be that scandals influence images of politicians as a group or that the cumulative impact of many politicians involved in scandal influences impressions not only of politicians but also of judgments about scandal in a specific case. For example, public images of the honesty and integrity of female officeholders tend to be higher than that of male officeholders (Alexander & Andersen, 1993). If more female politicians are involved in scandal allegations over time, the cumulative impact may influence judgments about the subgroup of female politicians. Cumulative impact of particular scandals may also influence changes in social norms about what is acceptable behavior; this, in turn, would likely influence whether specific scandal charges are serious and ultimately would lead to a redefinition of what is scandalous. For example, charges made during the 1992 campaign that Bill Clinton had smoked pot during his younger days (but not since then) have been followed by other politicians openly admitting their past use of marijuana. The cumulative impact of these kinds of admissions may also influence public reaction to a case such as George W. Bush's, where there were repeated suggestions of prior alcohol overuse and perhaps other drug use in his earlier days.

Scandals Unfold in Complex and Dynamic Ways

Public response to scandals is complex in part because the scandal situations themselves are complex. Most scandals can be loosely divided into at least four phases as they move from privately to publicly known behavior through various media outlets. Public reaction to the scandal is likely to be different in each phase of the scandal.

The first phase occurs when the charges or allegations are made public. In this phase there is always some degree of uncertainty regarding the truth of the allegations. The second phase entails initial reaction to the charges by the implicated politician. Typically, there is a separation in time between the initial charges and this second phase of reaction to the charges, but sometimes they occur almost simultaneously in the news cycle. A third phase occurs when media and public reactions to the initial charges begin emerging. These reactions often are directly related to the perceived truth of the charges and the perceived seriousness of the behavior. As with the phenomenon of rally-round-the flag effects for presidential performance during times of crisis, the reaction of other politicians is a key factor in public reaction (Brody, 1991). The absence of condemnations by politicians, especially in the same party, is typically an important influence on public response. By this time, new facts are often known, and the politician involved may have made numerous public statements about his or her behavior. By the fourth phase of the scandal, some degree of truth is known about the charges, and there has been a continuation, and perhaps evolution, in how media coverage portrays the scandal and in how other politicians respond to the scandal. This changing context for information is also likely to influence public reactions to the scandal.[3]

Even these four broad phases overly simplify many scandal situations. One major omission is the role of other "players" in the drama that unfolds related to the scandal. The politician is not the only person in the spotlight. Most scandals involve a host of other people who played a role in the scandalous behavior, in keeping it from the public eye, or in making it public knowledge. Evaluations of Clinton's behavior, for example, are formed in the context of impressions of other key figures such as Ken Starr, Linda Tripp, Monica Lewinsky, and even Paula Jones or Gennifer Flowers. Public impressions of the honesty, fairness, and motives of these other figures are likely to influence judgments about Clinton's behavior. These judgments can have far-ranging effects; for example, Alan Abramowitz (2001) suggests that public response to Ken Starr was a critical influence on the outcome of the 1998 midterm elections.

Other Factors in Public Reaction to Scandal and Candidate Electoral Fortunes

As discussed above, there are several major factors that determine public reaction to scandal. These include whether prior images of the politician were established at the time of the scandal, whether prior images of the politician are consistent or inconsistent with the scandal, the nature of the scandal including the presence of and perceived motives of other "players" in the scandal, and the response to the scandal from other politicians and media figures. Next, I consider three other factors in determining public reaction to the scandal: the politician's response to the scandal, the partisan inclinations, and the political expertise of the public. And last, I consider the role of elite politics and policy and performance considerations in determining the electoral fortunes of candidates involved in scandal.

The Politician's Response. A politician accused of scandal has a number of options in how to respond to these charges. For example, he or she may avoid any public comment, actively deny the charges, immediately confess to wrongdoing, or argue that his or her behaviors have been misunderstood. The politician's response can directly influence public response. For example, public concern in 2001 over the possible involvement of U.S. Representative Gary Condit in the death of his office intern appeared to grow largely in reaction to his tight-lipped denials of involvement or information about the missing intern. This reaction, whether just or unjust in the case of Mr. Condit, is consistent with experimental findings that show that people who confessed and apologized for a moral transgression were held less accountable for their actions than were people who denied the behavior (Weiner, Graham, Peter, & Zmuidinas, 1991). Similarly, reaction to politicians' accounts for controversial policy decisions depends on the account provided. Controlled experimental tests by Kathleen McGraw and colleagues (1990, 1991; McGraw, Timpone, & Bruck, 1993) have shown that some accounts can actually backfire, leading to less favorable views of the official. This is the situation implied by the Gary Condit case, when a CNN poll showed that 67 percent of those who had seen his televised interview with Connie Chung were more suspicious of his actions, and 16 percent reported being less suspicious, as a result of the interview. A number of judgments are affected by the account given for controversial behaviors, not just overall evaluations; judgments of blame and specific impressions of character traits such as integrity and empathy are also influenced by the politician's account. Reaction to a politician's account for scandalous behavior is not determined just by the words used but also by the emotion shown. A politician responding to charges of scandal with outrage or anger, sadness, and regret also influences public judgments related to the scandal (Tiedens, 2001).

Partisan Inclinations of the Public. One of the most powerful influences on public reaction hinges on whether or not one is a fellow partisan with the accused. Party affiliation or identification has long been a strong predictor of public reaction to officeholder performance. Experimental studies continue to underscore the importance of political party in evaluations of candidates (see Fischle, 2000; Rahn, 1993; Riggle, Ottati, Wyer, Kuklinski, & Schwartz, 1992; Lodge, Taber, & Galonsky, 1999). It is not surprising, then, that partisanship has a strong influence on judgments related to political scandal. Fellow partisans are more likely to give a politician the benefit of the doubt when scandal charges arise and consequently are less likely to believe in the veracity of the charges. Beyond that, partisanship is also associated with other mediating judgments such as the importance of the scandal. In reevaluating an already liked presidential candidate, fellow partisans are less likely to rely on character weakness judgments in their overall assessments of him than are those of the other party (Goren, 2002). Partisan reactions were key in response to Gary

Hart's alleged affair with Donna Rice during the 1998 presidential nomination campaign (Stoker, 1993). Michael Dimock and Gary Jacobson (1995) found a similar partisan effect in response to the House banking scandal. It's no surprise, then, that a key factor in explaining support for President Clinton in 1998 hinges on high levels of support from fellow Democrats (see Zaller, 2001). It's unclear exactly why these partisan effects occur. It could be a result of simply maintaining prior positive impressions of a candidate, or it may be a more motivated or biased attention to information. Partisans, in essence, put the best possible spin on their judgments of the candidate under the circumstances. If there is ambiguity about the truth of the charges, fellow partisans are more likely to belief in his or her innocence. When the truth is known, partisans are more likely to downgrade the importance of the behavior for job performance evaluations or the seriousness of the behavior as a breach of moral code.

Political Expertise of the Public. In addition to partisan reactions, those who follow politics more closely may respond to scandal information differently. Differences in political expertise among citizens hold a number of implications for exposure to and awareness of political information (e.g., Zaller, 1992). Past research has shown that political experts are better able to integrate complex political information into their judgments (Hamill & Lodge, 1986; Fiske, Kinder, & Larter, 1983; Fiske, Lau, & Smith, 1990; Judd & Downing, 1990; McGraw & Pinney, 1990). This ability may mean that those with more expertise are more likely to weigh scandal information against other considerations in judgment. Experimental studies have shown that other factors being equal, those with greater political knowledge were more likely than those with less expertise to rely on competence trait qualities in their overall candidate evaluations, discounting at least some types of scandal information (Funk, 1997, 1996b).

Elite Politics. It is important to recognize that public response to a scandal is not the only influence on candidate fortunes after a scandal. Elite politics can be the determining factor in at least two ways. First, politicians decide whether to "stay and fight" after a scandal or opt out of public life. Many officeholders choose not to run for reelection after they have been implicated in a scandal. For example, studies on the electoral impact of check overdrafts by members of the U.S. House in the early 1990s found that incumbents associated with that scandal were more likely to retire from public office (Alford, Teeters, Ward, & Wilson, 1994; Groseclose & Krehbiel, 1994; Jacobson & Dimock, 1994). Second, the support of other elites in party politics can be critical to the electoral fortunes of the candidate. Support from party activists has tangible effects on funding and other resources needed for an election campaign and influences the strength of the competition in the upcoming election. When Joe Biden was running for the Democratic nomination for president in 1988, he was accused of plagiarizing parts of a speech from a British politician. The storm that followed ultimately led Biden to step down from the nomination race. A number of other contenders were already in the race at the time. Those supporting Biden could readily transfer their allegiance to another Democratic candidate. The situation was quite different when Bill Clinton was accused of having an extramarital affair with Gennifer Flowers during the 1992 nomination race. Party activists had few other contenders for the nomination in place, giving Clinton a behind-the-scenes advantage in being able to maintain a higher degree of party and donor support. When news of George W. Bush's previous arrest on drunk driving charges surfaced, there was literally no time for elite support to wither; after all, it was just days before the general election.

Policy and Performance Considerations Offsetting the Impact of Scandal. Judgments of overall candidate evaluation are built on multiple considerations. This is one reason why the depth and breadth of impact of the scandal on candidate evaluations can vary considerably. Other information about an officeholder can offset the negative impact of scandal information, thereby acting as a buffer on overall candidate images and evaluations. Past studies suggest that policy and performance considerations can offset the impact of negative trustworthiness information conveyed by scandal, acting as a buffer on overall candidate images and evaluations. For example, a study by Rundquist et al. (1977) found evidence in a hypothetical campaign context that information about policy opinions can outweigh corruption information about an initially preferred candidate. In this case, the policy position of the candidate related to support for Nixon's policy on Vietnam. Those with strong feelings on this issue were more likely to continue support for a corrupt candidate with a preferred position on this issue than were individuals with less intense positions on this issue. Similarly, in a real political context, Stoker's (1993) analysis of change in public opinion toward Gary Hart before and after his relations with Donna Rice became widely known demonstrated that the negative effects of scandal can be moderated by policy concerns. Negative reactions to Hart after the scandal were muted for issue voters, in general, and for those who based more of their initial support for Hart on policy criteria. Similarly, Zaller (1998, 2001) argues that evaluations of Clinton's performance on peace and prosperity issues strongly influenced his unusually high job performance ratings. This is consistent with experimental findings using hypothetical candidates, which showed that candidates who are seen, in trait terms, as more competent are not as badly hurt by scandal information (Funk, 1996b, 1997). Policy and performance assessments, in essence, provide a buffer against negative reactions to scandal. Ultimately, this could make all the difference in the electoral fortunes of a candidate implicated in scandal.

Conclusion

Scandals are now commonplace in contemporary U.S. politics. The puzzle of scandals has centered on the variable impact of scandals on the electoral fortunes of candidates and elected officials. Scandals can influence a number of different judgments, however. In addition to overall candidate evaluations, scandals can influence judgments of a candidate's character traits, especially the honesty and integrity of the politician. A number of beliefs and affective reactions related to the scandal are also formed in response to news of the scandal; these can have important mediating effects on candidate images and overall candidate evaluations. More speculatively, the prevalence of scandals in U.S. politics may also influence broader judgments about the political system, the honesty of politicians, and the seriousness of moral breaches by public officials.

This chapter has looked across a number of different scandals in contemporary U.S. politics to highlight the common factors that influence public reaction to politicians involved in scandal. While every scandal situation is unique, there are a number of general principles that underlie public judgments in response to scandal. First, since established impressions are difficult to change, scandals tend to have a stronger negative impact on candidate images when the politician was not well known prior to the news of the scandal. Second, when the scandal itself is consistent with prior candidate images, it tends to have a stronger negative impact on candidate images. Inconsistent information is more likely to be discounted in judgment.

Responses to the scandal from the politician and other public figures have been shown to influence candidate images as well. The "best" response from the politician's perspective will vary depending on the circumstances of the scandal. Scandals unfold through media outlets in complex and dynamic ways. Public reaction typically evolves as more information becomes available about the scandal and about the role of other people in the scandal situation.

Politicians can play to their strengths, however, and those strengths can help offset the negative impact of scandal in many cases. Presidential candidates who have a strong performance record or are perceived to be more competent tend to experience a weaker negative effect of scandal. Public support for a politician involved in scandal tends to be stronger among that subset of citizens who either strongly support the policy positions of the candidate or are otherwise fellow partisans with him or her. The tendency for policy and performance considerations to offset the negative scandal information in judgments may be even stronger among those citizens who are relatively expert in following political affairs.

Scandal politics provides a fascinating look at how candidate images change in response to information suggesting image trouble for the candidate. These reactions are complex and wedded to the particular circumstances surrounding the candidate's prior image, the reaction to the scandal itself, and the political context. By focusing on the common factors that influence public reaction to scandal, this chapter has highlighted a number of general issues for understanding the dynamic aspects of candidate images, with or without scandal.

Notes

1. In practice, this distinction between more private scandal and more professional corruption is not always clear, especially for "scandals" involving complex sets of events such as Watergate or even the events leading to Clinton's impeachment trial. Much of the political debate surrounding these events centers on whether or not the behavior is related to the official duties of the officeholder and hence constitutes an abuse of power or is limited to a more personal realm of misbehavior.

2. In a related vein, see Kenneth Meier and Thomas Holbrook's (1992) analysis of what predicts the level of corruption in the states. Corruption was defined as the number of public officials convicted of illegal behavior per 100 elected officials in the state. Prosecution of corrupt public officials appeared to stem from partisan and racial targeting.

3. For a similar treatment of phases of scandal linked to the rhythms of news reporting, see Thompson (2000).

References

Abramowitz, Alan I. 1988. "Explaining Senate Election Outcomes." *American Political Science Review* 82: 385–403.

———. 1991. "Incumbency, Campaign Spending, and the Decline of Competition in U.S. House Elections." *Journal of Politics* 53: 34–56.

———. 2001. "It's Monica Stupid: The Impeachment Controversy and the 1996 Midterm Election." *Legislative Studies Quarterly* 26, no. 2: 211–226.

Alexander, Deborah, and Kristi Andersen. 1993. "Gender as a Factor in the Attribution of Leadership Traits." *Political Research Quarterly* 46, no. 3: 527–545.

Alford, John, Holly Teeters, Daniel S. Ward, and Rick K. Wilson. 1994. "Overdraft: The Political Cost of Congressional Malfeasance." *Journal of Politics* 45: 788–801.

Anderson, Norman H. 1965. "Primacy Effects in Personality Impression Formation Using a Generalized Order Effect Paradigm." *Journal of Personality and Social Psychology* 2: 1–9.

Arterton, F. Christopher. 1993. "Campaign '92: Strategies and Tactics of Candidates." In *The Election of 1992: Reports and Interpretations*, edited by Gerald M. Pomper et al., 74–109. Chatham, N.J.: Chatham House Publishers.

Brody, Richard A. 1991. *Assessing the President: The Media, Elite Opinion, and Public Support*. Stanford, Calif.: Stanford University Press.

Carlston, D. E. 1980. "The Recall and Use of Traits and Events in Social Inference Processes." *Journal of Experimental Social Psychology* 16: 303–328.

Dimock, Michael A., and Gary C. Jacobson. 1995. "Checks and Choices: The House Bank Scandals Impact on Voters in 1992." *Journal of Politics* 57, no. 4: 1143–1159.

Fackler, Tim, and Tse-min Lin. 1995. "Political Corruption and Presidential Elections, 1929–1992." *Journal of Politics* 57, no. 4: 971–993.

Feather, Norman T. 1993. "The Rise and Fall of Political Leaders: Attributions, Deservingness, Personality, and Affect." *Australian Journal of Psychology* 45, no. 2: 61–68.

———. 1994. "Attitudes toward High Achievers and Reactions to Their Fall: Theory and Research Concerning Tall Poppies." In *Advances in Experimental Social Psychology*, vol. 26, edited by Mark Zanna, 1–69. San Diego, Calif.: Academic Press.

Fischle, Mark. 2000. "Mass Response to the Lewinsky Scandal: Motivated Reasoning or Bayesian Updating." *Political Psychology* 21, no. 1: 135–159.

Fiske, Susan T. 1980. "Attention and Weight in Person Perception: The Impact of Negative and Extreme Behavior." *Journal of Personality and Social Psychology* 38: 889–906.

Fiske, Susan T., Donald R. Kinder, and W. M. Larter. 1983. "The Novice and the Expert: Knowledge-based Strategies in Political Cognition." *Journal of Experimental Social Psychology* 19: 381–400.

Fiske, Susan T., Richard R. Lau, and R. A. Smith. 1990. "On the Varieties and Utilities of Political Expertise." *Social Cognition* 8: 31–48.

Fiske, Susan T., and S. L. Neuberg. 1990. "A Continuum of Impression Formation, from Category-Based to Individuating Processes: Influences of Information and Motivation on Attention and Interpretation." *Advances in Experimental Social Psychology* 23: 1–74.

Funk, Carolyn L. 1996a. "Understanding Trait Inferences in Candidate Images." In *Research in Micropolitics: New Directions in Political Psychology*, vol. 5, edited by Michael X. Delli Carpini, Leonie Huddy, and Robert Y. Shapiro, 97–123. Greenwich, Conn.: JAI Press.

———. 1996b. "The Impact of Scandal on Candidate Evaluations: An Experimental Test of the Role of Candidate Traits." *Political Behavior* 18, no. 1: 1–24.

———. 1997. "Implications of Political Expertise in Candidate Trait Evaluations." *Political Research Quarterly* 50, no. 3: 675–697.

———. 1999. "Bringing the Candidate into Models of Candidate Evaluation." *Journal of Politics* 61, no. 3: 700–720.

Gilbert, Daniel T., Brett W. Pelham, and D. S. Krull. 1988. "On Cognitive Busyness: When Person Perceivers Meet Persons Perceived." *Journal of Personality and Social Psychology* 54: 733–739.

Goren, Paul. 2002. "Character Weakness, Partisan Bias, and Presidential Evaluation." *American Journal of Political Science*. 46, no. 3: 627–641.

Groseclose, Timothy, and Keith Krehbiel. 1994. "Golden Parachutes, Rubber Checks, and Strategic Retirements from the 102d House." *American Journal of Political Science* 38: 75–99.

Hacker, Kenneth L. 1995. "Introduction: The Importance of Candidate Images in Presidential Elections." In *Candidate Images in Presidential Elections*, edited by Kenneth L. Hacker, xi–xix. Westport, Conn.: Praeger.

Hamill, Ruth, and Milton Lodge. 1986. "Cognitive Consequences of Political Sophistication." In *Political Cognition: The 19th Annual Carnegie Symposium on Cognition*, edited by R. R. Lau and D. O. Sears, 69–93. Hillsdale, N.J.: Lawrence Erlbaum Associates.

Hellweg, Susan A. 1995. "Campaigns and Candidate Images in American Presidential Elections." In *Candidate Images in Presidential Elections*, edited by Kenneth L. Hacker, 1–17. Westport, Conn.: Praeger.

Hendrick, C., and A. F. Constantini. 1970. "Effects of Varying Trait Inconsistency and Response Requirements on the Primacy Effect in Impression Formation." *Journal of Personality and Social Psychology* 15: 158–164.

Higgins, E. Tory, and Jonathon A. Bargh. 1987. "Social Cognition and Social Perception." *Annual Review of Psychology* 38: 369–425.

Holbrook, Allyson L., Jon A. Krosnick, Penny S. Visser, Wendi L. Gardner, and John T. Cacioppo. 2001. "Attitudes toward Presidential Candidates and Political Parties: Initial Optimism, Inertial First Impressions, and a Focus on Flaws." *American Journal of Political Science* 45, no. 4: 930–950.

Iyengar, Shanto, and Donald R. Kinder. 1987. *News that Matters*. Chicago: University of Chicago Press.

Jacobs, Lawrence R., James N. Druckman, and Eric Ostermeier. 2001. "A Political Theory of Candidate Strategy: Nixon's Use of Polling Information on Policy Issues and Candidate Image." Paper presented at the annual meetings of the American Political Science Association, August 30–September 2, San Francisco, California.

Jacobs, Lawrence R., and Robert Y. Shapiro. 1994. "Issues, Candidate Image, and Priming: The Use of Private Polls in Kennedy's 1960 Presidential Campaign." *American Political Science Review* 88 (September): 527–540.

Jacobson, Gary C., and Michael A. Dimock. 1994. "Checking Out: The Effects of Bank Overdrafts on the 1992 House Elections." *American Journal of Political Science* 38, no. 3: 601–624.

Judd, Charles M., and J. W. Downing. 1990. "Political Expertise and Development of Attitude Consistency." *Social Cognition* 8: 104–124.

Just, Marion R., Ann N. Crigler, Dean E. Alger, Timothy E. Cook, Montague Kern, and Darrell M. West. 1996. *Crosstalk: Citizens, Candidates, and the Media in a Presidential Campaign*. Chicago: University of Chicago.

Kagay, Michael R. 1999. "Public Opinion and Polling during Presidential Scandal and Impeachment." *Public Opinion Quarterly* 63, no. 3: 449–463.

Kaid, Lynda Lee, and Mike Chanslor. 1995. "Changing Candidate Images: The Effects of Political Advertising." In *Candidate Images in Presidential Elections*, edited by Kenneth L. Hacker, 83–97. Westport, Conn.: Praeger.

Kanouse, David E., and L. R. Hanson. 1972. "Negativity in Evaluations." In *Attribution: Perceiving the Causes of Behavior*, edited by E. E. Jones, D. E. Kanouse, H. H. Kelley, R. E. Nisbett, S. Valins, and B. Weiner, 47–62. Morristown, N.J.: General Learning.

Kern, Montague. 1989. *Thirty-Second Politics: Political Advertising in the Eighties*. New York: Praeger.
Klein, Jill G. 1991. "Negativity Effects in Impression Formation: A Test in the Political Arena." *Personality and Social Psychology Bulletin* 17: 412–418.
———. 1996. "Negativity in Impressions of Presidential Candidates Revisited: The 1992 Election." *Personality and Social Psychology Bulletin* 22: 288–295.
Lau, Richard R. 1982. "Negativity in Political Perception." *Political Behavior* 4: 353–377.
———. 1985. "Two Explanations for Negativity Effects in Political Behavior." *American Journal of Political Science* 29: 119–138.
Lodge, Milton, Charles Taber, and Aron Chase Galonsky. 1999. "The Political Consequences of Motivated Reasoning: Partisan Bias in Information Processing." Paper presented at the annual meetings of the American Political Science Association, September 2–5, Atlanta, Georgia.
McGraw, Kathleen M. 1990. "Avoiding Blame: An Experimental Investigation of Political Excuses and Justifications." *British Journal of Political Science* 20: 119–142.
———. 1991. "Managing Blame: An Experimental Test of the Effects of Political Accounts." *American Political Science Review* 85, no. 4: 1133–1158.
McGraw, Kathleen M., and Neil Pinney. 1990. "The Effects of General and Domain-specific Expertise on Political Memory and Judgment." *Social Cognition* 8: 9–30.
McGraw, Kathleen M., Richard Timpone, and Gabor Bruck. 1993. "Justifying Controversial Political Decisions: *Home Style* in the Laboratory." *Political Behavior* 15, no. 3: 289–308.
Meier, Kenneth J., and Thomas M. Holbrook. 1992. "'I Seen My Opportunities and I Took 'Em: Political Corruption in the American States." *Journal of Politics* 54, no. 1: 135–155.
Mendelsohn, Matthew. 1996. "The Media and Interpersonal Communications: The Priming of Issues, Leaders, and Party Identification." *Journal of Politics* 58, no. 1: 112–125.
Moore, David W. 1995. *The Superpollsters: How They Measure and Manipulate Public Opinion in America*. New York: Four Walls Eight Windows.
Newman, L. S., and J. S. Uleman. 1990. "Assimilation and Contrast Effects in Spontaneous Trait Inference." *Personality and Social Psychology Bulletin* 16: 224–240.
Nimmo, Dan, and Robert L. Savage. 1976. *Candidates and Their Images: Concepts, Methods, and Findings*. Pacific Palisades, Calif.: Goodyear.
Peters, John G., and Susan Welch. 1978. "Political Corruption in America: A Search for Definitions and a Theory, or If Political Corruption Is in the Mainstream of American Politics Why Is It Not in the Mainstream of American Politics Research." *American Political Science Review* 72: 974–984.
———. 1980. "The Effects of Charges of Corruption on Voting Behavior in Congressional Elections." *American Political Science Review* 74: 697–708.
Rahn, Wendy M. 1993. "The Role of Partisan Stereotypes in Information Processing about Political Candidates." *American Journal of Political Science* 37: 472–496.

Riggle, Ellen D., Victor C. Ottati, Robert S. Wyer, James Kuklinski, and Norbert Schwartz. 1992. "Bases of Political Judgments: The Role of Stereotypic and Nonstereotypic Information." *Political Behavior* 14: 67–87.

Rundquist, Barry, Gerald D. Strom, and John G. Peters. 1977. "Corrupt Politicians and Their Electoral Support: Some Experimental Observations." *American Political Science Review* 71: 954–963.

Sabato, Larry J., Mark Stencel, and S. Robert Lichter. 2000. *Peepshow: Media and Politics in an Age of Scandal.* New York: Rowman & Littlefield.

Salmore, Barbara G., and Stephen A. Salmore. 1989. *Candidates, Parties, and Campaigns.* Washington, D.C.: CQ Press.

Shea, Daniel M. 1999. "All Scandal Politics is Local: Ethical Lapses, the Media, and Congressional Elections." *Harvard International Journal of Press-Politics* 4, no. 2: 45–62.

Skowronski, J. J., and D. E. Carlston. 1989. "Negativity and Extremity Biases in Impression Formation: A Review of Explanations." *Psychological Bulletin* 105: 131–142.

Stoker, Laura. 1993. "Judging Presidential Character: The Demise of Gary Hart." *Political Behavior* 15: 193–223.

Thompson, John B. 2000. *Political Scandal: Power and Visibility in the Media Age.* Malden, Mass.: Blackwell.

Tiedens, Larissa Z. 2001. "Anger and Advancement versus Sadness and Subjugation: The Effect of Negative Emotion Expressions on Social Status Conferral." *Journal of Personality and Social Psychology* 80, no. 1: 86–94.

Uleman, James S., and Gordon B. Moskowitz. 1994. "Unintended Effects of Goals on Unintended Influences." *Journal of Personality and Social Psychology* 66: 490–501.

Weiner, Bernard, Sandra Graham, Orli Peter, and Mary Zmuidinas. 1991. "Public Confession and Forgiveness." *Journal of Personality* 59, no. 2: 281–312.

Zaller, John R. 1992. *The Nature and Origins of Mass Opinion.* Cambridge: Cambridge University Press.

———. 1998. "Monica Lewinsky's Contribution to Political Science." *PS* 31, no. 2: 182–189.

———. 2001. "Monica Lewinsky and the Mainsprings of American Politics." In *Mediated Politics*, edited by W. Lance Bennett and Robert M. Entman, 252–278. Cambridge: Cambridge University Press.

4

The "Authentic Candidate": Extending Candidate Image Assessment

Allan Louden and Kristen McCauliff

POLITICS IS A CURIOUS BUSINESS. When predictability seems assured, voters (and candidates) are notorious for confounding pundits and academics alike. The 2000 election cycle was no exception. Al Gore, progeny of peace and booming economy, should be president, and George W., the political straggler, should be planning his retirement as Texas governor. Even more confounding is that Bill Clinton, the procurer of "lies," would likely have defeated all pretenders. Even today, suggestions of a third term engender not laughter but serious reporting on constitutional possibilities. Conventional wisdom, whether packaged in election models or known evaluative standards, often gets it wrong. It is not a reach to argue that Gore's demise was met, among ordinary voters, with resignation rather than outrage; that Bush's measured detachment and resolve have risen to "presidential" stature; and that credulity is not agonizingly stretched to imagine another Clinton term.

Other presidents and candidates have similarly perplexed predictions. If the approach by which we understand the formation of candidate image is substantial, then we could expect voters to punish "out-of-step" supplicants. Yet the media, and some researchers, remained bewildered that Ronald Reagan's policies were an affront to polled opinion even as the Great Communicator "hoodwinked" voters. And who can fully explain the observable success of a Jesse Ventura or Jesse Helms given the principles of positive image?

The realities of social science rightly concede that not every exception is accounted for. It is sufficient to find dominant influences among a variety of contributing causes. Yet electoral anomalies are often glaring and of great importance given the enormity of each election cycle. None of this is to say that the innumerable studies examining candidate image are without merit. Most of the time, most of the factors isolated in the research accurately reflect voters' ruminations. It is to suggest, however, that the notion of what is traditionally thought of as "image" has limitations, that current measures only tap aspects of voters' calculus. This chapter is designed to explore a slightly altered approach to the study of candidate assessment. Specifically, *authenticity* is examined as a lens for extending current conceptions.

Contemporary Image Research

The purpose of this chapter is not to review the range of research on candidate image, as excellent summaries are available in this volume and elsewhere (Hellweg, Dionisiopoulos, & Kugler, 1989; Hellweg, 1995), but rather to present a more nuanced reading of evaluative variables. The standard criteria for assessing image lend themselves to data retrieval and are well known. While progress has been made, the subtleties of how learned facts and inferences are reached has yet to be fully explored (Hacker, 1995).

Candidate image is a complex construct that can be conceived as message projection or auditor's reception, composed of discrete judgments or holistic blends, as idiosyncratic or stable tendencies. For the purpose of this chapter we, somewhat generically, view image as an evaluation negotiated and constructed by candidates, voters, and the media in a cooperative venture (Louden, 1990a). Samuel Popkin (1991) and Kenneth Hacker (1995) assume that voters reason about campaigns and candidates. Information about the candidate is gathered from three primary sources: mass media, individual thinking and opinion, and interpersonal conversations. Popkin (1991) states, "People use shortcuts which incorporate much political information; they triangulate and validate their opinions in conversations with people they trust and according to the opinions of national figures whose judgments and positions they have come to know" (p. 7).

As a starting point, we have taken the liberty of collecting, from a variety of research traditions, image variables found to contribute to voter assessment (for example, Hellweg, 1979; Kaid & Chanslor, 1995; Kinder, 1986; Miller, Wattenberg, & Malanchuk, 1985, 1986; Rosenberg, Bohan, McCafferty, & Harris, 1986; Shamir, 1994; Smith & Kidder, 1996; Tannenbaum, Greenberg, & Silverman, 1977; Trent, Mongeau, Trent, Kendall, & Cushing, 1993; Trent, Trent, Mongeau, & Short-Thompson, 1997), organizing those factors into "similar" groupings (see table 4.1). We understand that the categories are to some extent arbitrary, contain overlap within and between categories, include incommensurate levels of abstraction, and are not equally probative. They also vary from election to election, from constituency to constituency (Trent, Short-Thompson, Mongeau, Nusz, & Trent, 2001) and are modified in order to accommodate the qualities displayed by "real" candidates (Hellweg, King, & Williams, 1988; Kinder, Peters, Abelson, & Fiske, 1980; Nimmo & Mansfield, 1986). Nonetheless, there remains solidity to the judgments that echo categorizations existent in the literature and become useful when discussing the influence of character evaluations.

Initially the major categories can be thought of as reflecting the standard issue and image dichotomies that "afflict" much of image research (we discuss the issue/image distinction below). The most striking feature is the copious judgments that are directly or indirectly measures of character: personal qualities, abilities, and manner. This is not surprising, as many observers have concluded that the most important considerations utilized by voters are the candidate's character. Kathleen Kendall and Scott Paine (1995) remark, "Researchers have consistently confirmed that voters are far more interested in candidate characteristics than in party identification or specific issues and are more likely to vote on the basis of the candidate's image" (also see Miller et al., 1985, 1986). Placing character at the evaluative forefront is not misplaced. Assessing future performance is one of the voters' primary concerns. Bruce Buchanan (1988) reminds us that character

> begins as "personal attribute" because it radiates initially from within, in the form of such raw natural attributes as charm, personal magnetism, chemistry, or "vibrations." Call it what you will, presidents' way of being themselves has great impact on their fortunes in office. (p. 251)

TABLE 4.1
Categorized Image Variables

Issue Stance	Attitude homophily, ability to talk about the nation's problems, have solutions or favorable issues stances, sense of security
Personal Qualities and Traits	Calm and cautious, character, compassion, genuine, honest, just, fair, faithful to spouse, gender, good will, likable, moral integrity, personality homophily, persistence, physical attraction, respect, sacrifice, sincere, sophisticated, trustworthy
Competence	Competence, deep, experienced, expertise, intelligent, leader, independent, original, powerful, qualified, reliable, responsible, sense of mission, strong, successful, wise
Communicative Behavior	Ability as a communicator, active, aggressive, appearance believable, demeanor, composure, energetic, extroversion, friendly, humor, gender norms, good smile, humble, personal attraction, sensitivity, sociability, speaking ability

The Role of Issues

Below we address "character" in candidate assessment, and more specifically authenticity, issue knowledge should not to be dismissed as secondary. Simply stated, voters learn from campaigns (Jamieson et al., 2000) and issue homophily often accounts for preference (Kendall & Yum, 1984). The acquisition of issue knowledge is undoubtedly uneven and fine-tuned by campaign strategic choices, but auditors do get it (Page & Shapiro, 1992). Many issue trails, however, lead back to character in some manner; that is, awareness of candidates' issue position is elemental to the construction of character.

Issues are not "standalone" judgments. Issue positions and actions expressed as decisions made are *also* "evidence" of the quality of person. The obvious level is in terms of consistency across time, issue similarity, and ideological grounding, but it is more than a literal consistency, understood solely in terms of issues procurement and application. Candidates' actions and proclamations are constituent elements of their very being, an attribution field day of "what kind of person acts in this way." Actions and issues are a window into the enacted self, at once historical and accumulating.

Barbara Mackoff (2000), writing for the *Christian Science Monitor*, summarizes the meeting point of issues and character:

> What we're really talking about is the source of conviction—that busy intersection where a leader's position on the issues and his character meet. Because we understand that leadership is not a role or a party platform, it is a point of view that results from creating meaning from the events and relationships of a lifetime.

The Intersection of Issue and Character Evaluations

Nearly every article in the last decade has joined a chorus recognizing the limitation of the issue/image dualism, calling for an abandonment of viewing these as independent elements in voter's decision making. Kenneth Hacker, Walter Zakahi, Maury Giles, and Shaun McQuitty (2000) summarize, "The sustained bifurcation of issue and persona perceptions has led researchers to neglect the ways in which messages affect multiple types of candidate image content and how various forms of content affect each other and are interrelated" (p. 236).

The issue/image dichotomy continues to persist, grounded in the dualism's intuitive appeal, research constraints, and democratic idealism, yet progress has been made. More recent empirical findings have started to document the ways in which issue and image data are interrelated. The strongest evidence to emerge is that voters routinely engage in an "issue-to-image transformation."

That is, when voters are presented with issue content, they habitually infer image-based judgments. Initial findings examined political advertising, illustrating that auditors easily and automatically make character assessments even when these attributes were overtly absent in the messages (Helms, 1987; Johnston, 1989; Louden, 1990b, 1994). In the news domain, Doris Graber (1984) found that viewers engage in an "alchemy" whereby issues serve as the basis for making assessments of candidates as capable or compassionate, or smart, or likable.

A series of recent studies, directly measuring traditional image components, have begun to confirm interactions between issue and character reasoning. For example, Hacker et al. (2000) found that issue positions and persona impressions are not independent but rather highly correlated from each other, such that issue knowledge leads to image impressions. Ronald Rapoport, Kelly Metcalf, and Jon Hartman (1989) found "strong evidence of voter inference from trait to issues, and vice versa" (p. 917). Boas Shamir (1994) illustrated that image formations are collections of issue and persona impressions that combine to form an image impression, inseparable and mutually reinforcing. Finally, William Husson, Timothy Stephen, Teresa Harrison, and B. J. Fehr (1988) noted that voters ground their evaluations of traits in specific candidate behavior. The overarching point is that issue informs image, providing the details for auditors reading of candidates' character.

Honesty/Integrity/Trustworthiness

As illustrated in table 4.1, numerous factors have been identified as salient in candidate judgments. Of particular interest to this chapter are factors that, at face value, ally with authenticity. We argue later that most, if not all, of the image components have import when gauging the "authentic" candidate, yet intuitively honesty, integrity, and trustworthiness appear to be very similar, if not identical.

In its various formulations, *honesty* surfaces as a primary character dimension. For example, Roberta Siegel (1966) found that honesty was ranked number one, intelligence was the second factor, and the third consideration was independence. Judith Trent, Cady Short-Thompson, Paul Mongeau, Andrew Nusz, and Jimmie Trent (2001) reported that the public and media agreed that the most important characteristics were that "the candidate be honest, be a person of the highest moral integrity, and be able to talk about problems facing the country" (p. 2126). There was greater emphasis in 2000 than in previous elections, but the essential evaluative standards held among elections.

Graber's (1984) in-depth interviews with voters in Evanston, Illinois, found that "judgments about people's [candidates and officeholders] honesty were especially common" (p. 161), concluding that "while honesty is no assurance of other good qualities, lack of honesty presumably depreciates sharply the value of other good qualities" (p. 162). One index for assessment of honesty appeared to be consistency between a person's actions and statements.

Others have also found honesty and its semantic cousins to be central when assessing candidates. A more complete understanding of candidate image must account for these central character evaluations. Moreover, we argue later that honesty and related terms are part of what we mean by authentic, *but only part*. Variable measures like honest-dishonest and sincere-insincere are treated in current research as self-evident dichotomies with little discussion of what is actually measured. It is indeed an act of faith to believe that these measures are commensurate with authenticity. The following sections begin to sketch a larger framework for assessing authenticity in the political context.

Authenticity

Authenticity is most often a term of art adopted by pundits and the popular press. When authenticity is addressed in academic circles, it is more likely to be found in rhetorical traditions than in social science inquiry. Part of the reason rests in the indeterminate nature of the construct. At face value, the term lacks precision either in describing candidate attributes or voters' evaluative dimensions. And, as noted above, some would see presently examined variables (for example, believability, honesty, humor, fairness, faithfulness, justice, genuineness, independence, reliability, sincerity, and trustworthiness) as capturing, separately or as a class, the relevant judgments constituting "authenticity."

From our reading of the literature, it is less than clear what is being measured by "authenticity variables." Are they prototypes applied across the spectrum to candidates, are they extensions of the daily interpersonal evaluations we make about friends and foes, or are they responses to isolated instances of observed behavior or reflections of core character for any given candidate? And to what extent do they fail to capture relevant evaluations that voters employ in assessing a candidate's authentic self?

Media and Authenticity

Authenticity is hardly an isolated term in the political world. Newspaper reporters routinely assess candidates in terms of their presumed authenticity or lack thereof. Entire administrations and elections are condensed into a knowing appraisal, as with Ralph Nader's estimate that Gore lost in 2000 because he "didn't project authenticity during the campaign, and that he didn't project conviction" (Givel, 2001). Pundits in the 2004 presidential election cycle are quick to offer up John McCain's unique candor, much as they had praised in past elections the "authentic" John Anderson in 1980 and Eugene McCarthy in 1968. McCain, it is recounted, brazenly rejected that candidates have to be scripted. And some reporters are quick to note that the Democratic candidates in 2003 were falling "over themselves in an attempt to convince voters that they are 'more McCain' than the other guy" (Schatz, 2003).

Authenticity as portrayed in the media is often problematic. Not only are campaigns reported as a horse race, inviting cynical speculation for every decision and utterance, but they are also invested in "revealing" the person behind the public persona, turning nearly every reporting encounter into the drawing-aside-the-screen scene in the *Wizard of Oz*. A poignant example was a *Newsweek* cover story that purported to celebrate the search for the authentic candidate. Matt Taibbi (1999) reported on an *Adweek* article commenting on *Newsweek*'s article. Caricatures of Bill Bradley and John McCain were introduced on the cover with the striking headline "Straight Shooters: How Bradley and McCain are Scoring with the Politics of Authenticity." The story that follows inside, however, does not say they were authentic, but were in fact political. Taibbi reports, "When you look inside the actual lead article, here's what it says in the sub-headline: Bradley and McCain are *selling* this year's hottest *commodity*: the *aura* of authenticity that comes from a life that starts outside politics" (emphasis added). Calculated authenticity is not authentic, but rather evidence of the opposite. The media's cynical reading seldom strays far from the assumed duplicity of campaign behavior, assessing the *appearance* of authenticity.

The media's addiction to strategic implications invites responses from campaigns, where choruses of "spinners" become similarly fixated on *fashioning* an "appropriate" image. Their successes are calculated in terms of "effortless" connection with voters. Kathleen Jamieson and Paul Waldman (2003) speak of image construction in terms of *performance*.

> Unlike the grand nineteenth-century rhetoric, this form of political communication [the ability to connect to individuals through the televised medium] demands "sincerity" and "authenticity." Candidates whose performance is stilted or uncomfortable—Michael Dukakis, George H. W. Bush, Al Gore—are punished for appearing insincere, while those who enact the rituals of politics with ease and comfort are judged successful. Such comfort is taken as proof that the persona the politician represents is real and true, while the persona represented by the awkward politician is false and contrived. (p. 29–30)

We acknowledge that smooth, personable, sophisticated, self-conscious staging contributes to winning; yet leaving it there invites a reading of voters as "easily taken in" and fails to account for the abundance of successful politicians who lack these very qualities. As we argue below, authenticity is more than being apt.

Campaigns and Authenticity

Paul Theroux (2003), one of America's foremost travel writers, recounts one culture he encountered that welcomed "foreigners with a mixture of banter, hearty browbeating, teasing humor, effusiveness, and the sort of insincere familiarity I associate with people trying to become intimate enough with me to pick my pocket" (p. 7). He could as easily have been speaking of Americans' instinctive response to "politicians." Politicians as a class are presumed to be self-serving and are granted only provisional trust. Graber's (1984) respondents saw politicians as "a breed apart—power hungry, double dealing, unscrupulous" (p. 163). An important assumption of the suspect category—politician—was the expectation that such people put getting elected ahead of moral behavior.

The news media can feed this prejudice, as Jamieson and Waldman (2003) note with Vice President Gore in 2000:

> Journalists' portrait of Gore was so damaging in part because it fitted him in a mold their over-arching storyline assigns to politicians in general: Politicians are assumed to be dishonest schemers who present a false image to the public in order to advance their quest for power. (p. 30)

To avoid the damning classification of *politician*, campaigns routinely move to (re)establish their authenticity. Matthew Cooper (1999) provides a typical journalist's account, "Gore has explicitly said he's 'throwing away' his prepared text. To broadcast his soul searching, he has released his Vietnam letters. His campaign has even released Gore's handwritten text of an ad to show he's not consultant driven."

Campaigns can be thought of as unfolding stories, as narratives constructed through the actions and interactions of candidates, voters, and media. Story lines are massaged by various actors and, as Jamieson and Waldman (2003) persuasively argue, color the interpretation of most every happening in the election. A disquieting example from the 2000 presidential race involved the "seemingly unscripted smooch" (Anderson, 2000). Jamieson and Waldman (2003) suggest:

> Even if a politician's performance accurately represents reality, it remains a performance and thus in some sense artificial. When Al Gore gave wife Tipper a passionate kiss before ascending to the podium to deliver his acceptance speech at the 2000 Democratic convention, some commentators complained that the moment must have been planned in order to humanize Gore's image—after all, he knew that the cameras were on him. While no one questioned that the Gores have a strong and loving marriage, the genuineness of "The Kiss" was hotly debated. The question of whether the kiss was "real" or whether it was a perform-

ance could be raised because Gore's authenticity was itself in question. Bush could freely wear different types of clothing at different times without notice, but sartorial alterations on Gore's part became part of an ongoing discussion on his degree of authenticity. Just as Bush's intellect was subject to continual examination, and reevaluations, the question asked of Gore's performance was usually some form of: "Was it real?" (p. 27)

The very nature of a campaign, in addition to the media's cynical contribution, makes establishing authenticity a difficult assignment. Elections are definitionally win/lose, oppositional in nature. Elections call forth an opponent(s) whose task is to subvert. Additionally, campaigns are deeply tied to candidates as the central actor; it is not surprising that pitting two personas against one another promotes the embodiment of evil in the opponent. Finally, competition for voter approval asks candidates to fulfill voters' wishes and to invest in their identities, often creating tensions with their own personalities and agendas.

Not withstanding the pressures that undermine authenticity, many candidates (as least compared to their opponent) manage to establish a reliable identity. Often those office seekers (and office holders) we "come to know" are exempted from the stereotype of politician, and many candidates, even in introduction, are seen as genuine. It appears to us that the anomalous diversions from the "ideal candidate" require a closer look at the judgments that surround authenticity.

Authenticity Defined

Jamieson and Waldman (2003), in their recent book *The Press Effect*, provide a helpful discussion of the role that media narratives play in establishing and undermining candidate's authenticity. Their perspective draws upon Erving Goffman, viewing authenticity as a minimal difference between the frontstage persona presented to the public and the backstage persona presented to intimates. The search for the "real" candidate" by the media "is an effort to drag the backstage personal up to the front." (p. 29)

Voters, undoubtedly aided by the media filter, engage in similar frontstage and backstage comparisons. We take the position, however, that voters' judgments are more than press renderings or campaign offerings and are more expansive than the fit of public and private. In an earlier section, we claimed that issue positions and actions offer clues to credibility; below, we consider how core character evaluations impact authenticity.

To be authentic can mean a number of comparisons, the question being "in reference to what?" To be authentic is to be genuine, real, valid, bona fide, true, reliable, dependable, existent, unaltered, legitimate, faithful, and surely more expressions. These labels imply a correspondence between what is shared and one's actual positions, actual responsibilities, and, most importantly, actual self. It also suggests that voters make assessments even more fundamental than a simple correspondence with presentation. Voters draw upon their own experience and heuristic mapping (Lupia, McCubbins, & Popkin, 2000) much as they judge others every day, assessing the substance of every "interpersonal" encounter with a candidate (Husson et al., 1988). These judgments are subtle, complex, and integrated. From our perspective, minimally voters would look for (1) transparency, (2) dependability, and (3) consistency, all of which ask if the candidates are who they say they are. In other words, the authentic candidates are those who know who they are and behave consistently with themselves.

Authenticity: An Extension

Our contention is that the prior research efforts have not measured if auditors see candidates as *true to themselves*. To begin a discussion of what questions a researcher might pose to voters, we ground our thinking upon two influential rhetorical theorists.

Walter Fisher (1989) argues in his book *Human Communication as Narration* that humans come to understand their world via the narratives they encounter. Of particular interest is Fisher's notion of *characterological coherence*. He posits:

> Whether a story is believable depends on the reliability of characters, both as narrators and as actors. Determination of one's character is made by interpretations of the person's decisions and actions that reflect values. In other words, character may be considered an organized set of actional tendencies. If these tendencies contradict one another, change significantly, or alter in "strange" ways, the result is a questioning of character. Coherence in life and in literature *requires that characters behave characteristically.* (p. 47) (emphasis added)

He argues that "without this kind of predictability, there is no trust, no community, no rational human order" (p. 47). Fundamentally the judgment is an inquiry into motivation, the avenue to adherence for message and messenger. Fisher summarizes, "Determining a character's motive is prerequisite to trust, and trust is the foundation of belief" (p. 47).

As Fisher (1989) points out, this view of character "overlaps but is not exactly synonymous with traditional concepts of ethos" (p. 148). He reminds us that

> Ethos, in Aristotle's theory of rhetoric, is a kind of proof that establishes a speaker's intelligence, integrity, and goodwill. Credibility, in recent communication research, is a function of an audience's attribution of such traits as expertise, trustworthiness, and dynamism to a source. (p. 148)

That these traditional factors are mirrored in current research on candidate image is not surprising or inappropriate. Yet the traditional measures are thought of in terms of audience predisposition and candidate projection, neither of which requires a match with the actor's fundamental character. Fisher's characterological coherence goes beyond. His notion is more elemental; the fit with the person's central self, his or her fundamental value structure. When voters reach a sense of this authentic self and judge that orientation to be dependable with one's own way of being in the world, consent follows.

Michael Hyde (2001), in his examination of Heidegger and Levinas's writings, *The Call of Conscience*, discusses authenticity as *elemental* to humans. He observes:

> For any human being this ability [being one's "Own Self"] is uniquely his or her "own" (*eigen*); it defines the "authenticity" (*Eigentlichkeit*), the most primordial truth, of human being. Hence, in the truest and most authentic sense of the term, this self activity can be claimed by any persons to be personally and properly "mine." It forms the temporal basis of a persona's historically situated and thus "finite" freedom, which is always anchored to and constrained by past decisions, present involvements, one's biological condition, and existing environmental factors. (p. 42)

The call of conscience discloses the "self-constancy" of this challenging nature of our existence. Even as candidates are caught up in everyday campaign interactions and overwhelmed by demands of presenting the winning face, there is still something there that is their own. Hyde (2001) talks of this fundamental nature as "the source of what Heidegger defines as a human being's 'authenticity'" (p. 57). It is what, in the end, anchors choice.

Certainly a candidate's public face is not exactly the same as the private, but there is a core, a framework that underwrites their public presentation. Hyde (2001) holds that

> people can be so good at putting on a face, at engaging in the socially circumscribed rituals of "face-work" so as to maintain for themselves and others a "positive self-image" that what they offer us is essentially nothing but a successful cover-up of who they really are and what they truly believe. (p. 111)

Voters have as their central task unearthing insincerity and stealing a look through to that central self.

Are Voters Able to Evaluate "Authenticity"?

Fisher and Hyde's works point to fundamental judgments that underwrite authenticity: acting in concert with one's elemental being. That voters engage in such judgment surely will be greeted with considerable skepticism. Many argue that voters are little more than pawns to the unfolding campaign and media saturation. Our perspective is more forgiving, holding not only that voters have the ability and opportunity to make these more intricate assessments of authenticity, but also that the processes are inescapable.

In recent years, there has been a resurrection of voter "rationality" among researchers (Lupia et al., 2000). The trend in the literature is increasing affirmation of voter equanimity, whether in reasoned cognitive shortcuts (Popkin, 1991), issue knowledge (Page & Shapiro, 1992), or affective precursors to alignments (Marcus, Neuman, & MacKuen, 2000). Voters are never fully hostage to campaigns and media. Inherently, they make "reasoned" interpretations of the political environment that are their own. As one consultant reminded Clinton in a campaign memo, "Bill, voters are not stupid. They make complicated decisions they can't explain but they always have reasons" (Strother, 2003, p. 213).

Unquestionably the media are powerful in setting agendas and framing candidates' character. What is not predictable is how campaigns and candidates react in the face of prevailing narratives and events. The reality is that candidates continue to appear on television, proffer messages, and make strategic decisions. In other words, the central characters in the narrative *act* and their choices are windows to judging motive.

Our position is that voters have ample opportunity to observe candidates' tendencies. Most have watched the candidate "handle crowds, speeches, press conferences, reporters, and squabbles," all of which provides "information with which they imagine how he or she would be likely to behave in office" (Popkin, 1991, p. 62). Patterns emerge from the enormous amount of information that voters filter. The decisional process is described by Jamieson and Waldman (2003): "When one enters the world of personality profiling, the question asked is not did the event happen, but rather, is there a pattern, and if so, what does it mean?" (p. 39).

Additionally, not all coverage is uniform, and periodically the prevailing campaign stories are challenged. Not every instance of formulaic packaging of candidate attributes finds resonance, and lapdog conformity cannot be guaranteed among voters. The political landscape is littered with candidates who the pundits and press anointed as plausible contenders (e.g., Senator John Connelly of Texas, Senator Edmund Muskie of Maine, or even Senator Gary Hart of Colorado). The awareness of a candidate's fit with self may be so primary as to be a priori to media priming.

Appraising if candidates are "true to themselves" is admittedly a probability statement. Auditors can never fully know what others will do, let alone predict with precision their own behavior, yet having a sense of "who the candidate really is" seems elemental. And it is more than assessing truth telling regarding some policy domain or the threshold of a candidate's liberty with the "truth." Rather, it is a sense of having access to their very core or, minimally, that the candidate has such access. Voters do not require exposure to their naked private selves, but more an anticipation that they will act in accordance with "who they are." Minimally, the "better" candidates would know who they are, would be comfortable in their own skin, and would have a center guiding their dealings.

One implication of seeking authenticity would be auditing those situations in which the candidates are unfettered or, minimally, less constrained. Robin Anderson (2000) argues that viewers want to see the candidates in "casual, unscripted settings" where they can be themselves. That such conditions *ever* exist in a campaign is arguable, yet there are moments when authenticity is expected or thought to be more transparent. Perhaps the convention acceptance speech, arguably penned by the candidate, or the debates in which an aspirant "stands alone" with his or her intellect and soul bared to the world represent such times. A strong case can be made that the presidential debates in 2000 were pivotal in the election, the apex where Gore's inauthenticity was "fixed" and George W.'s constancy "affirmed."

Finally, even when candidates engage in "campaign behavior," that, too, provides clues to their inner selves. It is impossible to communicate without character leakage, however oblique. Campaigns are designed to massage an "image," moves that are from time to time intentionally disingenuous. It is almost a requisite that candidates be able to make the moves of a "skilled politician." Carefully brokered statements, omission, reticence, misappropriation, and a self-conscious brazenness become the measures of leadership skills. And all this is done with an obligatory seriousness yet retains a "tongue-in-cheek" quality wherein the candidate is aware that he or she is simply meeting role expectations. They *are* authentic when being "inauthentic" in their enacted behaviors. For candidates to not appreciate the difference brings their essential character into question. If Gore had embraced his exaggeration, had appropriated campaign excess as his own, then the very acts of exaggeration would endorse his character rather than reveal his duplicity. To be skilled at political moves has a certain authenticity, especially if that reveals skills and boundaries of core character. Voters perhaps tolerate, even invite, a degree of deception as long as it is "authentic."

Image Revisited

There is a flavor above that a candidate's authenticity is a trump card, providing critical background to understanding policy positions, campaign strategies, and personal worth/trust. This suggestion is intentional. Standard character measures tend to emphasize how issue or image, reliability or uncertainty, honesty or insincerity becomes the signature for a given campaign. The seductive element is to then miss how voters might reasonably endorse the "dishonest" or "incompetent" candidate.

In the 1996 presidential cycle, for example, William Flanigan and Nancy Zingale (1998) reasoned, "Dole successfully portrayed himself as having better integrity than Clinton, but integrity was not what voters were most concerned about in this election." As plausible as this may be, it follows that Clinton's integrity was found wanting and that he was not authentic yet electable. If one were to view authenticity in terms of the candidate's fits with their true self, then Clinton's demeanor cannot be simply dismissed as flawed. Voters knew what they were getting when they endorsed Clinton. Jamieson and Waldman (2003) recount that "few were truly surprised to learn that Bill Clinton had been unfaithful to his wife, behavior he had acknowledged, albeit obliquely, in a *60 Minutes* interview during the 1992 primaries" (p. 173).

Clinton was "inauthentic" but there was a self-awareness, even transparency, with his ambition and skills. His appetites were part and parcel of the ambition, charm, compassion, and engagement that warranted voters' assent. *Clinton was Clinton.* If voters, as we have argued, assessed Clinton via our expanded notion of authenticity—the fit with self—then his support is more understandable. This is in stark contrast to Gore's 2000 effort in which he likely possessed integrity, yet voters never got the sense that he was true to himself. He became a "politician" whose chameleon disposition left him without a central core the voters could trust; he was authentically inauthentic.

To ask what is new with our advocacy is reasonable. Although we do not have a firm answer, we believe there is potential to appreciate some of the anomalies that populate every election cycle. A direct solicitation of voter's assessments of candidate authenticity directs our thinking to connections among constituent elements of image that have yet to be systematically explored, for example, looking at instances in which candidates are evaluated negatively via traditional measures but still command elections. Inquires might include, for example, "Can candidates be viewed as less than honest yet trustworthy?" "How does sincerity interact with approval?" "How do the factors intersect with issues, such that we reject their ideas but embrace the person and vice versa?" and "Does viewing an actor's consistency across time suggest commonality in assessment of caution, compassion, persistence, and other judgments?"

We conclude with revisiting the questions typically asked in social science research. Questions presently posed take the form of "Do you agree with the candidate?" "Do you like the candidate?" "Do you trust the candidate?" and

"Does the candidate have high ethical standards?" Inquiries extending image to an authenticity frame would ask more than knowledge of candidate's biography, policy positions, and affective response. That is, versions of how "real" is the candidate would become a focal inquiry. Table 4.2 provides potential questions for each of the categories defined earlier.

Looking to Future Elections

Elections inevitably defy prediction. As we write, the 2004 presidential election is particularly unsettled. Events are driving the election in a way not seen since 1968, yet the election will nonetheless be influenced by the candidates' "fit with self."

George W. Bush, bolstered by fears of national (in)security, has firmly positioned his reelection effort. George W., arguably, is "lite" on image staples: competence, knowledge, or even "good will." Nonetheless, *there is a there there*. And it is more than being personable or common or even privately assessable. One has the sense that Bush has accommodation with self, that he can be trusted to act in accordance with his own limitations, principles, and vision. Of course, those very conclusions "scare the hell" out of many voters. Regardless, Bush's conviction/core simultaneously assures foe and friend alike that he passes some threshold of authenticity.

Bush's opponent, John Kerry, is more perplexing, and the authenticity jury is still out. Kerry, originally seen as reasoned yet distanced, has been able to sustain a more engaged and empathic persona. He is, at once, the militaristic dove, flexibly rock-solid, and the experienced outsider. His ability to traverse the emerging events may be successful *if* his political acumen follows from the

TABLE 4.2
Authenticity Judgments

Personal Qualities and Traits Are they who they say they are?	Do the candidates know who they are? Do the candidates reveal their true selves? Is the candidate consistent with his or her core self? Is the candidate comfortable in his or her own skin? Are candidates an enactment of themselves?
Competence Can they be counted on?	Do they believe in what they say they believe? Is the candidate consistent with his or her central beliefs? Do the candidates do what they say? Are the texts authentic?
Communicative Behavior Is their interaction authentic?	Is public and private character authentic? Can we trust our interpretation? Is the candidate too political?

"real" John Kerry and not the indecisive interpretation offered by the GOP ad makers. That John Kerry be John Kerry, even with potential limitations, seems advisable. One can adapt too much. Even when particular candidates do not embody our ideal, we often *respect* them. We believe that this has something to do with their being authentically authentic.

Surely events, money, issues, and the ability to rally the base, along with a myriad of other factors, will contribute to the 2004 decision. In the end, however, these factors are influenced by an ability to do more than *appear* authentic. The candidate who emerges surely will be aided if he *is* authentic. The candidates might well be advised to not try and be "John McCain," wearing excitable access and openness on their sleeve, but rather to celebrate those qualities that match up with who they are.

Political consultant Raymond Strother (2003), in his enjoyable new book *Falling Up*, narrates a lesson leaned in the making of his award-winning film *The Fight for Louisiana* for the Russell Long Senate campaign in 1982:

> I found that the Long campaign was changing my attitude about political communication. . . . Perhaps it was my great respect for him and his office . . . but I began to understand that all of my preconceived ideas about how to prepare candidates for filming were simply knee-jerk conventional wisdom. I didn't try to talk Long into hiring tailors for perfectly cut suits and I didn't rehearse lines with him. Russell Long was what he was, and it was my job to communicate the best parts of his character and not to try to change anything. He wore expensive but baggy suits, so I filmed him in baggy suits. He occasionally stuttered, and I recorded his stutters. . . . When a consultant tries to change a candidate, the result is a cardboard figure. (p. 124)

For many, "authenticity" will remains too "indeterminate" and "lacking in precision" for empirical investigation. Our submission, however, is that this key constituent of candidate image not continue to be ignored. Resourceful researchers should consider developing the means to measure voters' assessment of "candidate's fit with self."

References

Anderson, R. 2000. "The Marketing Is the Message." www.mediachannel.org/views/oped/andersen.shtml.
Buchanan, B. 1988. "Sizing up Candidates." *PS: Political Science and Politics* 21 (1988): 263–268.
Cooper, M. 1999. "The Search for Authenticity." www.cnn.com/ALLPOLITICS/time/1999/10/25/view.html.

Fisher, W. R. 1989. *Human Communication as Narration: Toward a Philosophy of Reason, Value, and Action.* Columbia: University of South Carolina Press.

Flanigan, W. H., and N. H. Zingale. 1998. *Political Behavior of the American Electorate,* 9th ed. Washington, D.C.: Congressional Quarterly Books.

Givel, M. 2001. "Dems Say Gore's Presidential bid Ruined by Populist Message." http://civic.net/civic-values.archive/200101/msg00169.html.

Graber, D. A. 1984. *Processing the News: How People Tame the Information Tide.* New York: Longman.

Hacker, K. L. 1995. *Candidate Images in Presidential Elections.* Westport, Conn.: Praeger.

Hacker, K. L., W. R. Zakahi, M. J. Giles, and S. McQuitty. 2000. "Components of Candidate Images: Statistical Analysis of the Issue-Persona Dichotomy in the Presidential Campaign of 1966." *Communication Monographs* 67: 227–238.

Hellweg, S. A. 1979. "An Examination of Voter Conceptualizations of the Ideal Political Candidate." *Southern Speech Communication Journal* 44: 373–385.

———. 1995. "Campaign and Candidate Images in American Presidential Elections." In *Candidate Images in Presidential Elections,* edited by K. Hacker, 1–17. Westport, Conn.: Praeger.

Hellweg, S. A., G. N. Dionisiopoulos, and D. B. Kugler. 1989. "Political Candidate Image: A State-of-the-Art Review." In *Progress in Communication Sciences,* vol. 9, edited by B. Dervin and M. J. Voight, 43–78. Norwood, N.J.: Ablex.

Hellweg, S. A., S. W. King, and S. E. Williams. 1988. "Comparative Candidate Evaluation as a Function of Election Level and Candidate Incumbency." *Communication Reports* 1: 76–85.

Helms, L. 1987. "Candidate Impressions: A Combination of Candidate Images and Issues." Master's thesis, Wake Forest University, Winston-Salem, North Carolina.

Husson, W., T. Stephen, T. M. Harrison, and B. J. Fehr. 1988. "An Interpersonal Communication Perspective on Images of Political Candidates." *Human Communication Research* 14: 397–421.

Hyde, M. J. 2001. *The Call of Conscience: Heidegger and Levinas, Rhetoric and Euthanasia Debate.* Columbia: University of South Carolina Press.

Jamieson, K. H., M. G. Hagen, D. Orr, L. Sillaman, S. Morse, and K. Kirn. 2000. "What Did the Leading Candidates Say, and Did It Matter?" *Annals of the American Academy of Political and Social Science* 572: 12–16.

Jamieson, K. H., and P. Waldman. 2003. *The Press Effect: Politicians, Journalists, and the Stories that Shape the Political World.* New York: Oxford University Press.

Johnston, D. D. 1989. "Image and Issue Information: Message Content or Interpretation." *Journalism Quarterly* 66: 379–382.

Kaid, L. L., and M. Chanslor. 1995. "Changing Candidate Images: The Effects of Television Advertising." In *Candidate Images in Presidential Elections,* edited by K. Hacker, 81–97. New York: Praeger.

Kendall, K. E., and S. C. Paine. 1995. "Political Images and Voting Decisions." In *Candidate Images in Presidential Elections,* edited by K. Hacker, 19–36. Westport, Conn.: Praeger.

Kendall, K. E., and J. O. Yum. 1984. "Persuading the Blue-Collar Voter: Issues, Images, and Homophily." In *Communication Yearbook 8*, edited by R. N. Bostrom, 707–722. Beverly Hills, Calif.: Sage.

Kinder, D. R. 1986. "Presidential Character Revisited." In *Political Cognition: The 19th Annual Carnegie Symposium on Cognition*, edited by R. R. Lau and D. O. Sears, 233–255. Hillsdale, N.J.: Lawrence Erlbaum.

Kinder, D. R., M. D. Peters, R. P. Abelson, and S. T. Fiske. 1980. "Presidential Prototypes." *Political Behavior* 4: 315–337.

Louden, A. 1990a. *Image Construction in Political Spot Advertising: The Hunt/Helms Senate Campaign, 1984.* Ph.D. diss, University of Southern California. Dissertation Abstracts, DAI-A 51/04.

———. 1990b. "Transformation of Issue to Image and Presence: Eliciting Character Evaluations in Negative Spot Advertising." Paper presented at the meeting of the International Communication Association, Dublin, Ireland, June.

———. 1994. "Voter Rationality and Media Excess: Image in the 1992 Presidential Campaign." In *The 1992 Presidential Campaign: A Communication Perspective*, edited by R. Denton, 169–187. Westport, Conn.: Praeger.

Lupia, A., M. D. McCubbins, and S. L. Popkin. 2000. *Elements of Reason: Cognition, Choice, and the Bounds of Rationality.* New York: Cambridge University Press.

Mackoff, B. 2000. "A Question of Experience." *Christian Science Monitor*, October 11. www.nandotimes.com/election2000/story/0,3977,500267715-500416094-502566581-0-nandotimes,00.html.

Marcus, G. E., W. R. Neuman, and M. MacKuen. 2000. *Artificial Intelligence and Political Judgment.* Chicago: University of Chicago Press.

Miller, A. H., M. P. Wattenberg, and O. Malanchuk. 1985. "Cognitive Representations of Candidate Assessments." In *Political Communication Yearbook—1984*, edited by K. R. Sanders, L. L. Kaid, and D. Nimmo, 183–210. Carbondale: Southern Illinois University Press.

———. 1986. "Schematic Assessments of Presidential Candidates." *American Political Science Review* 80: 521–540.

Nimmo, D., and M. W. Mansfield. 1986. "Change and Persistence in Candidate Images: Presidential Debates across 1976, 1980, and 1984." Paper presented at the meeting of the Speech Communication Association, Chicago, November.

Page, B. I., and R. Y. Shapiro. 1992. *The Rational Public: Fifty Years of Trends in Americans' Policy Preferences.* Chicago: University of Chicago Press.

Popkin, S. L. 1991. *The Reasoning Voter: Communication and Persuasion in Presidential Campaigns.* Chicago: University of Chicago Press.

Rapoport, R. B., K. L. Metcalf, and J. A. Hartman. 1989. "Candidate Traits and Voter Inferences: An Experimental Study." *Journal of Politics* 51: 917–932.

Rosenberg, S., L. Bohan, P. McCafferty, and K. Harris. 1986. "The Image and the Vote: The Effect of Candidate Presentation on Voter Preference." *American Journal of Political Science* 30: 108–127.

Schatz, A. 2003. "Copycat Candidates." www.prospect.org/webfeatures/2003/01/schatz-a-01-28.html.

Shamir, B. 1994. "Ideological Position, Leaders' Charisma, and Voting Preferences: Personal vs. Partisan Elections." *Political Behavior* 16: 265–287.

Siegel, R. S. 1966. "Image of the American Presidency: Part II of an Exploration into Popular Views of Presidential Power." *Midwest Journal of Political Science* 10: 123–137.

Smith, A., and R. M. Kidder. 1996. *Political Attack Advertising*. Camden, Maine: Institute for Global Ethics. www.campaignconduct.org/research/White-Paper.html.

Strother, R. D. 2003. *Falling Up: How a Redneck Helped Invent Political Consulting*. Baton Rouge: Louisiana State University Press.

Taibbi, M. 1999. "Press Review: Site Shooters." www.exile.ru/pr/pr78.html.

Tannenbaum, P., B. Greenberg, and F. Silverman. 1977. "Candidate Images." In *The Great Debates: Background, Perspective, Effects*, edited by S. Kraus, 271–288. Bloomington: Indiana University Press.

Theroux, P. 2003. *Dark Star Safari*. New York: Houghton Mifflin.

Trent, J. S., P. Mongeau, J. Trent, K. Kendall, and R. Cushing. 1993. "The Ideal Candidate: A Study of the Desired Attributes of the Public and the Media across Two Presidential Campaigns." *American Behavioral Scientist* 37: 225–239.

Trent, J. S., C. Short-Thompson, P. A. Mongeau, A. K. Nusz, and J. D. Trent. 2001. "Image, Media Bias, and Voter Characteristics." *American Behavioral Scientist* 44: 2101–2124.

Trent, J. S., J. D. Trent, P. Mongeau, and C. Short-Thompson. 1997. "The Ideal Candidate Revisited: A Study of the Desired Attributes of the Public and the Media across Three Presidential Campaigns." *American Behavioral Scientist* 40: 1001–1019.

5

A Dual-Processing Perspective of Candidate Image Formation

Kenneth L. Hacker

DURING AND AFTER EACH PRESIDENTIAL ELECTION, journalists and other chattering heads in the mass media offer the public what they believe is serious analysis of voter behavior and motivation. While there are occasional insights in their comments, most of their comments are atheoretical and speculative. In *Newsweek* (August 28, 2000), Jonathan Alter wrote that Bush's problem and Gore's advantage was that "presidential campaigns are not about the tone of presidential campaigns.... They're about the lives and futures of the voters—in other words, the issues" (p. 26). Alter argued that the voters in 2000 wanted vigorous debate about issues. In contrast, Anna Quindlen (*Newsweek*) wrote that this election like others was about the "cult of personality" in which voters assess and react to personalities of presidential candidates just like they do the personalities of their friends, spouses, coworkers, and neighbors (2000, p. 68). Alter argued that Reagan beat Carter in 1980 because of his charge that Carter had ruined the economy, while Quindlen said it was because the voters liked Reagan and his charm.

The literature on candidate images and image formation reveals a continual reference to issue position impressions and candidate persona impressions among other perceptions that end up constituting the presidential candidate images. Even if one adds other components as done in the study by Stephen, Harrison, Husson, and Albert (this volume), there are still two main types of voter impressions—either impressions about candidate issue positions or impressions about candidate traits. Candidate issues positions can include policy statements, actions on issues, record in office regarding issues, and arguments made about political changes. Candidate traits can include personality, communication behaviors, abilities, and leadership potential.

Since voters appear to process both avenues of perceptions (issues and traits) and persuasion theories indicate that human message reception involves dual routes of processing, there may be a parallel in the literature that can be useful in the service of producing more theoretical views of candidate images. Such a theoretical approach is not yet employed but is developed in this chapter in an effort to argue for a model of candidate image dual processing.

One possible dual-process model is a consolidative model, which is an alternative to the selective models like the elaboration likelihood model (ELM). A selective model assumes one route for message processing that operates in place of another route. With a consolidative model, persona and issue perceptions can have independent effects while also affecting each other. This does not refer to two processes occurring separately but rather simultaneously even if each process is doing different things and one is more active than the other at any given moment of communication. As will be shown later, this model is an alternative to the traditional dual-process and unimodal (single-process) models of message processing.

The discussion here about dual processing should not be confused with Cartesian dualism or what is known as Descartes' Error. Gilbert (1999) argues that the dual process models of psychology are less about specifying only two processes than about refuting that there is only one process operative in message processing. As early as Plato, there have been hunches that complex behaviors result from interactions of less complex processes (Gilbert, 1999). It is fairly common knowledge today in social and behavioral sciences that any explanation of human behavior must include the interaction and organization of multiple parts (Gilbert, 1999). Such a multiple-factor explanation must account for processes like cognition, emotion, reasoning, control, and consciousness. This chapter examines various ways to conceive of presidential candidate images with a general dual-process perspective. It concludes with a proposed consolidative model that attempts to account for such multiple factors as an explanation of the formation and component of candidate images.

Single-factor descriptions of human behavior are common in the social sciences and they are likely to be erroneous. This should have been easily evident in the journalists' explanations of the 2000 election described above. The reason why one list of causes may sound as good as another is that both are partially correct. This is why studies that say that votes are related to candidate issue positions are correct, and studies that say that votes are related to candidate persona impressions are correct even if they seem contradictory. Did Al Gore win the popular vote and Bush win the Electoral College votes because of issue differences or because of persona differences? Generally speaking, it appears that winning presidential candidates have the best candidate images with whatever mix of issue and persona impressions happen to constitute those images.

Gallup data from late July 2000 indicated that Bush led Gore in many key areas of both issue and persona evaluation. The data indicated that Bush led Gore on character perceptions of sharing values with voters (46–41 percent), being a strong and decisive leader (50–30 percent), being able to manage government effectively (49–37 percent), having a vision for the nation (45–38 percent), being someone people could be proud of as president (46–39 percent), and being honest and trustworthy (44–37 percent).[1] Of these candidate traits, voters indicated that the most important for them were strong and decisive leadership (94 percent), honesty and trustworthiness (92 percent), and a vision for the nation (91 percent).

The same Gallup data set regarding issues showed that Bush led Gore on the issues of the economy (47–40 percent), federal taxes (51–36 percent), national defense (58–31 percent), and handling the budget surplus (49–38 percent). On the other hand, Gore led Bush on the issues of creating jobs (44–40 percent), the environment (49–37 percent), and the cost of health care (47–41 percent). Of all these issues, the most important to the voters were the economy (86 percent), the costs of health care (84 percent), federal taxes (77 percent), and handling the budget surplus (77 percent). When looking at the most salient character traits and the most important issues in this data set, Bush was leading Gore on the most important traits and losing only on the issue of health care costs to Gore.

The Complexity of Voting Decision Making

The views of scholars regarding voting determinants have changed over the years and there is no consensus over what stable ordering, if there is one, exists with these determinants. Three factors stand out as clearly argued in some manner: partisanship, issues, and candidate character (Niemi & Weisberg, 1993). A problem facing statistical analyses, which sought to test relative importance of these three determinants, has been the fact that there are differences among voters in how they weigh them (Niemi & Weisberg, 1993). A presidential candidate is evaluated differently if the candidate is an incumbent rather than a challenger. The incumbents face retrospective voting processes to a large extent (Niemi & Weisberg, 1993).

Issues can change over time and if researchers do not ask about election-specific issues but only about generalized issues from past elections, the relative importance of issues will be underestimated (Niemi & Weisberg, 1993). Foreign policy matters are likely to affect voters more if candidates campaign on foreign policy. Some of this input on candidate image formation and decision making can be partially explained by Fazio's theory of attitude accessibility (Fazio & Roskos-Ewoldsen, 1994).

According to Fazio and Roskos-Ewoldsen (1994), attitudes can guide your behaviors with no thought about them. Individuals think about situations, and their interpretation of the situation determines the behavior that results. Defining the event consists of perceptions of the attitude object in the situation along with definition of the situation. Definition of situation activates schemata concerned with expected behaviors in situations. Attitudes vary in how accessible they are from memory. An attitude must be activated from memory when seeing the attitude object for the attitude to have an effect on behavior. Fazio and Roskos-Ewoldsen (1994, p. 79) argue that "attitude relevance cues" can be used to activate attitudes such that the individual considers the relevance of the attitude in a particular situation. Attitude accessibility refers to how easily an attitude comes to mind. Once attitudes are accessed, they affect how events in the situation are judged. With issues, then, voters are likely to bring issue-relevant schemata into play if there is substantial debating about issues. The same may be true for candidate traits.

The content of candidate images will vary in relation to what aspects of presidential candidacies are getting the most attention and what voters consider to be the most important differences between candidates. William Flanigan and Nancy Zingale (2002, p. 181) say, in reference to voter responses to National Election Studies questions, "Given the unusually high number of issue-related comments about Democratic candidates in recent elections, we need to be careful not to interpret candidate image as reflecting only personality traits." Many diverse factors affect these images, such as impressions of the opposing candidate, failure to keep promises, responsibility for events such as performance of the economy, traits such as honesty, and positions on issues like health care (Flanigan & Zingale, 2002).

While researchers agree that issues affect voting behavior today, there is no consensus on the exact nature of the effects. For example, there is evidence that issues that are weighted most heavily have the most effect on voting (Niemi & Weisberg, 1993). Gregory Markus (1993, p. 152) notes,

> Individual voting decisions . . . may be influenced by a myriad of factors: prevailing attachments to political parties, ideological and policy considerations, the personal characteristics and traits of contenders for office, regional loyalties, group memberships, candidate debates, media imagery, and more.

In his research on voter concerns with economic issues, Markus (1993) finds that voters are concerned with both macroeconomic conditions (sociotropic concerns) and personal economic circumstances (pocketbook issues).

Wendy Rahn, John Aldrich, Eugene Borgida, and John Sullivan (1993) state that voters form images of presidential candidates from information they receive and use to make judgments about candidate characteristics. Rahn et al. (1993, p. 190) say, "A wide variety of political cues and other kinds of information are abundantly available to the voters, and potentially all of it can be used when evaluating candidates."

Despite all of these claims about diverse input into voters' candidate evaluation processes, it continues to appear that voting is driven mainly by partisanship and candidate images with the latter being made up of candidate issue perceptions and candidate trait perceptions (Flanigan & Zingale, 2002).

Single-Factor Models of Presidential Candidate Images

Single-factor models of presidential candidate images are based on assumptions that voters process one main (or only) type of candidate attribute such as source credibility (see Hellweg, this volume), authenticity (Louden & McCauliff, this volume), and candidate issue positions (Benoit, 2003). William Benoit (2003, p. 110), while noting how important policy matters are for images, makes this important observation: "Future research could attempt to refine the analysis of candidate messages to go beyond this initial (crude) level of policy versus character." The fundamental problem with single-factor models of images is that they neglect other factors that also constitute content of candidate images.

Presidential candidate images develop over the course of a presidential campaign and are the basis of voters choosing one candidate over another. From a cognitive perspective, candidate images are cognitive representations of candidates that are held by voters. These representations are produced by the processing of messages from candidates, voters, journalists, and other sources of political stimuli such as advertising and debates (Trent & Friedenberg, 1991; Denton & Woodward, 1990; Nimmo & Savage, 1976). Neuman (1986) notes that voters can generally not process more than seven factors of consideration in the process of decision making and that most voters have to reduce campaign complexities to choose among candidates. Political parties and evaluations of issues are significantly related, and voters may bring preferred candidate's and their own issues positions more into alignment as they reach their voting decision (Neuman, 1986). Neuman (1986, p. 148) argues, "The citizen does not 'study' the candidates but rather picks up bits and pieces of information over time, gradually accumulating a composite picture of the prominent issues and candidates." In Neuman's view, voters' formation of images of candidates is a product of low-salience learning. Dan Nimmo (1990) notes that voters reduce some of the complexity of information processing in campaigns by making decisions about what sources of information they will pay attention to in order to orient themselves to the campaign.

Presidential candidate images are formed by voters or citizens as they process messages about the candidates in relation to their personal and social concerns. They do this in a crowded and overloaded environment of messages and rhetoric. Robert Denton and Gary Woodward (1998, p. 131) note, "Citizens select, sort, prioritize, and attend to messages that develop images of candidates." Kendall and Paine (1995) use a cybernetics approach to describe how voters form presidential candidate images in an environment of information overload. In their view, voters simplify their information-seeking strategies to cope with campaign environments. They also apply simplified rules of judgment to assess the presidential candidates. Candidate images provide the voters with economical ways of processing campaign information (Kendall & Paine, 1995).

Some scholars believe that candidate images only represent candidate persona variables such as source credibility. With this approach, candidate images are operationalized as voter impressions of the personal characteristics of candidates such as competence, honesty, leadership, and so on. Hellweg, Dionisopoulos, and Kugler (1989, p. 56) argue that research indicates that issue and image concerns are "two separate entities." Johnston (1989, p. 380) defines *image responses to political ads* as "thoughts referring to a candidate's character, personality, appearance or behavior." She defines issue responses to the ads as "those addressing the candidate's political role, political performance, issue stands or relevant experience" (p. 380).

On the other hand, some political communication scholars believe that images and issues are interconnected. Davis (1981), for example, states that issue-oriented messages may become part of images. Mendelsohn and O'Keefe (1976) argue that issue-related perceptions and candidate image perceptions show strong interaction effects on voting choice. McDonald, Ostman, and Glynn (1990) argue that "there is conceptual confusion as to where images originate and reside" (p. 10). Along with Aden (1988), they argue that images and issues are not separate, but rather are part of the same construct.

Press and Verburg (1988) refer to images as any type of subjective impressions that voters have of candidates. Hacker and Bergvall (1990) refer to images as cognitive representations of candidates that contain any impressions that voters maintain about the candidates. Kaid (1991, p. 148) notes, "Image and issue are not necessarily dichotomous concepts." Flanigan and Zingale (1991, p. 114) acknowledge that "candidate images and party images may be closely related to issues, and under some circumstances are indistinguishable."

Kenneth Hacker and Walter Zakahi (1994) tested the validity of separating issues from personality items in measuring candidate images in a 1992 presidential election study. They reasoned that if candidate images are to remain definable as persona traits as opposed to issue positions, we should find that persona evaluations are clearly independent of issue positions in voters' evaluations of candidates. If, however, personality items in voters' evaluations were correlated with issue positions, there would be reason to challenge the validity of dichotomizing issues and images. Furthermore, if candidate evaluations appeared to be constructed of both personality and issue items, there will be evidence suggesting that candidate image conceptual and operational definitions should include both personality and issue items. They found that there was no clear and total separation of specific issue and persona items. Their analysis found that issue and persona items are not independent enough to exclude issue items from a conceptualization of candidates' images as subjective perceptions of candidates. The next question is why this would be true.

Kenneth Hacker, Walter Zakahi, Maury Giles, and Shaun McQuitty (2000) tested the notorious issue-persona dichotomy in candidate image research with an examination of 1996 presidential election data. Their study found that candidate issue impressions (CII) and candidate persona impressions (CPI) are not orthogonal but rather are highly and significantly correlated. Thus, no support was found for the longstanding issue-persona dichotomy in candidate image research.

In a model of voter cognitive processing, Herstein (1985) argues that voting decisions begin with information acquisition. This information may be sought or simply encountered. According to Herstein (1985, p. 27), "For the voter this information may include each candidate's position on important issues, past performance, party, physical appearance, and so forth." As Herstein notes, voters draw upon various combinations of this stored information. It appears that there are two competing models of candidate image.

The first model assumes the issue-image dichotomy and separates personality from issue impressions as antecedents to voter decisions. The second does not dichotomize issues and personae. Instead, it accepts a variety of impression content dimensions. The first model is derived from source credibility studies. The second model is derived from studies of human cognition. Therefore, it may be reasonable to suggest that source credibility measures be labeled as simply candidate source credibility and that candidate personality measures simply be called that. Candidate image measures, in that case, would refer to measures that incorporate whatever dimensions of evaluations are used by voters to differentiate and choose among candidates. Celinda Lake (1989, p. 28), a campaign pollster, argues that "issues are a central way in which the contrasts between candidates are drawn."

While arguments by Neuman (1986), Herstein (1985), and others about the multiplicity of inputs into candidate images are useful, they do not provide explanations of how such diverse inputs are integrated into meaningful cognitive structures that guide candidate evaluation and eventual candidate selection.

A dual-process approach to presidential candidate images can offer some movement in that direction by specifying how both issue and persona impressions both drive the formation of candidate images. This view of candidate images can accommodate the widely held assertion that candidates take issue stands in order to generate perceptions of their persona, while also accounting for ways in which partisanship and personality considerations may affect how issue positions are processed.

Dual-Process Models

Dual-process models of persuasion assume that there are two differing mechanisms through which messages alter attitudes (Perloff, 2003). Unimodal theories assume that there is only one process generating attitude change and that process is reasoning to conclusions based on evidence, whether that evidence consists of arguments or whether it consists of cues (O'Keefe, 2002).

The Elaboration Likelihood Model and Political Persuasion

The postulates of the ELM have been widely accepted for over twenty years. One reason for the widespread acceptance of this theory by so many researchers is that prior to it there was a great deal of disarray in the persuasion literature (Petty & Wegener, 1999). Source credibility, for example, could be found to have both positive and negative effects on persuasiveness. The negative effects made no sense with traditional theories. The ELM was able to reduce persuasion down to a set of key variables and processes. The most critical process described by the ELM is elaboration, which is essentially a message receiver's scrutiny of the quality of arguments.

The first ELM postulate says that people are motivated to hold correct attitudes. People with higher need for cognition wish to know that there are good reasons to believe arguments other than who makes them (Petty & Wegener, 1999). Strategies vary in many ways in order to reach correct judgments. Some people may be low on need for cognition and find sources, even expert sources, untrustworthy, and thus evaluate the arguments on their own (Petty & Wegener, 1999). If the same people see the expert source as trustworthy, they may do little personal evaluation of the argument (Petty & Wegener,

1999). Because correctness is a "default goal," people seldom recognize their own biases as biases. They simply think they are right.

The second ELM postulate says that elaboration levels vary with individual and situation factors (Petty & Wegener, 1999). For example, issues that are considered important will create more need to be correct than issues that are not considered important (Petty & Wegener, 1999). All kinds of interesting variations can arise, all of which refute simple cookie-cutter approaches to persuasion. For example, the person who thinks an issue is important but cannot process it due to low knowledge may rely on expert sources. On the other hand, the person with high knowledge or confidence in this situation may rely on his or her own thinking rather than expertise of the sources (Petty & Wegener, 1999). Not only that, but the latter group of people can even be led to think that they are capable of doing this from a state where they doubt their processing abilities (Petty & Wegener, 1999).

One point of misunderstanding has been the elaboration continuum. For example, what do eight strong arguments do to persuasion? The low elaborator will have fewer impressions of good arguments than the high elaborator (Petty & Wegener, 1999). Source credibility and other factors have often been categorized incorrectly in terms of the content characteristics when what is most important is how the message receiver uses something like source credibility. It may be a cue but it may also be an argument (Petty & Wegener, 1999). When elaboration is low, source credibility will be a cue; when high, it may be an argument (Petty & Wegener, 1999). High self-monitoring teenagers may process models as arguments, not simply as cues, when receiving smoking ad content (Petty & Wegener, 1999). Source credibility varies in nature by level of how source credibility is judged. This may also be true for political candidate traits.

The third ELM postulate says that persuasion variables can affect arguments, cues, and direction of elaboration. Persuasion variables can come from source, message, context, or any part of the receiver (Petty & Wegener, 1999). Relevance of visuals to arguments is high for high elaboration and not important for low elaboration. In the second case, inconsistent visuals have cue effects like classical conditioning. (Petty & Wegener, 1999). With high elaboration a good visual also has positive effects but in a different way, being processed as arguments and added to other arguments to increase persuasion (Petty & Wegener, 1999).

Communication researchers have noted that a central thesis to the ELM is that cognitive responses mediate between incoming messages and attitude change related to those messages (Stephenson, Benoit, & Tschida, 2001). Communication researchers testing various propositions of the ELM have also found that, as predicted, high-quality arguments produce more favorable cognitive responses and those responses are significantly related to attitude change (Stephenson et al., 2001).

A central theme to the ELM is also that of personal relevance: the higher the relevance of a subject, the more the elaboration done by the receiver. The central thought is thoughtful, but the theorists admit that what is a good argument to one person may be a bad one to someone else (Petty & Cacioppo, 1981). The process of elaboration entails understanding and evaluating arguments and having either favorable or unfavorable responses to them (Petty & Cacioppo, 1981). In the peripheral route, attitude change can occur without any active evaluation of the issues or objects that are the subject of the messages (Petty & Cacioppo, 1981). For high-relevance conditions, subjects experience more attitude change with strong arguments than weak ones. The opposite is true for those with low relevance (Petty & Cacioppo, 1981).

For those who have high relevance, strong argument stimuli should produce more attitude change than weak argument stimuli. Thus, argument quality is the determinant of attitude change but is most important for those who are high in elaboration. The origins of the ELM are partially in the realization of Petty and Cacioppo (1981) that there appeared to be two types of persuasion identified in studies of message reception, one being thoughtful consideration of the merits of arguments (central route) and the other being persuasion that occurred without such evaluation (peripheral route). The problem of the ELM lies in this original dualism. It appears to imply or assume that there are not combinations or parallel processing at the same moment.

Petty and Cacioppo (1986) give the following campaign example of how the ELM may apply to election campaigns. They say that a voter may support a candidate because he or she gave money to the campaign, liked the background music in the candidate's TV spot, or analyzed and appreciated the candidate's stand on issues (elaboration). The more peripheral types of political influence are affective and the influence involving evaluation of arguments is cognitive, according to these theorists (Petty & Cacioppo, 1986).

Here is where the linkage between dual-process models of persuasion and models of candidate image formation may emerge. Studies show that candidate issue impressions and candidate persona impressions are highly correlated (Hacker & Zakahi, 1994; Hacker et al., 2000). The ELM and other dual-process models can help to explain why both candidate issue positions and candidate personality impressions are correlated and heavily related to vote selection. Of course, we have very little knowledge as yet of how and in what stages one set of impressions outweighs the others. However, this is where knowledge about voter behavior becomes useful. If voters have little salience for issues or personae, they are likely to base their vote on partisanship alone

(Flanigan & Zingale, 2002). If voters are heavily concerned about issues, know how candidates stand on the issues, and see differences between candidate choices on issues, issue processing is more likely than in the case of these three conditions being absent (Flanigan & Zingale, 2002). By looking at the ELM for a guide to possible dual processing of images, we can see that images can be formed by either issue message or character messages:

Central route → issues focus → CI formation
Peripheral route → persona focus → CI formation

The most obvious connection between the ELM and candidate image formation is that (1) campaign communication is persuasion and the ELM is a useful theory of persuasion, and (2) images are formed by the cognitive responding of message receivers to campaign, news, or interpersonal senders (Hacker, 1995). However, this representation might be inaccurate and the following may be more useful:

Central route →
Issues or persona focus → CI formation
Peripheral route →

We have to now ask more about the validity of asserting that there is issue processing and persona processing that parallel what the ELM specifies as argument processing and cue processing and then what the nature of these routes are in relation to the formation of images.

The ELM, for whatever reasons, has been scarcely employed by political communication researchers. One possible area of fruitful application is in explaining some of the phases that voter decision making entails. For example, when voters first encounter candidates in person or in media presentations and lack information about their issue positions, they may be most likely to process cues more than arguments and hence have more persona input than issue input in their candidate images. If motivation and ability to process details about candidate issue positions are low in the early stages of an emergent campaign, voters are left with low elaboration potential and are processing candidate messages such as personality, likeability, social proof (who else is supporting the candidate), decision rules (perhaps related to ideology), and so on. Voters will most likely begin with person-based images that increasingly integrate persona impressions with policy impressions later. We must remind ourselves that the ELM does not a priori tell us what constitutes a cue or an argument. Those things are determined by the cognitive responses of the voter. Levels of elaboration are probably going to fluctuate in response to how motivated and able receivers are to think about the quality of candidates' arguments.

Testing the utility of the ELM for candidate image research might begin with these types of hypotheses. First, when elaboration is low for the voter, more persona information or impressions will become content in the candidate image. When elaboration is high for the voter, more issue impressions than persona impressions will become content in the candidate image. In the case of parallel processing where elaboration is fluctuating or middle-range in elaboration, the candidate image will have both issue and persona content in nearly equal amounts (no significant differences in levels). Attitudes toward candidates can result from images made of varying mixes of persona and issue impressions. One of the most important postulates of the ELM that can correct some of what we have seen in candidate images studies of the past says that what is argument or what is a cue is not determined by the senders of messages (and not by researchers) but rather by the receivers of the messages. This realization might make the hypotheses stated above seem like oversimplifications. It could be that those voters who are elaborating the most are most likely to form candidate images based on evaluations of candidate arguments about issues, while those who are doing low elaboration (peripheral route processing) are more likely to have images with assessments based on cues such as the personal traits of the candidates that are not treated as arguments. Source credibility operationalizations of images may succeed when voters are using those traits as arguments and fail when they are using them as cues while elaborating on candidates' issue arguments. Richard Petty, Aland Strathman, John Cacioppo, and Joseph Priester (1994, p. 143) make this important argument about those message receivers who may be moderate in elaboration: "In many situations, the elaboration likelihood is moderate, and the persuasion is determined in part by the central route and its processes and in part by the peripheral route and its processes." This highlights the importance of dual-process views of candidate image formation. For the moderately elaborating voter, images may contain strong inputs from both issue stands and personality perceptions.

An alternative to the ELM we should consider is the heuristic-systematic model (HSM). The HSM assumes dual processing like the ELM but with the important difference of not seeing the heuristic (peripheral) route and the systematic (central) route function in mutually exclusive ways (Perloff, 2003). Accordingly, a voter could process information about a candidate in both heuristic and systematic ways. This fits the assumption of a dual-process model of candidate images that says that voters can process both issue and persona messages at the same time.

A review of the voting behavior literature shows a constant identification of three major voting determinants—party identification, candidate issue positions (CII), and candidate persona impressions (CPI) (Flanigan & Zingale, 2002; Niemi & Weisberg, 1993). Yet little is yet conclusively known about how these three factors act together to shape both images and votes (Niemi & Weisberg, 1993). Our concern here is with the two short-term factors, that is, CII and CPI. David Hamilton, Steven Sherman, and Keith Maddox (1999) observe that some scholars have suggested that a test for whether cognitive processing truly involves two mechanisms or routes is to see if they occur simultaneously rather than sequentially as with verbal and visual processing. In this view, two systems can be seen as coacting subsystems of the larger cognitive system and can operate simultaneously and independently of each other. Hamilton et al. (1999, p. 616) argue that person judgments are made with what they call "integrative processing" in which most of the information about the person perceived is integrated in an "online" manner. A schema is developed that stores the online impressions and serves to filter later messages. They contrast this to "retrospective processing," which is memory-based judgments of persons (Hamilton et al., 1999, p. 618). While integrative processing and retrospective processing do not occur contemporaneously, they argue that the two processes constitute a dual-process system (Hamilton et al., 1999).

Unimodal Processing Models

It is all too easy to recognize empirically that voters, like any other citizens, are often processing information in mindless ways with little cognitive effort. How do we know this? Quite simply, whenever any person cannot process the details of a complex set of messages, he or she resorts to processing on the basis of cognitive heuristics. Political party might serve as a heuristic as in the case when we hear of someone voting only by party line to simply the voting process. However, if this is truly the easy way out, the independent voters who take more time perhaps to decide on candidates should turn out to be more informed or knowledgeable. This is not what studies indicate (Flanigan & Zingale, 2002).

Studies of person perception are relevant for candidate image research since candidates are largely viewed and evaluated as individuals. Research shows that people often process others in quick mindless ways using stereotypes and other shortcut devices (Bargh, 1999). This type of stereotyping often occurs without awareness. This does not suggest that voters cannot be informed and mindful, but only that there are cases where voting or surveying of campaign stimuli can suffer from automaticity.

Arie Kruglanski, Erik Thompson, and Scott Spiegel (1999) argue that the ELM and HSM both assume that high elaboration encourages thoughtful evaluation of message, while low elaboration encourages a more mindless kind of processing. While the HSM assumes less separation of routes than the ELM, it allows for orthogonal processing at times (Kruglanski et al., 1999). These researchers propose a unimodal model of persuasion as an alternative to the ELM and HSM. They argue on the basis of what they refer to as lay epistemic theory (LET).

The LET view, a unimodel theory of persuasive message processing, says that judgments about messages are made in a process of hypothesis testing and inference (Kruglanski et al., 1999). In the LET view, important messages or evidence are what is subjectively relevant to a conclusion (Kruglanski et al., 1999). This operates like a syllogism. It is also related to if-then rule-like situations in which the voter has a general belief such as "Candidates without foreign policy knowledge cannot be good presidents." The observation that candidate A has little such knowledge thus instantiates this belief and the candidate is negatively assessed. The dual modes are more unitary than in the ELM and HSM because the theorists argue that the difference between avenues of processing is how the contents of the message become evidence for conclusions (Kruglanski et al., 1999). For example, one person who hears an expert present an argument may link evidence to conclusions with argument scrutiny while another may link evidence to conclusions linking expertise to believability (Kruglanski et al., 1999). Thus, the LET theorists see the dual routes as more a matter of quantitative than qualitative differences (Kruglanski et al., 1999).

From the LET, it is inferred that there can be high or low arguments or cues (Kruglanski et al., 1999). This line of analysis says that the availability of relevant knowledge in the receiver of messages is important to message processing whether it is processed heuristically or systematically (Kruglanski et al., 1999). The LET considers cues and arguments to be functionally equivalent in persuasion (Kruglanski et al., 1999). The ELM, HSM, and LET all assume that judgment processes can differ in relation to the motivation of message receivers (Kruglanski et al., 1999).

The heuristic-systematic model (HSM) assumes dual processing like the ELM but with the important difference of not seeing the heuristic (peripheral) route and the systematic (central) route function in mutually exclusive ways (Perloff, 2003). Accordingly, a voter could process information about a candidate in both heuristic and systematic ways. This fits the assumption of a dual-process model of candidate images that says that voters can process both issue and persona messages at the same time.

Emotions versus Rational Process in Image Formation

There is evidence that emotion and cognition work simultaneously as two sides of message processing. References to emotional appeals in political discourse are at least as old as the ancient writings of Aristotle about ethos, logos, and pathos (Perloff, 2003; Petty & Cacioppo, 1981). The research of Robert Cialdini (2000) shows that there are powerful effects of the emotional responses that generate liking of persuaders. Psychologists have clearly found that social influence can direct behaviors and shape beliefs (cognitions). Cialdini (2000) explains how people can follow social "trigger" events and begin following sequences of social behaviors that are not consciously thought about in any critical sense. He calls these "fixed-action patterns" (Cialdini, 2000, p. 3).

Cognitive heuristics are likely to become part of the political information processing. When information environments are complicated and people in them feel overwhelmed, people are likely to use cognitive shortcuts to deal with messages (Cialdini, 2000; Vertzberger, 1990). One way of dealing with such complexity is to classify things according to a few features. Once information is processed as true, it forms a partial basis for evaluating new messages. This is due to the clear human tendency to seek general consistency among beliefs and other elements of the cognitive system. The more that the persuader appears similar in opinions, personality traits, and other factors, the more message receivers are prone to like the persuader (Cialdini, 2000).

This is true even when the persuaders are using rational appeals and those appeals may be getting processed by the receivers. Baldwin Way and Roger Masters (1996, p. 49) argue that "emotion and cognition are independent—and interdependent." Affective influence can occur without receiver awareness (Way & Masters, 1996). One striking finding from neuroscience studies is that emotional arousal can shape cognitive reactions without the awareness of a receiver (Way & Masters, 1996). There are different functions for cognitive processing and emotional processing.

The emotional system evaluates the personal significance of stimuli while the cognitive system computes and transforms incoming stimuli (Way & Masters, 1996). The affective system can operate independently of the cognitive system, yet can be related to cognitive responses at times.

The importance of these findings in our discussion about dual-process models of image formation is that there is repeated empirical confirmation that certain psychological processes often treated as opposite and independent can in fact be coactive, independent at times, and interrelated at other times. This again points to the possibility that issue processing and candidate character processing may be part of a dual-processing system of election message responding by which voters can think about candidates' policies alone, respond to candidates' traits alone, or respond to interactions between candidates' traits and policies. The lack of orthogonal independence of CII and CPI, along with the observations that CII can predict vote and CPI can predict vote, may indicate that voters may think in two ways about candidates while at the same time those two ways are influencing each other and melting into the same cognitive structure we know as images. For example, voters in 2004 may think retrospectively about President Bush's record on the economy and not assess it favorably, while at the same time consider the incumbent to have a plain-spoken style that they admire as a personal trait. Which will have the most influence on them?

Candidate Images and Cognitive Systems

From the view of a cognitive and sociocognitive system, the images are related to many other structures such as beliefs, attitudes, values, and schemata. While attitudes are very useful as constructs, particularly in persuasion research, we must recognize that they fall short of what candidate images do in the function of linking messages and perceptions in the study of political communication. But rather than trying to argue one cognitive structure against another, it is more useful to use each one in its own productive sense.

Thus, we see that political images (candidate images, party images, presidential images, presidential candidate images, and so on) are specific cognitive representations of political candidates or leaders. They are interconnected to the other structures in the cognitive system such as attitudes, schemata, values, and political ideology.

Earlier we noted how emotional reactions have been found to be very important to political message processing. While researchers have long thought of images in relation to cognitions or beliefs, we know today that more affective components may also be relevant. As Richard Perloff (2003, p. 47) notes, for example, political belief systems comprising prejudice, sexism, or attitudes about abortion are not simply made of "molecular beliefs," but also entail affect and affective responses to symbols.

There are basic elements of cognitive processing we know as beliefs or cognitions. Cognitions are interconnected and interdependent, thus forming a system of cognitions. A cognitive system is organized to be efficient and useful (Petty & Cacioppo, 1981). The idea of system incorporates a tendency toward equilibrium in the system. As far back as the 1940s, psychologists were discovering the tendency to keep one's cognitive system in balance, which meant to keep one's cognitions consistent with each other. A cognitive system involves structures, content comprising the structures, and processes that create or modify the structures. There are linkages between cognitions and emotions in the cognitive system. As Milton Rokeach noted in the 1960s, every affective state is tied to beliefs.

When candidate images are treated from operational points of view only and not related to theories of political perception and information processing, the linkages between images and other cognitive structures are likely to be missing. Researchers can ask voters how they think about candidates to gain information about candidate images since the construct generally refers to a cognitive representation of candidates in the minds of voters (however operationalized). Because there are many structures in the cognitive system that are related to message reception and reasoning about candidates and campaigns, there should be more study of how images are related not only to incoming messages but also to existing and interrelated elements other than images in the cognitive system. Decades of persuasion studies have shown that received messages are judged in relation to stored beliefs, attitudes, values, and schemata (O'Keefe, 2002).

In his work on political ideology, Teune van Dijk (1998) has described many interesting facts about the cognitive system that introduce possibilities for how political ideology can unify separate elements of the system. Older characterizations of ideology like "system of beliefs" remain so vague that the ideology construct can be interpreted in too many directions to be explanatory. Ideologies have specific political functions such as facilitating the political practices of groups. Ideologies are learned and internalized over time, and because they are cognitive structures, they require processes of construction and modification (van Dijk, 1998).

According to van Dijk, clusters of beliefs can be seen as stored in schemata. A political schema (singular) has sociocultural knowledge in categories with a hierarchy to the categories. To understand more about both political behavior and political communication, we need to know more about the rules or strategies used to connect structural units in the mind to various situations (van Dijk, 1998). Strategies for the use of ideologies could reveal more about political communication.

Van Dijk (1998) argues that like the other components of the ideological cognitive system, values are related to memory and consist of some type of specialized memory structure. Values are the most abstract of the ideological components. As decades of persuasion studies indicate, they are nearly impervious to change efforts instigated from external sources. Values are closely related to culture and cultural knowledge. This is why people who share the same culture are likely to have commonalities in values. This is as true for political culture as it is for general culture.

In political communication involving adversaries, both sides have competing value systems that, along with ideologies, present clashes among methods of message evaluation and also with moral positioning. Competing sides in a political conflict are likely to see themselves as "good people" fighting some form of "evil." We have value domains for each domain of human activity, such as values for physical attractiveness and values for interpersonal communication.

For politics, values are often single terms like democracy, freedom, self-determination, and so on.

The function of values within the ideological system is to monitor how things are evaluated in the lower levels of the system. The political values that are internalized into the cognitive system will be those of the groups that a person affiliates with as a member. Political values are therefore less likely to be personal as much as they are to be group-based and ideological. This is because politics is generally competition among groups for resources and each group will have its special set of values.

Another important function of the ideological cognitive system is to balance group interest with self-preservation in the face of competing or dominating social values (van Dijk, 1998). Thus, a true value may not be expressed and a social value may be articulated instead. Enough discourse may reveal this, however, as in the case of "I am not a racist, but I believe that those people are lazy and do not want to work."

Another important part of the cognitive system that van Dijk describes is that related to mental models. Mental models are cognitive structures that are most likely related to both schemata and candidate images. Mental models are cognitive representations that are less stable than schemata and that are closest to personal experience memory for any subject or activity that has our attention.

Variations in mental models show how ideologies are used in different ways by group members who have the same or similar ideology. They also help to explain how similar or same ideologies can emerge from variant social interactions, behaviors, situations, and events. People who share ideologies are likely to have similarities in key abstractions and some differences in applications of the ideology in various concrete circumstances.

When you participate in an event, your mind constructs a model of the event, and that is called a mental model. A mental model is totally subjective. It represents personal experience and interpretation. Political communication involves the construction of mental models by the communicators. Understanding political content (discourse) is related to the mental models formed in relation to received messages. Producing political discourse is also related to mental models since those models tell the speaker what the situation means. Each person forms mental models all day long in every situation. For any mental model, there is a connection to social knowledge. Social knowledge thus meets personal experiences in our mental models (van Dijk, 1998).

Central to an understanding of political communication is the realization that mental models organize how we understand political discourse, events, and communication, and such understanding is vital to the entire process of communication. We need the cognitive structures like mental models, schemata, images, and so on to understand various political situations and to generate responses to them. We build these structures by communicating and behaving in political situations or in response to political messages. When a person is engaged in political communication, she or he makes inferences from generated mental models that provide an interface between real-time events and more generalized political knowledge.

Mental models are made from schemata, activated stored models, beliefs, sociocultural beliefs about communication processes, and previous parts of discourse (van Dijk, 1998). This observation can begin to illuminate the connection between the complexity of the cognitive system and the formation of candidate images. Mental models constrain discourse production and discourse comprehension and processing (van Dijk, 1998). The construction or change of mental representations results from contents and structures in ongoing mental models.

An examination of the relationship between mental models and candidate images could help us to understand the social nature of images. Socially shared opinions are represented in social representations and stored in social memory. Socially shared attitudes are more abstract than personal opinions and are slower to form and also slower to change. The shared attitudes are likely to influence the processing of messages from candidates.

This discussion about the cognitive system is intended to highlight the importance of gaining knowledge about candidate image formation and change in ways that relate candidate images to other important structures that coact with images and other processes that coact with the image-formation processes.

All human information processing begins with information being physically perceived, and this process is a combination of data-driven processing and conceptually driven processing (Lindsay & Norman, 1977). Humans have what are known as internal representations of the external world (Lindsay & Norman, 1977). Candidate images are just one type of cognitive structure related to campaign communication.

Multiple Kinds of Processing with Variation

The extant literature on candidate images should inform us that voters are processing different types of candidate content in differing contexts. For example, we know that when events are stable or unimportant or when issues are not appreciably different between presidential candidates, voters are most likely to evaluate personality content. Thus, the presidential candidate images will contain more persona-based impressions than issue-based impressions.

A dual-process view of candidate image formation assumes that voters vary in how much thinking they do regarding the candidates and that they may be doing parallel processing of peripheral- and central-route messages. As the ELM predicts, there is theoretical support for the conclusion that voters will process cues about candidates when their motivation or ability to process argument quality is low.

An Argument for a Consolidative Dual-Process Model

As mentioned early in this chapter, Gilbert (1999) talks about the analogy of a soft drink machine being explained with competing models. He suggests that these models can be tested with numerous types of cognitive processing. The first is what he calls a selective design. This is the behaviorist's preferred model. The observer looks at regularities of a person thumping on the machine and it providing a beverage in response (Gilbert, 1999). For the mind, a selective design looks at behavioral variety in terms of one process being active and one dormant in a particular situation. The ELM may be looked at this way (Gilbert, 1999). Of course, a more interactive version of the ELM, including parallel processing as a third option, might not.

The second design Gilbert (1999) presents is the competitive design. Here we view the two routes of cola and H_2O in the coke machine as one winning out over the other. For the mind, the analogy is controlling and noncontrolling mental processes. A third design is the consolidative design. Later, I will argue that this design is promising for potential new knowledge about candidate image formation and the relationship of the candidate image construct to impressions from the two domains of persona perceptions and issue position perceptions.

In the consolidative model of the coke machine, the machine produces a beverage that is a product of both the coke and the H_2O processes operating at the same time. In this joint operation, there are instances in which system disturbances, like the machine being tilted, will make one process dominate the other (Gilbert, 1999). Applied to the mind, consolidative design implies that computations are performed in the mind by different modules and neural systems but that these are consolidated before we are conscious of them (Gilbert, 1999). For example, for analytical purposes, we can think about a person's nonverbal behavior separate from their verbal behavior, but in normal transactions of social interaction, we are processing nonverbal cues, verbal messages, and combinations or consolidations of the two simultaneously. This process of consolidation results in an "integrated impression" of the person (Gilbert, 1999, p. 6).

It is important to remember that in the consolidative process, one process of two (or more) may dominate and which dominates may vary by situation. This fits nicely with what we have learned over many decades of research regarding voting and candidate images. The variance in candidate images is easily identified in the history of presidential elections. In 1952, for example, Eisenhower's persona as a World War II general dominated his image. However, in 1956, when he ran for reelection, his performance on issues as president dominated his image (Flanigan & Zingale, 1991).

The fourth design presented by Gilbert is the corrective design. In the corrective design, we see a variant of the consolidative design. For the coke machine, the beverage will result from the H_2O and coke processes occurring at the same time again. However, now that disturbances change the domination of one over the other, one process begins first and the other reacts with its contribution to the state of the first process. Thus, the second process compensates for changes in the first. For the mind, this is popular in psychology because it explains how the system is kept stable by two processes (Gilbert, 1999). Gilbert acknowledges that there are more than four possible designs, but his set of four provides some useful theoretical and empirical model-building points of departure. They are also consistent with indications in political communication research that voting decisions do not result from single types of determinants.

Voting behavior researchers found that voters are concerned with both persona and issue factors of candidate discourse and presentation and that persona impressions and issue impressions are not orthogonal as is commonly assumed. Earlier qualitative research also showed that when voters talk with each other, they go back and forth between impressions of policy differences and personality differences (Hacker, 1995).

A consolidative model of candidate image formation can account for more than one route of candidate image processing and can also be used to explain how the relative contributions of two types of processing, like issue processing and trait processing, can occur simultaneously. A corrective version of the consolidative model might also account for how the two types of processing react to each other.

While candidate personal impressions (CPI) and candidate issue impressions (CII) are both important to the formation of presidential candidate images, studies continue to indicate that they may also be interrelated such that both are causal sources of candidate evaluation and resulting candidate images but also that both influence each other (see figure 5.1, below).

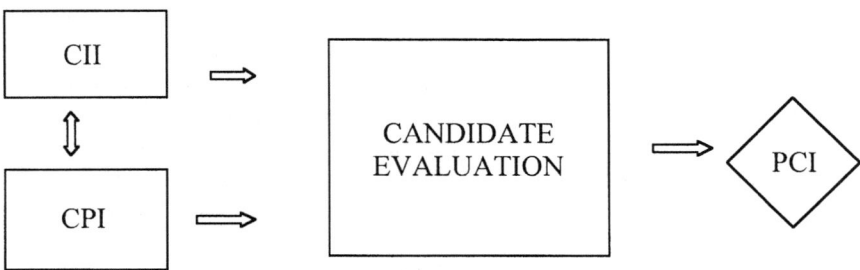

FIGURE 5.1
The Dual Influence of Issues and Personae

A Preliminary Dual Consolidation Principle

While there are specialized forms of message processing in various channels of message reception, there appear to be both independent and interdependent processes that may occur at the same time. Way and Masters (1996, p. 50) state, "Reason and passion do not exist in separate realms; in the normal brain, they are produced by separate systems that are interacting and interdependent." Emotional responses that are seen but not recognized or even known can occur (Way & Masters, 1996).

Way and Masters (1996) argue that the human brain processes information in parallel ways, which means that cognitive processing and emotional processing are more likely to occur simultaneously than sequentially. This implies that cognitions affect emotions and vice versa and also that beliefs and feelings about candidates are integrated (Way & Masters, 1996). For candidate images, this suggests that a variety of impressions are integrated into unified cognitive representations (Hacker et al., 2000).

Separate, but Parallel

Researchers discovered that emotions and cognitions can have separate but simultaneous effects on attitudes toward political leaders (Way & Masters, 1996). Way and Masters (1996) argue that emotional and cognitive data are integrated into the single structure known as attitude. While this is not the specific issue being addressed in this chapter, there does appear to be an analogous pattern, that is, that two routes or sets of impressions appear to have independent effects on candidate evaluation while also affecting each other. As cognitions and emotions appear to become united in attitudes, it may be that CII and CIP are integrated into the structures we call candidate images.

A review of voting decision literature is necessary to determine if the analogy is defensible. Paul Abrahamson, John Aldrich, and David Rohde (2001) argue that voting researchers have come to agree that (1) voting choices are closely related to candidate attitudes; (2) voters choose the candidate they believe will do the best job as president; and (3) three sets of attitudes shape the vote—candidate attitudes, party attitudes, and issue attitudes. Abrahamson et al. (2002) argue that attitudes toward candidates (candidate attitudes) are shaped by attitudes toward issues and toward parties. CII are formed in differing ways depending on whether or not the candidate is the incumbent president. The incumbent's record is judged by voters, while the incumbent's challenger is evaluated in terms of how good the alternative policies sound in replacing the existing policies (Abrahamson et al., 2002). Voters also compare candidate policy proposals to their own ideas about what policies should be implemented (Abrahamson et al., 2002). The challenger's policy proposals are not simply judged by their own merit but also in relation to perceptions of how that candidate's party did when it previously controlled the White House (Abrahamson et al., 2002).

Cross Effects between Dual Channels

Richard Perloff (2003) argues that when voters are low in involvement (in the ELM sense) with presidential elections, they focus on peripheral cues like candidate appearance, endorsements, slogans, and key phrases. Those voters who are more involved, Perloff argues, will be more prone to pay attention to the arguments made by the presidential candidates.

Studies on emotional processing and cognitive processing of political leaders have found that emotions are stronger predictors of leader approval (Way & Masters, 1996). There is also evidence that cognitions not only affect emotional responses but also that emotional reactions affect rational or cognitive processing (Way & Masters, 1996). If emotional processing and cognitive processing are dual channels or parallel-channel processes, there may be a cross effect of one channel on the other. If this link of thinking is extended to images, we should test to see if CIP affects CPP, as is commonly assumed, but also if CPP affects CII (not commonly assumed). This will probably require experiments as well as panel or longitudinal samples with path analysis procedures to test for causality.

Forming Images in 2004

In the 2004 presidential election campaign, which began in 2003, the incumbent president Bush and his would-be challengers gearing up for the Democratic primaries faced enormous challenges of assessing what Aristotle called *statis*, or the rhetorical environment in which they would do their persuasion work. Democrats would have to shape a candidate that could attack Bush and help make his public image doubtful and easy to reject while making the Democratic candidate look like a viable and strong alternative with clear plans to solve the problems that Bush was unable to solve. Once it was known that John Kerry was his opponent, the Bush campaign began to attack the challenger on traits that might contribute to a positive Kerry image and policy positions that might do the same. In turn, the Kerry campaign launched vigorous attacks on Bush's character and presidential record.

The models shown in figure 5.2 illustrates the following propositions about presidential candidate images formation that can be derived from a dual-processing perspective:

P1: When voters are highly involved with campaign issues and see them as personally relevant, they will be more likely to form candidate images that are constructed with candidate issue positions than candidate trait impressions.

P2: When voters are low in involvement with campaign issues and low in seeing them as personally relevant, they will be more likely to form candidate images that are more determined by candidate trait impressions than candidate issue positions.

P3: Voters with moderate levels of involvement and relevance will have more balanced issue-trait combinations of impressions than those voters who are either high or low in involvement and relevance.

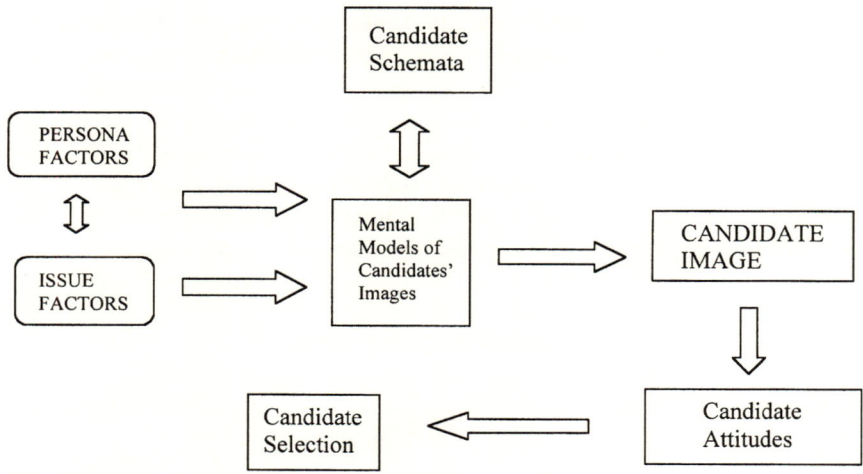

FIGURE 5.2
Preliminary Model of Candidate Image Formation

P4: Candidate persona impressions (CPI) and candidate issue impressions (CII) will be highly correlated despite the type of impression that dominates the process of image formation.

P5: CII and CPI will be significantly correlated with voting preference at the same time that they are significantly correlated with each other.

P6: Whether CII or CPI dominate the candidate image structure will be related to circumstances of news agenda setting, campaign framing, and voter selection of most relevant criteria for candidate evaluation.

P7: If there is disequilibrium in the cognitive system regarding a candidate, consistency will be restored in the image formation process by altering the routes of issue and traits input such that the images are corrected.

P8: Candidate issue perceptions will have effects on candidate issue perceptions.

P9: Candidate trait perceptions will have effects on candidate issue perceptions.

While it is widely asserted that candidate issue positions are used by campaigns to generate candidate trait perceptions, there are far fewer references to how candidate trait perceptions can affect issue perceptions. Flanigan and Zingale (2002, p. 187), however, make this interesting observation: "When voters agree on issues with the candidate they support, they may have adopted this position merely to agree with their candidate."

Presidential candidate image formation is a complex process involving many possible causal directions among many cognitive elements. Situational factors abound, and voters are likely to vary in how they form their images. The dual-process perspective advocated here may allow us to take closer looks at the variation among voters, candidates, and elections to the point that we are capable of identifying the patterns within the variation.

Note

1. These data come from the "Candidate Images" section of the Gallup Poll website (www.gallup.com), which is no longer available online.

References

Abrahamson, Paul, John Aldrich, and David Rohde. 2001 *Change and Continuity in the 2000 Elections*. Washington, D.C.: Congressional Quarterly Press.

Aden, R. C. 1988. "The 'Irrational' Voter: Toward a Realistic Model of Political Communication." Presented to the International Communication Association, New Orleans, May.

Alter, Jonathan. 2000. "Betting that Substance Sells." *Newsweek*, August 28, 26.
Bargh, John, A. 1999. "The Cognitive Monster: The Case against the Controllability of Automaticity Stereotype Effects." In *Dual-Process Theories in Social Psychology*, edited by Shelley Chaiken and Yaacov Trope, 361–382. New York: Guilford.
Benoit, W. L. 2003. "Topic of Presidential Campaign Discourse and Election Outcome." *Western Journal of Communication* 67: 97–112.
Cialdini, Robert. 2000. *Influence*. Boston: Allyn & Bacon.
Davis, D. K. 1981. "Issues Information and Connotation in Candidate Imagery: Evidence from a Laboratory Experiment." *International Political Science Review* 2: 461–479.
Denton, Robert, and Gary Woodward. 1998. *Political Communication in America*. Westport, Conn.: Praeger.
Fazio, Russell, and David Roskos-Ewoldsen. 1994. "Acting as We Feel." In *Persuasion: Psychological Insights and Perspectives*, edited by Sharon Shavitt and Timothy Brock, 71–93. Boston: Allyn & Bacon.
Flanigan, W. H., and N. H. Zingale. 1991. *Political Behavior of the American Electorate*. Washington, D.C.: Congressional Quarterly Press.
———. 2002. *Political Behavior of the American Electorate*. Washington, D.C.: Congressional Quarterly Press.
Gilbert, D. T. 1999. "What the Mind's Not." In *Dual-Process Theories in Social Psychology*, edited by Shelley Chaiken and Yaacov Trope, 3–11. New York: Guilford.
Hacker, K. 1995. "Interpersonal Communication and the Formation of Candidate Images." In *Candidate Images in Presidential Elections*, edited by K. Hacker, 65–82. New York: Praeger.
Hacker, K., and V. Bergvall. 1990. "A Discourse Analysis of Voters' 1988 Political Images Formulated in Linguistic Behaviors, Discourse Formulations, and Mental Models." Paper presented to the Southwest Social Science Association, San Antonio, Texas, March.
Hacker, K., and W. Zakahi. 1994. "Re-evaluating the Issue-Persona Dichotomy in Candidate Images: A Statistical Test." Presented to the mass communication division of the Western States Communication Association, San Jose, California.
Hacker, Kenneth L., Walter R. Zakahi, Maury J. Giles, and Shaun McQuitty. 2000. "Components of Candidate Images: Statistical Analysis of the Issue-Persona Dichotomy in the Presidential Campaign of 1996." *Communication Monographs* 67: 227–238.
Hamilton, David, Steven Sherman, and Keith Maddox. 1999. "Dualities and Continua: Implications for Understanding Perceptions of Persons and Groups." In *Dual-Process Theories in Social Psychology*, edited by Shelley Chaiken and Yaacov Trope, 606–626. New York: Guilford.
Hellweg, S. A., G. N. Dionisiopoulos, and D. B. Kugler. 1989. "Political Candidate Image: A State-of-the-Art Review." In *Progress in Communication Sciences*, Vol. 9, edited by B. Dervin and M. J. Voight, 43–78. Norwood, N.J.: Ablex.
Herstein, J. A. 1985. "Voter Thought Processes and Voting Theory." In *Mass Media and Political Thought*, edited by S. Kraus and R. M. Perloff, 15–36. Beverly Hills, Calif.: Sage.
Johnston, D. 1989. "Image and Issue Political Information: Message Content or Interpretation?" *Journalism Quarterly* 66: 379–382.

Kaid, L. 1991. "Ethical Dimensions of Political Advertising." In *Ethical Dimensions of Political Communication*, edited by R. E. Denton, 145–169. New York: Praeger.

Kendall, K. E., and S. C. Paine. 1995. "Political Images and Voting Decisions." In *Candidate Images in Presidential Elections*, edited by Kenneth Hacker, 19–36. Westport, Conn.: Praeger.

Kruglanski, Arie W., Erik P. Thompson, and Scott Spiegel. 1999. "Separate or Equal: Bimodal Notions of Persuasion and a Single-Process 'Unimodel.'" In *Dual-Process Theories in Social Psychology*, edited by Shelley Chaiken and Yaacov Trope, 293–313. New York: Guilford.

Lake, C. 1989. "Political Consultants: Opening up a New System of Political Power." *Political Science and Politics* (March): 26–29.

Lindsay, Peter, and Donald A. Norman. 1977. *Human Information Processing*. New York: Academic Press.

Markus, Gregory. 1993. "The Impact of Personal and National Economic Conditions on the Presidential Vote: A Pooled Cross-Sectional Analysis." In *Controversies in Voting Behavior*, edited by Richard Niemi and Herbert Weisberg, 152–166. Washington, D.C.: Congressional Quarterly Press.

McDonald, D. G., R. E. Ostman, and C. J. Glynn. 1990. "Media Orientations and Issue-Image Perceptions in the 1988 Presidential Election." Paper presented to the International Communication Association, Dublin, Ireland, May.

Mendelsohn, H., and G. F. O'Keefe. 1976. *The People Choose a President*. New York: Praeger.

Neuman, W. Russell. 1986. *The Paradox of Mass Politics*. Cambridge, Mass.: Harvard University Press.

Niemi, Richard, and Herbert Weisberg. 1993. *Controversies in Voting Behavior*. Washington, D.C.: Congressional Quarterly Press.

Nimmo, Dan. 1990. "Principles of Information Selection in Information Processing: A Preliminary Political Analysis." In *Mass Communication and Political Information Processing*, edited by Sidney Kraus, 3–17. Hillsdale, N.J.: Lawrence Erlbaum.

Nimmo, D., and R. Savage. 1976. *Candidates and Their Images*. Pacific Palisades, Calif.: Goodyear.

O'Keefe, Daniel. 2002. *Persuasion: Theory and Research*. Thousand Oaks, Calif.: Sage.

Perloff, Richard. 2003. *The Dynamics of Persuasion*. Mahwah, N.J.: Lawrence Erlbaum.

Petty, Richard E., and John T. Cacioppo. 1981. *Attitudes and Persuasion: Classic and Contemporary Approaches*. Dubuque, Iowa: Wm. C. Brown.

———. 1986. "The Elaboration Likelihood Model of Persuasion." *Advances in Experimental Social Psychology* 19: 123–205.

Petty, Richard, Alan Strathman, John Cacioppo, and Joseph Priester. 1994. "To Think or Not to Think." In *Persuasion: Psychological Insights and Perspectives*, edited by Sharon Shavitt and Timothy Brock, 113–147. Boston: Allyn & Bacon.

Petty, R., and D. Wegener. 1999. "The Elaboration Likelihood Model: Current Status and Controversies." In *Dual-Process Theories in Social Psychology*, edited by Shelley Chaiken and Yaacov Trope, 41–72. New York: Guilford.

Press, Charles, and Kenneth Verburg. 1988. *American Politicians and Journalists*. New York: Scott Foresman.

Quindlen, Anna. 2000. "It's the Personality." *Newsweek*, August 16, 68.
Rahn, Wendy, John Aldrich, Eugene Borgida, and John Sullivan. 1993. "A Social-Cognitive Model of Candidate Appraisal." In *Controversies in Voting Behavior*, edited by Richard Niemi and Herbert Weisberg, 187–206. Washington, D.C.: Congressional Quarterly Press.
Stephenson, Michael T., William L. Benoit, and David A. Tschida. 2001. "Testing the Mediating Role of Cognitive Responses in the Elaboration Likelihood Model." *Communication Studies* 52: 324–337.
Trent, Judith, and Robert Friedenberg. 1991. *Political Campaign Communication*. New York: Praeger.
Van Dijk, Teune. 1998. *Ideology*. London: Sage.
Vertzberger, Yaacov. 1990. *The World in Their Minds*. Stanford, Calif.: Stanford University Press.
Way, B. M., and R. D. Masters. 1996. "Emotion and Cognition in Political Information-Processing." *Journal of Communication* 46: 48–65.

6

The Effects of Political Advertising on Candidate Images

Lynda Lee Kaid and Mike Chanslor

A HALF-CENTURY HAS PASSED SINCE THE EISENHOWER CAMPAIGN of 1952 introduced televised political advertising on a meaningful level to U.S. presidential campaigns. In the ensuing years, the televised political spot has become the predominant form of candidate-controlled communication for presidential hopefuls, and there are indications that advertising importance is on the rise, at least from the candidates' perspectives. Advertising spending went from a record $133 million in the 1992 presidential elections (Devlin, 1993), rose to almost $200 million in 1996 (Devlin, 1997), and hit the all-time high of $240 million in 2000 (Devlin, 2001).

The reliance of presidential hopefuls on well-produced, visually arresting 30- and 60-second commercials to communicate their major ideas has been a cause of great concern to political commentators. At the heart of the concern with political commercials is the notion that their appeal relies on images rather than issue information. There is no doubt that the rise of televised political ads has helped generate research interest in the images of political candidates. While scholars have dealt with images in a general way, trying to determine what components constitute a voter's image of a candidate and what effect these images might have on political actions, this chapter explores televised political commercials and how their image components can affect voter perceptions and vote intentions. After reviewing previous research on political spots and candidate image, the chapter applies a particular definition of candidate image to the 1988, 1992, 1996, and 2000 presidential campaign spots.

Conceptualizations of Candidate Images

Because *image* can be an elusive concept, it is not surprising that some political commentators are concerned about the effects of image on the democratic process. Bruce Newman (1999) writes, "Washington has become the Hollywood of the East, where image is more important than substance and the intensity of a politician's charisma determines his power with the people" (p. 13). He refers to the modern president as "America's celebrity-in-chief" (Newman, 1999, p. 13).

It is likely that the concern with image as it applies to political candidates centers in part on a simplistic conception of that term. Image can be viewed as nothing more than a combination of physical attractiveness and surface-level communication skills, such as the ability to speak convincingly into a television camera.

However, image is a complex concept that includes more substantial dimensions than attractiveness or camera presence. Previous research warrants such a view of image. Dan Nimmo and Robert Savage (1976) found that the candidate characteristics of perceived strength, integrity, and empathy were important factors for voters as they formed images. Arthur Miller, Martin Wattenberg, and Oksana Malanchuk (1985, 1986) uncovered five dominant dimensions of candidate image—competence, integrity, reliability, charisma, and personal characteristics. They found that respondents make a substantially larger number of comments about the first three dimensions.

Such research does not support the elimination of appearance and performance dimensions from the concept of image, but it does lend credence to the definition of image adopted here. Candidate image is defined as a combination of appearance dimensions and candidate characteristics relevant to job performance (honesty, ability, qualified, and so on) as perceived by voters and interacting with the voter's own characteristics and predispositions. These substantive dimensions are at least as important, and probably more so, than their more superficial counterparts in voters' constructions of candidate images. Seen in this way, candidate image is clearly a concept that encompasses Nimmo and Savage's (1976) notion that candidate image is a transactional process in which images result through the interplay of candidate information and voter predispositions.

The concept of image may have been oversimplified because of the tendency to categorize political information in terms of an image-issue dichotomy. This conceptualization almost certainly leads to image information being viewed superficially in relation to issue information. The more complex conceptualization of image that is outlined above calls for the rejection of a strict issue-image dichotomy to describe political communication. It is often impossible to clearly delineate between information that moves from being image-oriented to being issue-oriented. For example, in the 1992 presidential campaign, George Bush made Bill Clinton's trustworthiness a campaign "issue." Allan Louden (1990) has made a more detailed case for the blending of these two concepts, and recent analyses of issue and image content in presidential ads further suggest the overlap and covariance of these two factors (Johnston & Kaid, 2002).

The Political Commercial–Candidate Image Relationship

Like the concept of image in general, the specific relationship between televised political commercials and candidate image has been a cause for concern. The basic reason for this concern is derived from the belief that television's inherent predispositions to drama and visual imagery make it a natural playground for superficial image portrayal.

Much research effort has been spent on clarifying the role that image plays in televised political advertisements. These earlier findings can be divided into work focusing on political advertising image *content* and that aimed at discovering the *effects* of political ads on voter perceptions of candidate images.

Content

Content studies of the relationship between televised political advertising and image date back to impressionistic work by Duane Tucker (1959), who analyzed radio and television ads from the 1956 Oregon Senate campaign. Tucker concluded that part of the winning candidate's success was his superior ability to project positive "personality" characteristics. In similar work, Ernest Rose and Douglas Fuchs (1968) found that the winning candidate in a California gubernatorial race used more issue-oriented spots.

Later work more systematically tried to assess television ad content. Although Richard Joslyn's (1980) study of 156 ads used a convenience sample, this early effort found that 57.7 percent of the ads contained issue content while only 47.4 percent mentioned candidate qualifications. In their studies of the 1972 presidential campaign, Thomas Patterson and Robert McClure (1976) and C. Richard Hofstetter and Cliff Zukin (1979) found that a majority of television ads, in the latter study 85 percent, contained issue information. Taken together, the bulk of this early systematic work seemed to dispel the notion that television ads are "afflicted" with a preponderance of image information.

Later research (Benoit, 1999; Kaid, 1994, 1998, 1999a; Kaid & Johnston, 1991, 2001; Kaid & Tedesco, 1999a; Kern, 1989) has confirmed that political advertisements are more issue than image oriented. For example, Lynda Kaid and John Tedesco's (1999b) analysis of the 1996 campaign showed that 65 percent of Bob Dole's ads were issue oriented while 87 percent of Bill Clinton's spots focused on issues, and similarly high percentages of issue spots were dominant in the 2000 campaign (Kaid, 2002). In an extensive study of 1,204 1952–1996 presidential election spots, Kaid and Anne Johnston (2001) found that a strong majority of 66 percent focused on issues.

However, in a content analysis of 196 ads, John Boiney and David Paletz (1991) found that 71 percent mentioned one candidate quality and 51 percent mentioned two. In contrast, 76 percent of the ads mentioned one issue while only 10 percent mentioned two. While this work points to the prevalence of image information in ads, it is important to note that more ads overall contained issue than image information.

In-depth discussion of image content in political spots is provided by Leonard Shyles (1984a, 1984b, 1986), who specifically described image content in order to determine if there are distinct issue and image presentational styles in political advertisements. Shyles defined his concept of image as references to a candidate's character traits rather than appearance. In 140 presidential primary ads, he found 383 image-related references with over 30 percent related to experience. Other popular image-type mentions included competence, "other special qualities," honesty, leadership, and strength. Shyles's content work also found that image-oriented ads featured stills, indirect camera contact, celebrity and citizen testimonials, and fast-cut editing. This work is interesting because it supports the idea that image information is related to substantial candidate characteristics but at the same time shows that image spots rely on "slicker" production values, which has been one criticism of them.

Several researchers (Kaid & Davidson, 1986; Kaid & Johnston, 2001; Kaid & Tedesco, 1999a) have attempted to account for the uniqueness of visual presentation with their work on candidate commercial videostyle, which is defined as the verbal content, nonverbal content, and film/video production techniques used by candidates for self-presentation through television. Kaid and Johnston's (2001) analysis showed that aggressiveness was the most common personal characteristic stressed in presidential advertising, being utilized in 45 percent of spots. Other popular characteristics stressed were competency (23 percent), performance/success (18 percent), and activeness (15 percent).

In Kaid and Dorothy Davidson's (1986) videostyle analysis of fifty-five senatorial ads, coders ranked the extent to which several issue- and image-related variables were present in the audio and video segments. Associating a candidate with a positive issue was ranked first or second in the audio portions of 60 percent of the ads, but issue information was not substantial in the video portions of the ads. Trust was ranked first or second in the video content of almost half of the ads, with competence ranked first or second in 57 percent of the audio content. These findings indicate that television advertising may indeed uniquely qualify as a medium for carrying substantial image information.

Effects

Research concerning the effects of political advertisements on candidate image has taken many forms. Patterson and McClure (1976) used survey research to conclude that voters learned more about campaign issues than candidate images from political advertising exposure in the 1972 presidential campaign. Hofstetter, Zukin, and Terry Buss (1978) concurred that television ad exposure resulted in little effect on candidate images. However, early researchers did find positive correlations between ad exposure and candidate image evaluations in races below the presidential level (Atkin & Heald, 1976; Mulder, 1979). More recently, Darrell West (1993) has used a variety of survey results to show that political advertising exposure does have significant effects on perceptions of presidential candidate qualities and traits.

The greatest success in identifying political advertising effects on candidate images has come from experimental research. Some researchers manipulated various commercial types to see if there were differing effects. Almost all of this work has relied on relatively simple definitions to describe ad content. Image ads are generally defined as those that focus on the personal characteristics and abilities of a candidate (Kaid & Sanders, 1978; Thorson, Christ, & Caywood, 1991). Issue advertisements are defined as those that predominantly provide information on candidate policy stands (Kaid & Sanders, 1978). An early effort by Kaid and Keith Sanders (1978) found issue ads superior to image spots in producing higher candidate evaluations, although image ads elicited better information recall. Work by Esther Thorson, William Christ, and Clark Caywood (1991) and Seth Geiger and Byron Reeves (1991) supports the notions that issue ads are superior to image spots in eliciting better attitude toward the candidate and better candidate evaluations. Kaid, Mike Chanslor, and Mark Hovind (1992) found that an issue commercial produced higher candidate image evaluations than an image ad, though the image ad was better at eliciting greater likelihood of voting for the candidate. Robert Rudd (1989) produced evidence that specific issue appeals in radio ads resulted in higher candidate image ratings than ambiguous issue appeals.

Other research has focused more on the effects on candidate image ratings as the result of television advertising exposure. Donald Cundy (1986) provided general evidence that political advertising results in significant increases in ratings for intelligence, strength under pressure, dependability, fairmindedness, honesty, and liking. Kaid, Chris Leland, and Susan Whitney (1992) have also demonstrated experimentally that advertising exposure positively enhanced the image of George Bush in 1988. Research by Gina Garramone (1983, 1986) has focused on differences in the processing of advertisements based on respondent's orientation or motivation for watching ads. In similar work, Deirdre Johnston (1989) produced evidence supporting the notion that people bring to political advertisements image or issue information-processing orientations. Garramone (1983, 1986) found that image-motivated respondents use more general concepts to process commercial information than issue-motivated subjects. They also pay more attention to the video channel and are more confident in their ability to recall video information. Her effort with Michael Steele and Bruce Pinkleton (1991) confirmed her earlier work in that they found that image processors encode more visual information. They also discovered that candidate attractiveness is more related to vote likelihood for image processors than issue processors. These findings point to a strong relationship between image and visual advertising information, and highlight the need for studies to focus on the visual presentation that makes television unique.

Other research (Kaid, 1997, 2001; Kaid, McKinney, & Tedesco, 2000; Kaid & Tedesco, 1999b) has found evidence not only that advertising exposure can affect candidate image ratings, but also that those effects may change over the course of the campaign. In their analysis of the 1996 campaign, Kaid and Tedesco (1999b) found that subject exposure to spots in a late September experimental session resulted in a significantly more positive image rating for Bob Dole but did not affect Bill Clinton's rating. However, in a late October session, Dole's image rating actually dropped significantly as a result of subject spot exposure while Clinton's image rating rose significantly. Such research suggests the possible elasticity of candidate image during a campaign and the potential importance of advertising in molding that image.

Another aspect of political advertising research has been related to the interest in negative advertising. Brian Roddy and Garramone's (1988) results showed that issue-attack ads resulted in significantly higher evaluations of both the candidate's commercial and his character than image-attack ads. In work with predominantly issue-attack spots, Garramone, Charles Atkin, Pinkleton, and Richard Cole (1990) found that negative ads resulted in greater image discrimination and attitude polarization between candidates.

These findings would indicate some usefulness in the running of negative spots, particularly those that are issue oriented. However, work by Michael Basil, Caroline Schooler, and Byron Reeves (1991) found that positive ads resulted in candidates being liked more and being perceived as stronger, though the liking finding was not statistically significant. There was a connection between ads and vote intent, with subjects more likely to vote for candidates they liked and thought would be a strong leader. This work supports the notion that positive ads are better than negative ads for raising some image ratings.

There is also evidence that independently sponsored negative advertising may be effective in changing candidate images. Independently sponsored ads have been shown to result in lower image ratings and less likelihood of voting for the targeted candidate than candidate-sponsored negative ads (Garramone, 1985). Kaid and John Boydston (1987) also found that an independently sponsored negative ad lowered image ratings of the target. Other work supports the existence of indirect effects. Independent sponsorship has been shown to affect image ratings by affecting sponsor trustworthiness ratings, which affects commercial evaluations, which affects image (Garramone & Smith, 1984).

Political advertising may have similar effects across cultures. Kaid's (1991) cross-cultural comparison between U.S. and French presidential hopefuls shows that television-induced perceptions in both countries are similar, with respondents focusing more on images than issues after political television viewing. She also found that political broadcasts eliciting the emotions of optimism, confidence, security, and patriotism were positively related to better images for candidates in both countries. Similar findings have been noted when measuring political advertising effects on candidate images in Germany (Kaid & Holtz-Bacha, 1993), and research in several other countries has shown that there are indeed effects on candidate image, sometimes positive and sometimes negative, as a consequence of viewing political television broadcasts (Kaid, 1999b; Kaid & Holtz-Bacha, 1995).

Taken as a whole, research supports the view that candidate image is a complex concept that is made up of substantive (honesty, ability, qualifications, and the like) as well as appearance and performance dimensions. Probably the most important finding from effects research is that political advertisements do have an effect on candidate image ratings, including effects on substantive dimensions. There is evidence that there may be relationships between image and the visual information in televised ads and between image and issue information. This latter relationship is supported by findings on the superiority of issue ads in building candidate images. In some instances negative advertising, particularly when independently sponsored, may be important in affecting candidate image.

In recent years political theorists have conceded that candidate image plays a very important, perhaps determinative, role in voting decisions (Miller et al., 1986). The fact that researchers are increasingly able to substantiate a relationship between political advertising exposure and candidate image effects is certainly one of the most important components of current political communication theory.

However, these findings have not done enough to expand our understanding of *how* campaign commercials actually configure and reconfigure candidate images. Researchers have begun also to isolate the specific image components that are affected by political spots and to assess the relationships between image characteristics and other aspects of voter information processing. Earlier research by us has demonstrated that exposure to political ads may affect the structure or dimensions of the image that voters hold in their minds about political candidates. In an analysis of the 1988 campaign, for instance, the researchers found that exposure to campaign ads resulted in a compression of the dimensions of Michael Dukakis's image, while George Bush's image remained similar from pre- to post-test (Kaid & Chanslor, 1995). In 1992, however, Bush's image was affected by the spot viewing in a manner similar to the Dukakis situation in 1988. That is, after viewing, voters had a more concentrated, less differentiated view of Bush. Clinton, on the other hand, had more success in 1992 as the spot viewing served to reconfigure his image to provide more emphasis on a performance/credibility factor that may have accounted for the successful interpretation voters gave him after viewing his spots (Kaid & Chanslor, 1995).

Because campaign spots continue to be such an important part of the U.S. political process, it is important to look at the effects of spots on images across time and elections to be sure that any given set of effects are not situation specific. The research project reported below uses experimental data from four presidential elections to replicate earlier findings and to explore additional relationships.

Approach to 1988–2000 Political Commercials

The research reported here is the result of experimental studies conducted in the fall of 1988, 1992, 1996, and 2000, allowing data to be gathered in the context of the actual presidential campaigns. In the 1988 and 1992 campaigns, subjects were 93 undergraduate students enrolled in communication classes at a large southwestern university during the fall 1988 ($n = 43$) and 1992 ($n = 50$) semesters. In 1996 and 2000 the study benefitted from the data of a large national study that allowed simultaneous data gathering at several universities throughout the United States. In 1996, 525 subjects participated at 19 different universities located in different regions of the United States.[1] In 2000 the subjects consisted of 906 respondents at 26 different universities located throughout the United States, representing all regions and parts of the country.[2] Most of the participants were students, but the sample included some nonstudents who participated in the study.

The design of the study in all years was the same; subjects were randomly assigned to groups as part of a larger study of television spots; each group filled out a pretest questionnaire, viewed a series of political spots, and then completed a post-test questionnaire. All studies took place in late October or early November of their respective election years, just prior to Election Day.

In 1988 the stimulus material consisted of three spots for George Bush and three spots for Michael Dukakis, in alternating order.[3] The same basic approach was used in 1992, with subjects viewing three George Bush spots and three Bill Clinton spots.[4] In 1996, the groups viewed a series of four spots for Clinton and four spots for Dole,[5] and again in 2000, a series of four spots was used for each of the presidential contenders, George W. Bush and Al Gore.[6]

In order to control for any predispositions toward the candidate, subjects completed a pretest questionnaire before viewing their respective ads. The pretest questionnaires consisted of simple demographic data and a semantic differential on each of the two major party candidates in each of the four presidential election years. The semantic differential consisted of twelve bipolar adjectives rated on a seven-point scale.[7] Subjects were instructed to record their reactions to the candidates on each adjective. The instrument used here was an adaptation of an instrument that is the result of extensive research and testing since 1968. Originally developed to measure candidate image but also used to evaluate news commentators (Kaid & Boydston, 1987; Kaid & Sanders, 1978; Kaid, Singleton, & Davis, 1977; Sanders & Pace, 1977), the scale has consistently achieved high reliability for nearly four decades (Kaid, 1995). In the studies reported here, the Cronbach's alpha for the pretest/post-test image scales were .90/.92 for Bush and .86/.91 for Dukakis in 1988, .92/.93 for Bush and .88/.88 for Clinton in 1992, .81/.83 for Clinton and .78/.84 for Dole in 1996, and .80/.83 for G. W. Bush and .65/.85 for Gore in 2000. The post-test repeated the pretest semantic differential scales, adding a three-point rating scale (*a lot, a little*, or *not at all*) designed to measure how much the advertisements evoked nine feelings or emotions in the respondents (e.g., confident, anxious, optimistic, and the like).

Image Findings from 1988 to 2000

Effects on Candidate Image of Television Ad Exposure

One of the most important findings from these data is the confirmation that exposure to political advertising messages does appear consistently to have a direct effect on candidate image evaluations. Summing the semantic differential image scales and comparing the before-after measures, table 6.1

TABLE 6.1
Comparison of Presidential Images before and after Viewing Television Spots

	Before	After
1988 (N = 34)		
Bush*	4.88	5.12
Dukakis	4.08	4.05
1992 (N = 50)		
Bush*	4.57	4.78
Clinton*	4.38	4.58
1996 (N = 525)		
Clinton*	4.51	4.59
Dole*	4.48	4.34
2000 (N = 906)		
Gore	4.63	4.66
G. W. Bush*	4.65	4.72

* Indicates t test is significant at $p \leq .01$.

shows that respondent evaluations of the images of at least one of the presidential candidates was affected significantly in each of the four presidential campaigns. This increase in positivity of the post-test score after viewing the ads was true for Bush in 1988, for both Bush and Clinton in 1992, for Clinton in 1996, and for G. W. Bush in 2000. In two cases, Dukakis in 1988 and Gore in 2000, the viewing of the political commercials had no effect on the image of the candidate. In one case, Dole in 1996, the spots had the effect of reducing significantly the image evaluation of the candidate.

This image effect from spot exposure is also related to other important aspects of the voter's judgment process. For instance, in earlier reports on the 1992 study, there was a significant correlation between the post-test image scores and the likelihood of voting for the candidate for both Bush ($r = .86$; $p \leq .01$) and for Clinton ($r = .73$; $p \leq .01$) (Kaid & Chanslor, 1995). The post-test image scores for the presidential candidates were also related in all four years to the emotional feelings elicited by viewing the spots. In all years, respondents were asked to indicate the extent to which viewing the spots for each candidate elicited various emotions. The amount of each emotional feeling elicited was then correlated with the post-test image evaluation of each candidate. As table 6.2 indicates, these relationships were generally strong ones. For instance, across all candidates in all years, the more *optimistic, confident, excited, secure,* and *patriotic* the spots made voters feel, the higher their evaluations of the candidate images. Conversely, the generation of feelings of *boredom* and *fear* resulted in a negative evaluation of candidates. Interestingly, in contrast to the uniformity of other correlations across candidates and time, the generation of *anxiety* seemed to work in Bush's favor in 1992.

TABLE 6.2
Correlations of Post-Test Image Scores and Emotional Feelings

	1988		1992		1996		2000	
	Dukakis	Bush	Bush	Clinton	Clinton	Dole	Bush	Gore
Emotions								
Optimistic	.56*	.58*	.60*	.69*	.44*	.51*	.61*	.58*
Confident	.72*	.63*	.79*	.71*	.54*	.50*	.65*	.50*
Anxious	−.01	.20	.30*	−.03	.01	.07	−.01	−.05
Excited	.30*	.60*	.67*	.55*	.34*	.27*	.41*	.45*
Secure	.63*	.71*	.72*	.71*	.52*	.47*	.37*	.59*
Fearful	−.66*	−.55*	−.20	−.49*	−.45*	−.35*	−.50*	−.49*
Bored	−.56*	−.41*	−.54*	−.49*	−.20*	−.37*	−.40*	−.34*
Patriotic	.41*	.58*	.50*	.52*	.40*	.38*	.46*	.34*
Concerned	−.19	−.18	−.21	−.36*	−.27*	−.05	−.18*	−.24*

*Indicates that Pearson correlation is significant at $p \leq .01$.

Relationship of Ad Effects to Ad Content

Finally, a look at the importance of candidate image and political spots would not be complete without some reference to the image content of political spots. Content analysis[8] of major party candidate spots in these four elections reveals some interesting aspects of image content. When spots are coded for mentions of particular candidate qualities, there are some interesting differences among candidates. Table 6.3 shows the most frequently mentioned character themes in the spots for these years. For instance, honesty was a strong content category for Dukakis in 1988 and for Bush in both 1988 and 1992. Clinton was reluctant to mention it in his subsequent campaigns. Only Dole in 1996 gave any particular emphasis to this important quality, mentioning it in 32 percent of his spots. Competence was stressed by both Bush and Dukakis in 1988 and by Clinton in 1992, but given less emphasis by Bush in 1992. Clinton took maximum advantage of this image quality in his 1996 spots, however, mentioning it in 72 percent of all his ads. For Clinton, the competence quality, along with performance/qualifications, served to provide the ideal mix of qualities for an incumbent president seeking to reinforce his accomplishments. Amazingly, George Bush ceded performance claims to Clinton in 1992, when Bush had the advantage of incumbency. It is less surprising that Dole in 1996 and even G. W. Bush in 2000 gave these qualities less emphasis. However, it is surprising that Al Gore did not take advantage of the accomplishments of his years with Clinton. Gore emphasized performance/qualifications in only 5 percent of his 2000 ads. Thus, there may be some relationship between the positive effects on the candidate's image and the image qualities emphasized in the spots they use during the campaign.

TABLE 6.3
Emphasis on Image Qualities in Presidential General Election Spots

	1988		1992		1996		2000	
Candidate	Bush (N = 37)	Dukakis (N = 44)	Bush (N = 32)	Clinton (N = 39)	Clinton (N = 61)	Dole (N = 41)	Bush (N = 46)	Gore (N = 115)
Image Mentions								
Honesty	60%	61%	59%	33%	20%	32%	15%	10%
Strength	65	59	34	21	54	22	4	37
Compassion	22	39	6	39	48	27	39	20
Competence	87	57	25	64	72	17	7	7
Performance	78	46	19	49	80	17	4	5
Aggressiveness	16	59	16	18	51	24	48	9
Activeness	19	68	13	8	26	7	4	5

Conclusion

The review of prior research on the relationship of political television advertising to candidate image indicated that research has uncovered some strong linkages. The unique research reported here provided a rare opportunity to consider results over time using similar research designs and measurement techniques. Although subject to the usual limitations of experimental research (student subjects, artificial viewing situations, one-time measurement), these data still suggest some consistent findings.

In line with prior research, several overall conclusions seem warranted:

1. Political television advertising exposure can lead to changes in candidate image ratings. Generally, the direction of that change is a positive one, although this is not always true, as the Dole campaign demonstrated in 1996.
2. Candidate image ratings resulting from spot viewing are also strongly related to the generation of emotional feelings in respondents.
3. There may be a relationship between candidate image effects and the specific image qualities that candidates stress in their television ads.

Taken together, these results suggest an important role for political advertising in the construction of presidential candidate image during presidential campaigns. It may be that while image construction is a transactional process (Nimmo & Savage, 1976), candidate information projection, particularly through political television advertising, can play a bigger image formation role than voter predispositions in certain instances. More research is needed to answer the broad question of how images are formed. Considerable work also needs to be done to isolate more fully the nature of changes in candidate image that might result from exposure to political advertisements. Particular attention also needs to be given to the interrelationship between spot content and resulting image changes and reconfigurations, particularly by associating changes more directly with the specific spots to which viewers are exposed.

Notes

1. The nineteen universities were located in the following states: Maryland, Pennsylvania, Florida, Alabama, South Carolina, Illinois (two locations), Indiana, Ohio, Minnesota, Arkansas, Iowa, Missouri, Oklahoma (two locations), Texas, California (two locations), and Oregon.

2. The states in which the universities were located included Arkansas, California, Colorado, Florida, Idaho, Illinois, Indiana, Iowa, Kansas, Massachusetts, Missouri, Ohio, Oklahoma, Pennsylvania, Texas, Virginia, and South Carolina.

3. The spots used for the 1988 study for Dukakis were (1) a commercial detailing Dukakis's record on crime, (2) a spot that contained excerpts from the Democratic Convention and a general discussion of Dukakis's leadership potential, and (3) the negative "Quayle Empty Seat" ad questioning Bush's vice-presidential selection. Bush's spots were (1) the negative "revolving door" furlough spot, (2) an ad known as "The Future" that implied that Bush is a family man, and (3) a general qualifications spot detailing Bush's public service record.

4. The 1992 spots used for Bush were (1) "What I Am Fighting For," featuring a forceful candidate speaking on a variety of issues he felt important; (2) "Gray Dot/Unfortunately," that attacked Clinton for making contradictory statements and featured two Clintons on a split screen with the faces covered by gray dots; and (3) "Agenda," an edited version of a five-minute spot in which Bush spoke to his ability to lead and his vision for the future. Clinton's spots were (1) "Welfare to Work," outlining his welfare reform plan; (2) "Jobs," attacking Bush for allegedly false statements made in the past; and (3) "Hope," a predominantly biographical spot.

5. The spots for the 1996 experimental sessions were (1) a Dole spot called "Truth on Spending" that attacked Clinton's support for big-money projects like $48 million for Alpine Slides and Midnight Basketball; (2) a Clinton negative ad with split screens of Bob Dole saying he was fighting against Medicare and the creation of the Department of Education; (3) a Dole positive Dole ad called "From the Heart," in which Elizabeth Dole talks about her husband keeping his word and commitment to a 15 percent tax cut; (4) a Clinton positive spot titled "Second" in which Jim Brady endorses Clinton as a man of strong character for supporting gun control legislation; (5) a Clinton negative ad attacking Dole as "Wrong in the Past," capturing Dole's Washington insider status by showing Dole's actions in the 1960s, 1970s, and 1980s against such legislation as Medicare, the Brady Bill, Family and Medical Leave, the Department of Education, and the creation of the drug czar; (6) a Dole ad called "Riady," which is a negative ad playing on Clinton's creation of a large government bureaucratic health care system and his tax increase and using clippings to emphasize his ethical uncertainties; (7) a Dole spot called "Nicole," which describes an editorial from the *New York Times* about a teenage girl named Nicole who thinks it's okay to smoke marijuana because the president did it; and (8) a Clinton spot titled "Look," which emphasizes how "risky" the Dole tax scheme is and accuses Dole of voting for legislation that would total $900 million in higher taxes.

6. The spots used in the 2000 experimental sessions, in the order of their appearance, were (1) a positive Bush spot titled "Trust," in which Bush talks about trusting America and renewing America's purpose; (2) a positive Gore ad, "College," in which Gore's college tuition tax deduction for middle-class families is featured; (3) a negative Bush ad, "Gore-Gantuan," that attacks Gore's spending plan and says it will wipe out the surplus and increase governmental spending; (4) a Gore ad titled "Down" that uses a graphic of a dissolving dollar bill to attack Bush's tax cut plan, ending with the message that Gore will pay down the debt, protect Social Security, and give a tax deduction for college tuition; (5) a Bush ad titled "Education Recession" that suggests that there is a Clinton/Gore education recession and that Bush raised education standards in Texas, and tells the viewer how to obtain the "Bush blueprint for education"

that features accountability, high standards, and local control; (6) a Gore ad titled "Apron" that attacks Bush on the minimum wage in Texas and promotes the "Al Gore plan" of increasing the minimum wage, investing in education, middle-class tax cuts, and a secure retirement; (7) a Bush ad called "Big Relief vs. Big Spending" that compares Bush's tax cut plan with Gore's spending plan, stating that Gore's spending plan threatens America's prosperity; (8) a negative Gore ad called "Needle" that opens with a foggy Houston skyline, attacks Bush on his environmental policies in Texas, and ends with a foggy Seattle skyline, asking the viewer to "imagine Bush's Texas-style environmental regulations" in Seattle.

7. The twelve bipolar adjective pairs used were qualified-unqualified, sophisticated-unsophisticated, honest-dishonest, believable-unbelievable, successful-unsuccessful, attractive-unattractive, friendly-unfriendly, sincere-insincere, calm-excitable, aggressive-unaggressive, strong-weak, and active-inactive.

8. The procedures and category development are similar to that described in earlier research by Kaid and Johnston (1991, 2001). The number of ads used in each year's sample is listed in table 6.3. Using Holsti's formula (North, Holsti, Zaninovich, & Zinnes, 1963), intercoder reliability averaged + .86 across all categories.

References

Atkin, C., and G. Heald. 1976. "Effects of Political Advertising." *Public Opinion Quarterly* 40: 216–228.

Basil, M., C. Schooler, and B. Reeves. 1991. "Positive and Negative Political Advertising: Effectiveness of Ads and Perceptions of Candidates." In *Psychological Processes*, vol. 1 of *Television and Political Advertising*, edited by F. Biocaa, 245–262. Hillsdale, N.J.: Lawrence Erlbaum.

Benoit, W. L. 1999. *Seeing Spots: A Functional Analysis of Presidential Television Advertisements, 1952–1996.* Westport, Conn.: Praeger.

Boiney, J., and D. L. Paletz. 1991. "In Search of the Model Model: Political Science versus Political Advertising Perspectives on Voter Decision Making." In *Psychological Processes*, vol. 1 of *Television and Political Advertising*, edited by F. Biocaa, 3–26. Hillsdale, N.J.: Lawrence Erlbaum.

Cundy, D. T. 1986. "Political Commercials and Candidate Image: The Effect Can Be Substantial." In *New Perspectives on Political Advertising*, edited by L. L. Kaid, D. Nimmo, and K. R. Sanders, 210–234. Carbondale: Southern Illinois University Press.

Devlin, L. P. 1993. "Contrasts in Presidential Campaign Commercials of 1992." *American Behavioral Scientist* 37: 272–290.

———. 1997. "Contrasts in Presidential Campaign Commercials of 1996." *American Behavioral Scientist* 40: 1058–1084.

———. 2001. "Contrast in Presidential Campaign Commercials of 2000." *American Behavioral Scientist* 44: 2338–2369.

Garramone, G. M. 1983. "Issue versus Image Orientation and Effects of Political Advertising." *Communication Research* 10: 59–76.

———. 1985. "Effects of Negative Political Advertising: The Roles of Sponsor and Rebuttal." *Journal of Broadcasting & Electronic Media* 29: 147–159.

———. 1986. "Candidate Image Formation: The Role of Information Processing." In *New Perspectives on Political Advertising*, edited by L. L. Kaid, D. Nimmo, and K. R. Sanders, 235–247. Carbondale: Southern Illinois University Press.

Garramone, G. M., C. K. Atkin, B. E. Pinkleton, and R. T. Cole. 1990. "Effects of Negative Political Advertising on the Political Process." *Journal of Broadcasting & Electronic Media* 34: 299–311.

Garramone, G. M., and S. J. Smith. 1984. "Reactions to Political Advertising: Clarifying Sponsor Effects." *Journalism Quarterly* 61: 771–775.

Garramone, G. M., M. E. Steele, and B. E. Pinkleton. 1991. "The Role of Cognitive Schemata in Determining Candidate Characteristic Effects." In *Psychological Processes*, vol. 1 of *Television and Political Advertising*, edited by F. Biocaa, 311–328. Hillsdale, N.J.: Lawrence Erlbaum.

Geiger, S. F., and B. Reeves. 1991. "The Effects of Visual Structure and Content Emphasis on the Evaluation and Memory for Political Candidates." In *Psychological Processes*, vol. 1 of *Television and Political Advertising*, edited by F. Biocaa, 125–143. Hillsdale, N.J.: Lawrence Erlbaum.

Hofstetter, C. R., and C. Zukin. 1979. "TV Network News and Advertising in the Nixon and McGovern Campaigns." *Journalism Quarterly* 56: 106–115, 152.

Hofstetter, C. R., C. Zukin, and T. F. Buss. 1978. "Political Imagery and Information in an Age of Television." *Journalism Quarterly* 55: 562–569.

Johnston, A., and L. L. Kaid. 2002. "Image Ads and Issue Ads in Presidential Advertising: Using Videostyle to Explore Stylistic Differences in Televised Political Ads from 1952 to 2000." *Journal of Communication* 52: 281–300.

Johnston, D. D. 1989. "Image and Issue Political Information: Message Content or Interpretation?" *Journalism Quarterly* 66: 379–382.

Joslyn, R. A. 1980. "The Content of Political Spot Ads." *Journalism Quarterly* 57: 92–98.

Kaid, L. L. 1991. "The Effects of Television Broadcasts on Perceptions of Presidential Candidates in the United States and France." In *Mediated Politics in Two Cultures: Presidential Campaigning in the United States and France*, edited by L. L. Kaid, J. Gerstle, and K. R. Sanders, 247–260. New York: Praeger.

———. 1994. "Political Advertising in the 1992 Campaign." In *The 1992 Presidential Campaign*, edited by R. E. Denton, Jr., 111–127. Westport, Conn.: Praeger.

———. 1995. "Measuring Candidate Images with Semantic Differentials." In *Candidate Images in Presidential Election Campaigns*, edited by K. Hacker, 131–134. New York: Praeger.

———. 1997. "Effects of the Television Spots on Images of Dole and Clinton." *American Behavioral Scientist* 40: 1085–1094.

———. 1998. "Videostyle and the Effects of the 1996 Presidential Campaign Advertising." In *The 1996 Presidential Campaign: A Communication Perspective*, edited by R. E. Denton, 143–159. Westport, Conn.: Praeger.

———. 1999a. "Political Advertising: A Summary of Research Findings." In *The Handbook of Political Marketing*, edited by B. Newman, 423–438. Thousand Oaks, Calif.: Sage.

———. 2001. "Technodistortions and Effects of the 2000 Political Advertising." *American Behavioral Scientist* 44: 2370–2378.

———. 2002. "Videostyle and Political Advertising: Effects in the 2000 Presidential Campaign." In *The 2000 Presidential Campaign: Communication Perspectives*, edited by R. D. Denton, 183–197. Westport, Conn.: Praeger/Greenwood.

———, ed. 1999b. *Television and Politics in Evolving European Democracies*. Commack, N.J.: NovaScience Publishers.

Kaid, L. L., and J. Boydston. 1987. "An Experimental Study of the Effectiveness of Negative Political Advertisements." *Communication Quarterly* 35: 193–201.

Kaid, L. L., and M. Chanslor. 1995. "Changing Candidate Images: The Effects of Television Advertising." In *Candidate Images in Presidential Election Campaigns*, edited by K. Hacker, 83–97. New York: Praeger.

Kaid, L. L., M. Chanslor, and M. Hovind. 1992. "The Influence of Program and Commercial Type on Political Advertising Effectiveness." *Journal of Broadcasting and Electronic Media* 36: 303–320.

Kaid, L. L., and D. K. Davidson. 1986. "Elements of Videostyle: Candidate Presentation through Television Advertising." In *New Perspectives on Political Advertising*, edited by L. L. Kaid, D. Nimmo, and K. R. Sanders, 184–209. Carbondale: Southern Illinois University Press.

Kaid, L. L., and C. Holtz-Bacha. 1993. "Audience Reactions to Televised Political Programs: An Experimental Study of the 1990 German National Election." *European Journal of Communication* 8: 77–99.

———, eds. 1995. *Political Advertising in Western Democracies: Parties and Candidates on Television*. Thousand Oaks, Calif.: Sage.

Kaid, L. L., and A. Johnston. 1991. "Negative versus Positive Television Advertising in U.S. Presidential Campaigns, 1960–1988." *Journal of Communication* 41, no. 3: 53–64.

———. 2001 *Videostyle in Presidential Campaigns: Style and Content of Televised Political Advertising*. Westport, Conn.: Praeger.

Kaid, L. L., C. M. Leland, and S. Whitney. 1992. "The Impact of Televised Political Ads: Evoking Viewer Responses in the 1988 Presidential Campaign." *Southern Communication Journal* 57: 285–295.

Kaid, L.L., M. S. McKinney, and J. C. Tedesco. 2000. *Civic Dialogue in the 1996 Presidential Campaign: Candidate, Media, and Public Voices*. Cresskill, N.J.: Hampton Press.

Kaid, L. L., and K. R. Sanders. 1978. "Political Television Commercials: An Experimental Study of Type and Length." *Communication Research* 5: 57–70.

Kaid, L. L., D. L. Singleton, and D. Davis. 1977. "Instant Analysis of Televised Political Addresses: The Speaker versus the Commentator." In *Communication Yearbook I*, edited by B. Ruben, 453–464. New Brunswick, N.J.: Transaction Press.

Kaid, L. L., and J. C. Tedesco. 1999a. "Tracking voter reactions to the television advertising. In *The Electronic Election: Perspectives on the 1996 Campaign Communication*, edited by L. L. Kaid & D. G. Bystrom, 233–245. Mahwah, N.J.: Lawrence Erlbaum.

———. 1999b. "Presidential Candidate Presentation: Videostyle in the 1996 Presidential Spots." In *The Electronic Election: Perspectives on the 1996 Campaign Communication*, edited by L. L. Kaid & D. G. Bystrom, 233–245. Mahwah, N.J.: Lawrence Erlbaum.

Kern, M. 1989. *30-Second Politics: Political Advertising in the Eighties*. New York: Praeger.

Louden, A. D. 1990. "Transformation of Issue to Image Presence: Eliciting Character Evaluations in Negative Spot Advertising." Paper presented at the International Communication Association convention, Dublin, Ireland, June.

Miller, A. H., M. P. Wattenberg, and O. Malanchuk. 1985. "Cognitive Representations of Candidate Assessments." In *Political Communication Yearbook 1984*, edited by K. R. Sanders, L. L. Kaid, and D. Nimmo, 183–210. Carbondale: Southern Illinois University Press.

———. 1986. "Schematic Assessments of Presidential Candidates." *American Political Science Review* 80: 521–536.

Mulder, R. 1979. "The Effects of Televised Political Ads in the 1975 Chicago Mayoral Election." *Journalism Quarterly* 56: 336–340.

Newman, B. I. 1999. *The Mass Marketing of Politics: Democracy in an Age of Manufactured Images*. Thousand Oaks, Calif.: Sage.

Nimmo, D., and R. L. Savage. 1976. *Candidates and Their Images: Concepts, Methods and Findings*. Pacific Palisades, Calif.: Goodyear.

North, R. C., O. Holsti, M. G. Zaninovich, and D. A. Zinnes. 1963. *Content Analysis: A Handbook with Applications for the Study of International Crisis*. Evanston, Ill.: Northwestern University Press.

Patterson, T. E., and R. D. McClure. 1976. *The Unseeing Eye: The Myth of Television Power in National Politics*. New York: G. P. Putnam's Sons.

Roddy, B. L., and G. M. Garramone. 1988. "Appeals and Strategies of Negative Political Advertising." *Journal of Broadcasting & Electronic Media* 32: 415–427.

Rose, E. D., and D. Fuchs. 1968. "Reagan vs. Brown: A TV Image Playback." *Journal of Broadcasting* 12: 247–260.

Rudd, R. 1989. "Effects of Issue Specificity, Ambiguity on Evaluations of Candidate Image." *Journalism Quarterly* 66: 675–682, 691.

Sanders, K. R., and T. J. Pace. 1977. "The Influence of Speech Communication on the Image of a Political Candidate: 'Limited Effects' Revisited." In *Communication Yearbook I*, edited by B. Ruben, 465–474. New Brunswick, N.J.: Transaction Press.

Shyles, L. 1984a. "Defining 'Images' of Presidential Candidates from Televised Political Spot Advertisements." *Political Behavior* 6, no. 2: 171–181.

———. 1984b. "The Relationships of Images, Issues and Presentational Methods in Televised Spot Advertisements for 1980's American Presidential Primaries." *Journal of Broadcasting* 28: 405–421.

———. 1986. "The Televised Political Spot Advertisement: Its Structure, Content, and Role in the Political System." In *New Perspectives on Political Advertising*, edited by L. L. Kaid, D. Nimmo, and K. R. Sanders, 107–138. Carbondale: Southern Illinois University Press.

Thorson, E., W. G. Christ, and C. Caywood. 1991. "Effects of Issue-Image Strategies, Attack and Support Appeals, Music, and Visual Content in Political Commercials." *Journal of Broadcasting & Electronic Media* 35: 465–486.

Tucker, D. E. 1959. "Broadcasting in the 1956 Oregon Senatorial Campaign." *Journal of Broadcasting* 3: 225–243.

West, D. M. 1993. *Air Wars: Television Advertising in Election Campaigns*. Washington, D.C.: Congressional Quarterly Press.

7

Presidential Debates and Candidate Image Formation: 1992, 1996, 2000

Walter R. Zakahi

IN THIS CHAPTER I WILL EXAMINE THE CONTRIBUTION of presidential debates to the formation of candidates' images during the 1992, 1996, and 2000 elections. First, I will examine and explore how candidate image is linked to the debate about debates that seems to occur in every presidential campaign. Second, I will examine the unusual strategy of lowering expectations employed by candidates leading up to the debates. Finally, I will consider the contribution of debates' defining moments to candidate image.

Value of Presidential Debates

While presidential debates are important to the democratic process for a number of reasons, a key factor is in their ability to influence voters who remain uncommitted or weakly committed at the time of the debates (see, for example, Pfau & Kang, 1991). Several recent elections that have included presidential debates have been so close as to argue that their outcomes may have turned on the outcomes of the debates. John Kennedy, the clear winner of the 1960 debates, beat Nixon by less than 0.2 percent of the popular vote. Jimmy Carter, the winner of the 1976 debates, beat Gerald Ford by less than 2 percent of the popular vote. Most recently, George W. Bush actually received more than 539,000 fewer popular votes than Al Gore (CNN, 2000b) but was a controversial winner in the Electoral College.

Debate about Debates

In recent years the process of negotiating whether to debate, the number, the format, and even minute details about such things as the type of microphones, the height of the podium or stools, lighting, and room temperature have been the subject of extensive negotiation. This process often begins with public challenges from the candidate who is trailing in the polls, but debate negotiations eventually move behind closed doors.

Since 1988, the bipartisan Commission on Presidential Debates has sponsored and scheduled the presidential debates. Although the commission has sponsored the last four series of presidential debates, their sponsorship has not been without controversy. Several candidates have objected to the commission having a role in the process. Most notably, George H. Bush rejected commission sponsorship in 1988, and George W. Bush challenged the commission's sponsorship in 2000. George W. Bush did, however, eventually agree to debate under the auspices of the Debate Commission. As the challenger in 1992, Bill Clinton embraced the Debate Commission's proposals. As the incumbent in 1996, however, he refused to participate in all the debates proposed by the commission.

Bush–Clinton–Perot

In June 1992, the Commission on Presidential Debates announced its proposal for three presidential debates and one vice presidential debate. The first debate would be held September 22 and the final debate on October 15. The three debates would each be ninety minutes long and have a single moderator instead of a panel of journalists (Schwarts & Babcock, 1992). The Clinton campaign decided during the Democratic National Convention to embrace the commission's proposal. Although the commission's proposal was not precisely what the Clinton campaign wanted, this was a strategic decision designed to avoid debate negotiations. James Carville, of the Clinton campaign, reports that he wanted to avoid negotiating with the Republicans in general and James Baker in particular. "Don't get me in a room with Jim Baker. That's all they can't wait for us to do [sic]. This is their whole life, is getting us in a room and negotiating debate terms [sic]" (Matalin, Carville, & Knobler, 1994, p. 323). The Democrats were able to claim the moral high ground by immediately accepting the commission's proposal while the blame for delaying or not having debates would be placed on Bush ("The War Room Drill," 1992).

Following the Republican National Convention on September 3, Bush's campaign chair, Robert Teeter, announced Bush's rejection of the commission's proposal for the debates. He indicated that the campaign was dissatisfied with the number and format for the debates. Teeter also signaled a desire to negotiate directly with the Clinton campaign (Balz, 1992). Bill Clinton responded, "They want to haggle behind closed doors. I think it's plain that for some reason open forums and free debates bother them" (Walsh, 1992a). Republican negotiating strategy for the last few presidential elections in which there was a Republican incumbent (or a sitting vice president) had been to agree to no more than two debates in order to limit the challenger's time on stage with the incumbent and to demand a panel of journalists, not a single moderator. Single moderators were a concern because they could follow a line of questions and make a candidate's evasions more apparent to the audience (Waldman, 1992).

In early and mid-September, the Bush campaign was operating under the assumption that as the challenger Clinton *needed* to appear on stage and debate President Bush. This was evident as late as mid-September, when Teeter wrote a letter to Mickey Kantor, Clinton's campaign chair, demanding debates "under the same terms and conditions" as in 1988. Teeter continued that if Clinton did not accept, "We will assume you do not wish to debate" (Broder, 1992, p. A8). The Clinton campaign, however, maintained its strategy of accepting the Debate Commission's terms and conditions and refusing to negotiate. This strategy was combined with a strategy of attacking President Bush for refusing to debate. For example, the Democrats placed campaign workers dressed in chicken costumes carrying signs that read "Chicken George" to heckle the president at his campaign appearances (Matalin et al., 1994).

The September 22 debate scheduled for Michigan State University and later the debate scheduled for Louisville on September 29 were cancelled. Just as the Democrats had hoped, President Bush received much of the blame for the cancellations. For example, a survey of newspaper editorials conducted by the debate commission failed to find one newspaper sympathizing with the president's position (Rosentiel & Gerstenzang, 1992). By the end of September, it was clear that President Bush, who had been trailing in the polls for weeks, was not gaining ground. For instance, *USA Today* reported on September 24 that in six national polls Clinton held anywhere from a 9 to a 21 percentage point lead over Bush (Nagourney, 1992). The president and his staff were searching for a way to shake up the election and the electorate (Goldman et al., 1992).

On September 29 President Bush challenged Clinton to debate on four consecutive Sunday evenings, beginning in October and running until just before Election Day. Bush's proposal had two single-moderator debates, two panel-of-journalist debates, and included Ross Perot (Rosentiel & Gerstenzang, 1992). Although the Democrats rejected the proposal, it allowed the two sides to begin negotiations. The negotiation process did, however, become a target for Bill Clinton. Even as his representatives were negotiating with the Bush campaign, Clinton complained about secrecy. "Those things are now being negotiated—*because* George Bush insisted—in private by politicians instead of in public by the nonpartisan debate commission" (Rosentiel, 1992, p. A26).

Eventually the campaigns agreed to three presidential debates. The first debate used a panel of reporters, the second debate used a town-hall format, and the final debate used a panel of reporters for the first half and a single moderator for the second half.

In 1992 the Clinton campaign seemed to recognize early that the debate about debates could provide an opportunity to shape both candidates' images. The Clinton campaign presented its candidate as eager to debate and open to the Debate Commission's proposal. The Clinton campaign seemed to succeed in casting Bush as fearful of debating, someone who wanted to manipulate a bipartisan process away from the kinds of forums he feared.

As in recent presidential elections (e.g., 1980, 1984, 1988) the Republicans counted on pressing their demands for debate formats they perceived as better suited to their candidate during face-to-face negotiations with the Democrats. Clinton's lead in the polls throughout September, however, meant that the Clinton campaign was in a position to reject any demands and continue to insist on the Debate Commission plan. While the debate about debates continued for much of September, the Bush campaign tried (see, for example, Clifford, 1992) but failed to convince the public that Clinton was at fault.

In the end the Bush campaign lost the debate about debates because it appeared that George H. Bush wanted to avoid debating or at least wanted to manage the format to his own advantage. Clinton won the debate about debates by insisting on the Debate Commission proposals.

Clinton–Dole

The story of the debate negotiations in 1996 was essentially written by the polls. In the week prior to the GOP convention, Senator Dole was trailing President Clinton by more than twenty percentage points in the Gallup Poll. Dole was able to close this gap to about seven percentage points as a result of his convention "bump" ("Dole Gains," 1996), but his bump evaporated following the Democratic National Convention. By September 1, Clinton's lead in the Gallup Poll was back to more than twenty points (Benedetto, 1996a), making Dole's negotiating position weak. He needed to debate more than Clinton did, and as a result he was not in a position to make demands.

Probably because of his double-digit poll deficit, the Dole campaign proposed adding an additional presidential debate and an additional vice-presidential debate to the series proposed by the commission on Presidential

Debate. This proposal was rejected by Clinton's negotiators (Richter, 1996). Apparently the issue of more debates was raised by Dole's negotiators throughout this period.

The primary point of contention in the 1996 debate about debates was whether Ross Perot would be allowed to participate. Janet Brown of the Commission on Presidential Debates signaled that consideration of Perot's bid for participation would be determined by objective criteria. "We have developed a strict set of criteria that we will apply to any candidate who appears on even one state ballot." In an apparent reference to Perot, she goes on to note, "The criteria don't automatically include parties that have taken part in the past" (Heller, 1996, p. 1A).

Having benefited from Perot's participation in the 1992 debates, the Clinton campaign was in favor of his participation in 1996. Comments from the Clinton campaign, however, focused on language of "inclusion." The *Washington Post* quoted a Clinton staff member as saying "Millions and millions of Americans voted for him [Perot in '92]. I find it difficult to exclude him" (Merida, 1996a, p. A11). The Dole campaign, by contrast, focused on Perot as a distraction. Carroll Campbell, Dole's debate negotiator, commented, "We think the American people deserve to see them [Dole and Clinton] unfettered answering questions . . . just the two of them" (Merida, 1996b, p. A16).

The Dole campaign, however, also used Ralph Nader as a negotiation ploy. When Perot's name was mentioned for inclusion in the debates, Dole's people would typically counter with Nader. Scott Reed, Dole's campaign manager, is quoted from *Evans & Novak* on CNN that "there is another part of this debate we need to talk about too—that's Ralph Nader's existence in the debates" (Associated Press, 1996a).

Although Perot's participation in the debates was an issue throughout the debate negotiations, the question was settled by the debate commission on September 17 when they formally excluded him from the debates since he did not have a "realistic chance to win" (Balz, 1996a).

With Perot's participation in the debates decided by the commission, the two campaigns quickly settled their differences and agreed to debate. Clinton prevailed on all major points in the negotiations, including fewer debates, a town-hall format debate, scheduling a debate against the baseball playoffs, and his desire to avoid a debate too close to the election (Balz, 1996b; Hohenberg, 1997).

Ironically the Clinton team appeared to be working from a Republican incumbent strategy. Two of Clinton's conditions for debating were identical to George H. Bush's conditions four years earlier. Bush had proposed two, not three, debates and that the debates be broadcast at the same time as the baseball playoffs. Clinton's conditions were designed (as were Bush's four years earlier) to limit any benefit to his opponent's image. Presidential debates are typically thought to favor the challenger (Schroeder, 2000). The common wisdom is that, by appearing on stage with the president, the challenger appears more presidential and elevates his or her stature (Waldman, 1992; Zakahi & Hacker, 1995). Incumbents will try to limit the number of debates or suggest times (such as the World Series or baseball playoffs) that will reduce the audience.

Gore–Bush

The 2000 presidential election will be remembered for the Florida recount rather than the presidential debates or the debate about debates. Yet the negotiations process leading up to the 2000 presidential debates may have been the most interesting and possibly the most strategic since the emergence of televised debates in 1960. Some might argue that the negotiation process was more important in influencing the candidates' images than the actual debates. Vice President Gore, trailing in the polls, attempted to initiate a debate discussion early. Once both candidates clinched their party's nominations in March, Gore challenged Governor Bush to twice-weekly debates beginning in March and running through the November election. He proposed this series of debates as an alternative to television advertising. Bush rejected Gore's proposal, indicating that he would be willing to debate in the fall ("Bush and Gore Wrap Up," 2000). He did, however, include Gore's early debate challenge as part of his negotiation strategy in the fall.

In January 2000, the Commission on Presidential Debates announced plans for three presidential debates and one vice presidential debate in October ("Debate Panel," 2000). Disagreement between the campaigns about the debates became apparent even before the conclusion of the Democratic National Convention. On August 17, the final day of the Democratic Convention and prior to Vice President Gore's acceptance speech, the Bush campaign announced the governor would agree to three presidential debates and two vice presidential debates but would not necessarily accept control of Commission on Presidential Debates in terms of location or format (Bruni, 2000a). Frontrunners often dictate or try to dictate many of the conditions under which debates will be held. At the time of this announcement Bush was still clearly leading in the polls, and he seemed to be in a position to dictate. The Gallup Poll of August 11 and August 12 indicated that Bush was leading by sixteen percentage points. Following Gore's speech accepting the nomination of the Democratic Party, Bush's lead in the polls evaporated. The August 18 and August 19 Gallup Poll indicated that the race had tightened and that Bush was actually trailing Gore by one percentage point (Gallup Poll, 2000). Although such "convention bumps" typically disappear within a few weeks (e.g., Dole in 1996), Gore stayed close to Bush throughout the fall campaign (see, for example, Langer, 2000; Holland, 2000d). The Gore campaign made it clear that the vice president would agree to additional debates but that they were committed to the debates proposed by the Commission on Presidential Debates (Bruni, 2000a). For the remainder of the month, the campaigns wrestled to take advantage of the ongoing disagreement. On August 29 the Gore campaign reiterated its commitment to the commission's proposal and asked Governor Bush to participate (Balz, 2000a).

The media and the campaigns seemed to play up several issues in the 2000 debate about debates. When the Bush campaign suggested that debates might take place during Sunday morning public affairs programs, the Gore campaign and the media suggested that Bush was afraid to debate in prime time (Balz, 2000a). Later, after Bush proposed accepting one of the commission debates and debating on *Larry King Live* and *Meet the Press* (broadcast in prime time), the Gore campaign charged that he was trying to limit the size of the audience since all of the major networks would not have access to, or would be unwilling to, broadcast another network's program (Finnegan & Brownstein, 2000).

The Bush campaign responded that they were concerned about the confrontational nature of the traditional moderator/podium debate. They felt that this format would not serve their candidate well. They preferred the idea of the two candidates sitting at a table with a moderator for a conversation or discussion, as in a Larry King–type program (Stevens, 2001).

The Bush campaign attempted to use the debate about debates in a larger campaign strategy that attacked Gore's honesty. A Bush ad that ran on September 6 indicated that the vice president agreed to debate on CNN and later on NBC; the announcer can be heard to intone that Gore said he would debate "anytime, anyplace, anywhere"; and Gore's rejection of the Bush debate proposal was attacked as another sign of Gore's dishonesty. The announcer ended, the ad by saying, "If we can't trust Al Gore on debates, why should we trust him on anything?" Apparently, however, the Bush campaign's argument wasn't working with the electorate. A CNN/*Time* poll taken in early September reported that 34 percent of respondents thought that George Bush was avoiding a debate while only 22 percent thought that Al Gore was avoiding a debate (Holland, 2000a).

By September 7, however, the Bush campaign was giving ground, possibly because of negative reactions from the press, the electorate, and even members of the Republican party. The *New York Times* quoted a member of the Bush campaign as saying that "the realization that people didn't buy their debate strategy that Gore was hiding from debates" (Bruni, 2000b, p. A 16) was responsible for the reversal. Consequently, Bush announced his campaign would enter into debate negotiations with the Gore campaign. Members of his staff now suggested Governor Bush would agree to two commission debates but continue to insist on the *Larry King Live* debate and the *Meet the Press* debate (Allen & Neal, 2000).

In the end, Governor Bush acceded to the original schedule established by the commission, including the debate at the University of Massachusetts, Boston, campus, which is situated across the street from the Kennedy Library. Governor Bush long claimed that this was not neutral territory (Balz, 2000b).

Stuart Stevens (2001), a member of the Bush campaign, details some of the minor issues that had to be settled once the two campaigns agreed to debate. Among the seemingly trivial issues were room temperature, lavaliere versus podium-mounted microphones, camera angles, and the option of a monitor visible to the candidates. The monitor was something that Gore wanted but Bush did not.

The events leading up to the presidential debates in 2000 reinforce the value of a big lead in the polls. Almost literally overnight, as a result of Gore's acceptance speech, George Bush went from being able to dictate the conditions for the debates to having to negotiate with Al Gore.

Summary of Debate about Debates

The 1992 and 2000 campaigns clearly demonstrate that the debate about debates has the potential, itself, to influence candidate image. In 1992 President Bush's campaign initially rejected commission sponsorship of the debates and wanted Bush to debate only under conditions they perceived favorable to him. They wanted to control the format, timing, and number of debates. By immediately accepting the proposal of the Commission on Presidential Debates and insisting that any debates conform to the commission's plan, the Clinton campaign succeeded in making it appear that President Bush was afraid to debate. Similarly, in 2000, Governor George W. Bush initially rejected the commission's proposal. Bush wanted to debate on public affairs programs such as *Larry King Live* and *Face the Nation*, and he wanted to have a conversation at a table rather than a traditional podium debate. The Gore campaign charged that Bush simply wanted to limit the size of the audience by avoiding prime time and by not broadcasting on all of the major networks. The Bush campaign attempted to make Gore look disingenuous for refusing to debate under Bush's terms since Gore had earlier said he would debate "anytime" and "anywhere." Gore, like Clinton in 1992, simply argued that both candidates should accept the Debate Commission's proposal. Gore had the polls behind him; they indicated that 34 percent of respondents thought Bush was avoiding debates versus 22 percent who thought Gore was avoiding debates (Holland, 2000a).

These three presidential campaigns demonstrate that the candidate who holds a large lead in the polls also has more power during the debate about debates. In 1992, the Bush campaign made demands about the debates while trailing heavily in the polls. Ultimately Bush agreed to much of what Clinton demanded. Bill Clinton entered the 1996 campaign with a large lead, and as a result he was able to insist on terms that limited the number of debates and limited the audience for at least one of the debates. Bob Dole was simply not in a position to argue because he trailed Clinton by such a wide margin. Finally, in the 2000 election, George W. Bush entered the month of August with a large lead in the polls and the power to insist that debates be held on his terms. When his lead disappeared in the middle of August, his ability to make demands also disappeared. The resulting debate about debates allowed the Gore campaign and the media to argue that Bush was afraid to debate.

Apparently, televised presidential debates have become a tradition. We have witnessed such debates in every presidential election since Carter and Ford in 1976. They have become such a tradition that a number of scholars argue that they are now inevitable (e.g., Hart & Jarvis, 1997; Schroeder, 2000) or institutionalized (e.g., Benoit, McKinney, & Holbert, 2001; Matera & Salwen, 1996). Arguing for inevitability or institutionalization ignores the lessons of relatively recent history. Johnson in 1964 and Nixon in 1968 and 1972 chose not to debate, despite the popularity of the Kennedy and Nixon debates in 1960. Standing in the polls probably explains the 1964 and the 1972 elections. Johnson in 1964 and Nixon in 1972 held poll leads of at least 30 percent into September (Zakahi & Hacker, 1995). With such commanding leads, neither Johnson nor Nixon had any reason to debate. It seems that a popular candidate who is holding a commanding lead could avoid debating. While any candidate who chooses not to debate would probably lose some of his or her lead in the polls, it is not hard to imagine a situation where such a candidate could and probably would still win. In fact, with a lead as high as thirty percentage points (especially by an incumbent), I would argue that engaging in televised debates could be considered reckless. The candidate with a large lead has nothing to gain from debating and an unfortunate word choice, a mistake, or simply a bad performance could put the election at risk.

In 1984, Ronald Reagan held a large lead in the polls but still chose to debate Walter Mondale. His lead of eighteen percentage points in late September ("Gallup Gives Reagan-Bush," 1984) was a much smaller lead than the lead held by Johnson in 1964 and Nixon in 1972 when they refused to debate. While Reagan may still have won reelection, it is not clear that an eighteen-percentage point lead was large enough to avoid debating. More important to

Reagan's decision was his confidence in his ability as a debater (Schroeder, 2000). In the end, Reagan received 59 percent of the vote (versus 41 percent for Mondale), and he received the electoral votes of forty-nine states.

In 1996 Bill Clinton held as high as a seventeen-percentage-point lead in September and as low as a nine-percentage-point lead (Lee & Wolf, 1996). As with Ronald Reagan in 1984, Clinton's lead was never high enough to seriously consider not debating. It is also clear (as I discuss in the next section) that the Clinton campaign never considered Dole a serious threat in the debates. In the end Clinton won the 1996 election by only 8 percent of the popular vote. While this was not a close election, his lead never compared to the kind of leads held by Johnson in 1964 or Nixon in 1972.

While thirty-point leads in presidential polls are obviously rare, a candidate who held such a lead in September would certainly receive advice from her or his handlers to consider not debating. Such recommendations should be seriously considered.

The Expectations Game

Alan Schroeder (2000) argues that the predebate strategy of trying to lower expectations for your candidate while simultaneously trying to increase expectations for the other candidate can be traced back to the 1976 Carter–Ford debates. The theory behind the practice is simple. If a campaign can minimize the electorate's expectation of a candidate's performance in a debate, then even a weak performance can be rationalized as a victory. On the other side of the argument, a campaign should make expectations so high for the opposition that even a strong performance in a debate can be explained away as simply meeting minimal expectations. The expectations game is a clear indication that candidates understand the link between their image and how their performance in the debates is perceived by the electorate. This is arguably the only time in a campaign where a candidate will try to play down his or her ability while praising the abilities of his opponent.

Unfortunately for the candidates, this strategy is now widely recognized by the media. Praising your opponent's debating prowess or diminishing your own ability as a debater is quickly labeled by the media as "playing the expectations game."

Clinton–Perot–Bush

Probably because the candidates were not sure there would be debates, neither candidate paid much attention to debate expectations until mid-September.

But even as the debate about debates continued, Bush started to work on expectations. In the surreal world of debate expectations, a top-notch education can be used against a candidate. Speaking in Detroit on September 10, President Bush referred to Clinton's time at Oxford University by saying, "I'll debate Governor Clinton. . . . [but] I'm not a professional debater. I'm not an Oxford man." ("Bush no 'Oxford man,'" 1992, p. 4A). Bush continued to use similar wording as a way of lowering expectations for him and raising expectations for Clinton for the next few weeks. Speaking on the Rush Limbaugh radio show on September 21, he indicated he would like to debate Clinton but qualified his statement by saying, "I'm not a professional Oxford debater" (Walsh, 1992b, p. A10).

Responding to Bush's consistent references to Oxford, Clinton commented,

> One day I'm a redneck from a little Southern state, the next day I'm an Oxford man. . . . He went to a country day school and prep school in Connecticut and Yale. Where does he get off looking up to me as an Oxford man? (Walsh, 1992b, p. A10)

I couldn't find an instance where Clinton denigrated his own debating abilities; rather, he chose to praise Bush's ability as a debater. In Toledo, Clinton noted that Bush "won every debate he's ever been in except that one debate where Reagan said he paid for the microphone. He's a good debater. I've seen the debates with Dukakis and all the others. He's won every one" (Berke, 1992, p. 1). Clinton aide Paul Begala echoed the governor's words a few days later, "Bush might be the most successful presidential-level debater in modern American history. . . . He's been doing this full time for 12 years" (Walsh, 1992c). Clinton also commented on Perot, "I think he'll do fine. He'll be at ease. You know, nothing to lose. I think he'll be very relaxed" (Rosentiel & Lauter, 1992).

President Bush and Governor Clinton seemed to follow a fairly standard scenario for managing expectations prior to the 1996 debates. The presence of a third-party candidate in the person of Ross Perot did not seem to make much difference to how the major party candidates dealt with expectations. It is noteworthy that I wasn't able to find any evidence that Perot played the expectations game in 1996. It may be that he did not engage in trying to manage expectations or, if he did, it is possible that the news outlets simply failed to report those efforts.

Dole–Clinton

In 1996, the Dole campaign worked hard to increase expectations for Bill Clinton. John Buckley, Dole's director of communications, seemed to be the point-man for increasing expectations for Clinton. In mid-September, he said that President Clinton was the greatest debater since the days of the Roman Senate (Harris, 1996). Toward the end of the month, he commented that "Clinton is the greatest debater since Benjamin Disraeli," and a few days later he said, "We're up against the greatest debater since Clarence Darrow, a master of the universe" (Kurtz, 1996). Although Buckley weighed in most frequently with comments about Clinton's debating prowess, other members of the Dole campaign also commented. Carroll Campbell, Dole's debate negotiator, indicated that Clinton "could charm birds out of the trees" (Richter, 1996). Nelson Warfield of the Dole campaign combined an attack on Clinton's veracity with an expectations comment: "[Clinton has] substantial advantages ... he's glib, he's agile and he's willing to stake out positions unrestrained by the truth" (Roth, 1996). Even Senator Dole contributed to the 1996 expectations game. He is quoted in early September as saying, "He's the heavyweight. ... He's the one all the media said, 'he'll wipe the floor with Bob Dole in the debate" (Associated Press, 1996b). In the last few days before the debate, he even joked, "If I can find Hartford [where the debate was to be held], I'll be all right" (Ball, 1996b). Apparently the Dole campaign was successful in decreasing expectations for their candidate. Wayne Woodlief (1996), in a *Boston Herald* editorial on September 26, commented that "Dole has his debate-performance expectations where he needs them. There's no place he can go but up" (p. 39).

It isn't clear if the Clinton campaign was really playing the expectations game in 1996. For example, Edward Walsh and Donald Baker of the *Washington Post* reported:

> The Clinton campaign clearly seemed confident, even cocky, about the prospect of pitting the quick-on-his-feet president against Dole. White House press secretary Michael McCurry sarcastically referred to Dole as "this titanic juggernaut of a debater ... we may be hanging our head because of Bob Dole's prowess as a debater." (1996, p. A18)

In the end, while the Clinton campaign made a few attempts to raise expectations for Dole (see for example, Ball, 1996a; Kurtz, 1996), they focused on lowering expectations for their candidate by indicating that he simply did not have time to prepare for the debates (Ball, 1996b).

Bush–Gore

In 2000, the Gore and Bush campaigns engaged in the kind of expectation setting that marked the last few elections. Members of the Gore campaign praised Governor Bush's skill as a debater on numerous occasions. Paul Begala, an adviser to Gore noted, "The governor has done a masterful job of spinning expectations. That's one of the reasons he beat Ann Richards and he beat John McCain. It would be very, very foolish to underestimate him" ("Gore and Bush Prep," 2000). Members of Bush's campaign praised Gore's debating abilities. For instance, communication director Karen Hughes characterized Gore as "the best debater in politics today," while campaign director Don Evans said, "The vice president spent the better part of his career debating" (CNN, 2000d). Usually campaigns try to elevate expectations for their opponents rather than decreasing expectations for their own candidate, yet Alison Mitchell (2000) quotes an unnamed Republican strategist as saying that rejecting the commission debates demonstrated that Governor Bush is "concerned about filling the full two-minute answer." While this comment may have been an attempt to lower expectations for Bush, it may have also reflected the frustration felt by many Republicans at Bush's apparent reluctance to debate.

Governor Bush also commented directly on Gore's debate prowess on several occasions. For instance, while campaigning on September 7, he commented, "This guy [Vice President Gore] is a very good debater. I hope I'll be able to hold my own" (CNN, 2000a). Bush made strikingly similar comments on August 5, when he described Gore as "a very good debater" (Associated Press, "Bring It On," 2000), and on a September 16 appearance on CNN's *Evans, Novak, Hunt & Shields* (CNN, 2000c) he indicated, "I understand that he's [Gore] a great debater."

George W. Bush may have taken the expectations game to a new level in the 2000 campaign. Several media outlets argued that Bush's protracted debate about debates may have been a strategic move on the part of his campaign where "Bush only want[s] to be seen as timid so he can lower expectations to the point where even a mediocre performance against Gore earns raves" ("Bush Play on Debates," 2000, p. 26A; see also "Not Debatable," 2000). Bush may have tied the debate about debates into the expectations game. If true, his apparent timidity about debates was part of a larger strategy to lower expectations about his debate performance. Yet such a strategy would appear to have been a huge gamble. As I noted earlier, the senior Bush's campaign suffered because he appeared reluctant to debate Clinton in 1992. In 2000, the polls for September and October showed Bush and Gore in a virtual tie. It seems strange that George W. Bush would take a risk on an untested strategy when the election seemed so close. It seems far more likely that the Bush campaign was simply trying to win the debate about debates rather than strategically positioning Bush with extremely low expectations. In other words, when the Bush campaign was pushing for debates in nontraditional forums and outside of prime time, they were trying to corner Gore on his willingness to debate "anytime, anyplace, anywhere." While the Bush campaign may not have won the debate about debates in the sense that both campaigns ended up signing onto the debate commission proposal, they were successful (perhaps purposefully, but probably by accident) in lowering voter expectations about Bush's performance.

Summary of the Expectations Game

The expectations game is, perhaps, the best example of how candidate image is tied to debating. By attempting to manipulate their own image and that of their opponents, candidates hope to affect the perceived outcome of a debate.

All three presidential elections we have discussed provide evidence of campaigns playing the expectations game. The Bush and Clinton campaigns in 1992, the Bush and Gore campaigns in 2000, and the Dole campaign in 1996 played the expectations game with gusto. All of these campaigns made serious attempts to raise expectations for their opponents. Only the 1996 Clinton campaign did not seem to make a serious attempt to lower expectations for its candidate.

Defining Moments

A number of presidential campaigns have been marked by debates that included what have come to be known as defining moments. A defining moment "is an occurrence during a debate that becomes the most memorable aspect of that debate series" (Zakahi & Hacker, 1995, p. 103). Those defining moments have, in a close election, the potential to swing the election to the beneficiary of the defining moment.

There has been a defining moment in most presidential campaigns that included presidential debates. For example, in 1976 President Ford mistakenly claimed that Eastern Europe was not under the control of the Soviet Union. In 1984, following a poor performance in his first debate versus Walter Mondale, Ronald Reagan was facing questions about his age. There were open questions about whether he was too old to serve another term. In the second debate in response to a question, Reagan responded, "I will not make age an issue of this campaign. I am not going to exploit for political purposes my opponent's youth and inexperience." This response combined with a strong performance in the second debate helped Reagan diminish concerns about his age. Following a strong showing in the first debate versus Bush, the Dukakis campaign was looking for a knockout punch in the second debate. Dukakis's response to the opening question from Bernard Shaw proved, however, to be *his* undoing. Shaw asked, "Governor, if Kitty Dukakis were raped and murdered, would you favor an irrevocable death penalty for the killer?" Dukakis proceeded to give a scripted, technical response that only served to reinforce his "ice-man" image. The *New York Times* ("Sure Loser," 1988) described his response as a "passionless laundry list" (p. 30).

Of the last three elections, the 1992 and 2000 elections contained examples of defining moments, but I would argue that the 1996 election did not seem to have a defining moment.

Clinton–Bush

In 1992 Governor Clinton entered the first of three debates with more than a twenty-percentage-point lead in the Gallup polls (Benedetto, 1992). The media argued that Clinton needed a strong performance in the debates to "close the sale" (e.g., Kurtz, 1992; Toner, 1992)—that is, to demonstrate to voters that he could be presidential. The second debate of the 1992 presidential election proved to be the most crucial, and while there is wide agreement of *a* defining moment, I would argue that several things occurred in the second debate that were all key to what was clearly a Clinton victory.

The second debate used a "talk show" format. That is, Carole Simpson, a journalist for ABC, moderated, and members of an audience made up of undecided voters asked the questions. Early in the debate, a member of the audience expressed concern about "the amount of time the candidates have spent in this campaign trashing their opponents' character and their programs." President Bush responded,

> Well, in the first place, I believe that character is a part of being president. I think you have to look at it. I think that has to be a part of a candidate for president or being president.... My argument with Governor Clinton—you can call it mud wrestling, but I think it's fair to put in focus is—I am deeply troubled by someone who demonstrates and organizes demonstration in a foreign land when his country's at war.

The very next question from the audience stayed on the same point. The questioner commented: "Can we focus on the issues and not the personalities and the mud? I think there's a need . . . I think there's a real need here to focus at this point on the needs." Even after the candidates each agreed with his point, the questioner persisted:

> Could we cross our hearts? It sounds silly here, but could we make a commitment? You know, we're not under oath at this point, but could you make a commitment to the citizens of the U.S. to meet our needs, and we have many, and not yours again? I repeat that. It's a real need, I think, that we all have.

It was clear from the first debate and from his response to the first audience member who was concerned about the time spent "trashing" opponents that President Bush wanted to continue to attack Clinton's character. The second audience member who asked the candidates to "cross our hearts" probably made any further discussion of character impossible. Goldman et al. (1994) describe Vice President Quayle watching the debate "and waiting for the president to start swinging" (p. 572). At one point it appeared that Bush would go on the attack, and Quayle exclaimed, "He's starting" (p. 572), but Bush never followed through. The importance of this part of the debate is that it constrained the president from pursuing what was apparently a strategy to continue to attack Clinton's character.

Another important moment in the debate occurred when President Bush was caught on camera, four separate times, looking at his watch (Von Drehle, 1992). The press widely viewed this behavior as Bush's boredom or lack of interest in the debate (e.g., Philips, 1992; Von Drehle, 1992) or impatience with discussions of domestic issues (e.g., Dowd, 1992). Roger Simon (1998) claims that this was no accident. It was the fallout of a strategy conceived by Clinton friend, television producer Harry Thomason. According to Thomason, Clinton practiced walking to a point onstage that would place Bush in the background when Clinton was speaking. The obvious goal was to catch President Bush unaware that he was on camera.

Finally, what is generally recognized as the defining moment of the 1992 debates started with an economic question from audience member Marisa Hall.

Marisa Hall: Yes. How has the national debt personally affected each of your lives? And if it hasn't, how can you honestly find a cure for the economic problems of the common people if you have no experience in what's ailing them?
Bush: Well, I think the national debt affects everybody.
Hall: You personally.
Bush: Obviously it has a lot to do with interest rates—
Moderator: She's saying, "you personally."
Hall: You, on a personal basis—how has it affected you?
Moderator: Has it affected you personally?
Bush: I'm sure it has. I love my grandchildren—
Hall: How?
Bush: I want to think that they're going to be able to afford an education. I think that's an important part of being a parent. If the question—maybe I—get it wrong. Are you suggesting that if somebody has means that the national debt doesn't affect them? . . . I'm not sure I get—help me with the question and I'll try to answer it.
Moderator: I think she means the recession, the economic problems today the country faces rather than the deficit.

> **Bush:** Well, listen, you ought to be in the White House for a day and hear what I hear and see what I see and read the mail I read and touch the people I touch from time to time. I was in the Lomax AME Church. It's a black church just outside of Washington, D C. And I read in the bulletin about teenage pregnancies, about the difficulties that families are having to make ends meet. I talk to parents. I mean, you've got to care. Everybody cares if people aren't doing well. But I don't think it's fair to say, you haven't had cancer. Therefore, you don't know what it's like. I don't think it's fair to say, you know, whatever it is, that if you haven't been hit by it personally. (Commission on Presidential Debates, n.d.)

What is remarkable about this exchange is that initially President Bush doesn't understand her question. This is apparent in the transcript, but it is also visible nonverbally in the president's expression. He sounds and looks lost during much of the exchange. Even when he finally grasps the question, he is unable to formulate a response that actually addresses Hall's question. This exchange left Bush looking like he was out of touch with average people, unable to understand the impact of a weak economy on their lives. This fed an existing image that George Bush was a man of privilege unable to relate to middle-class America.

Clinton seemed to grasp the question, and his response was immediate and direct. He walked toward Marisa Hall and seemed to converse with her.

> **Clinton:** Well, I've been governor of a small state for twelve years. I'll tell you how it's affected me. Every year Congress and the president sign laws that make us do more things and gives us less money to do it with. I see people in my state, middle class people—their taxes have gone up in Washington, and their services have gone down while the wealthy have gotten tax cuts.
>
> I have seen what happened in this last four years when—in my state, when people lose their jobs there's a good chance I'll know them by their names. When a factory closes, I know the people who ran it. When the businesses go bankrupt, I know them. . . . It is because we are in the grip of a failed economic theory. And this decision you're about to make better be about what kind of economic theory you want, not just people saying I'm going to go fix it, but what are we going to do? I think what we have to do is invest in American jobs, American education, control American health care costs and bring the American people together again.

The difference between the way Bush and Clinton handled this question was telling. Bush's failure to understand the question left the impression that he was out of touch with the average person. Clinton's response was direct and to the point and gave viewers the impression that he understood the plight of the average person in the midst of a recession. While all three parts of the debate I have highlighted were important to the general perception of a Clinton victory (e.g., Siegel, 1992), there is no doubt that the question about the "national debt" was the most important of the second debate and that the second debate was the most important of the three.

Bush–Gore

The defining moment of the 2000 presidential debates centered on the first debate, but its effects spilled over into the second debate. In the days following the first debate, news reports indicated that two claims made by the vice president turned out to be untrue or at least exaggerated (e.g., Miga & Battenfield, 2000; Robinson & Kornblut, 2000). These exaggerations were important for how they were interpreted after the debate and for how they influenced Gore's strategic decisions in the two debates that followed.

A key Bush strategy for the 2000 debates was to focus on Gore's honesty. In fact, the Bush campaign focused on Gore's honesty throughout the 2000 campaign; in that sense, the debate strategy was simply an extension of a basic Bush strategy for the campaign. As early as April, the Republicans were attacking Gore's honesty. The *Times-Picayune* quoted Republican staffer Mark Pfeifle as noting that "Al Gore has dished out more whoppers than a drive-through at Burger King" (Hillman, 2000). Questioning another presidential candidate's honesty is the kind of charge that is usually made by campaign staff or possibly the vice presidential candidate. For example, the *Daily News* quoted vice presidential candidate Dick Cheney as arguing that Gore would say "virtually anything" to win (Bazinet, 2000, p. 6). But even Governor Bush was willing to make such charges: "The Republican Party is putting people on notice that he [Gore] is willing to exaggerate in order to win" (Bruni & Mitchell, 2000). The focus on Gore's honesty was also evident in Bush's ad campaign. Lynda Kaid (2002) highlighted ads run by the Republican National Committee (RNC) that attacked Gore's honesty on claims such as "inventing the internet."

As I have already noted, similar attacks on Gore's honesty were also a consistent aspect of the campaign trail. So it was not a surprise that honesty was raised in the debates. Governor Bush brought this up indirectly in the first debate. In a discussion about a drug plan for seniors, Bush noted, "Look, this is a man who has great numbers. He talks about numbers. I'm beginning to think *not only did he invent the Internet*, [emphasis added] but he invented the calculator." By introducing Gore's Internet claim, Bush was able to reinforce the Republican claim that Gore was prone to exaggeration. This was, however, the only instance in the first debate that Bush seriously discussed Gore's honesty. Immediately following the debate, it appeared that Gore could claim at least a small victory from the debates. Polls by NBC and also by CNN indicated that viewers thought Gore won the debate (Balz, 2000c). This apparent victory was, however, short lived.

Just two days after the debate, Republicans were claiming that Gore exaggerated on several points in the first debate. First Gore presented the example of a Sarasota, Florida, high school student who was in a classroom so crowded that "they can't squeeze another desk in for her, so she has to stand during class." He also claimed during the debate, "I accompanied [FEMA chief] James Lee Witt down to Texas when those fires broke out." News reports in the days following the debate demonstrated that the Sarasota classroom was in the midst of a $100,000 renovation and the room was packed with boxes of new lab equipment at the time the student had to stand. News reports also noted that the vice president did not accompany Witt on the specific occasion mentioned in the debate (e.g., Connolly & Neal, 2000; Nichols, 2000). Gore spent time between the first and second debate trying to repair the damage from his apparent misstatements in the first debate (e.g., CNN, 2000e, 2000f; Sack, 2000). During this week, much was made of Gore's apparent tendency to stretch the truth. Internal memos warning Gore about exaggerating surfaced (Lawrence, 2000), and the media elaborated on examples of other exaggerations by Gore (e.g., Miga & Battenfield, 2000; Shepard, 2000).

Evidence that press reports and Republican claims that attacked Gore had some impact can be found in a CNN poll conducted October 4 and 5. When respondents were asked, "Will he say or do anything to get elected?" 60 percent indicated that this described Gore while just over 40 percent said it described Bush (Holland, 2000c). An ABC poll reported strikingly similar results (Balz & Deane, 2000).

Questions of honesty follow Gore into the second debate. By this time, concerns about Gore's mistakes had become so visible that moderator Jim Lehrer included it in one of his questions.

> **Lehrer:** Last question. For you, Governor. And this flows out of the Boston debate. You, your running mate, your campaign officials have charged that Vice President Gore exaggerates, embellishes, and stretches the facts. . . . Are you, do you believe these are serious issues? This is a serious issue that the voters should use in deciding which one of you two men to vote for on November 7.
>
> **Bush:** Well, we all make mistakes. I've been known to mangle a syllable or two myself, you know, if you know what I mean. I think credibility is important. It is going to be important for the president to be credible with Congress, important for the president to be credible with foreign nations. And yes, I think it's something that people need to consider. This isn't something new. I read a report, or a memo, from somebody in his 1988 campaign, I forgot the fellow's name, warning then Senator Gore to be careful about exaggerating claims. I thought during his debate with Senator Bradley saying he authored the EITC [Earned Income Tax Credit] when it didn't happen. . . . I found it to be an issue in trying to defend my tax relief package. I thought there was some exaggerations about the

numbers. But the people are going to have to make up their mind on this issue. ... And I have every right in the world to defend my record and positions. That's what debates are about and that's what campaigns are about.

Lehrer: Vice President Gore?

Gore: I got some of the details wrong last week in some of the examples that I used, Jim, and I'm sorry about that. And I'm going to try to do better. One of the reasons I regret it is that getting a detail wrong interfered several times with the point that I was trying to make. However many days that young girl in Florida stood in her classroom, however long, even if it was only one day, doesn't change the fact that there are a lot of overcrowded classrooms in America and we need to do something about that. There are seniors who pay more for their prescriptions than a lot of other people, more than their pets, sometimes. More sometimes than people in foreign countries. And we need to do something about that. ... I can't promise that I will never get another detail wrong. I can promise you that I will try not to, and hard. But I will promise you this with all the confidence in my heart and in the world, that I will do my best if I'm elected president, I'll work my heart out to get the big things right for the American people.

This is a momentous exchange. Lehrer notes that the Bush campaign has charged that the vice president "exaggerates, embellishes, and stretches the facts." This is a wonderful moment for Bush. He does not have to initiate the discussion of honesty in the debate; the moderator has done it for him; in fact, his first sentence "Well, we all make mistakes" followed immediately with self-deprecating humor about his problems with pronunciation sounds as if he is going to let Gore off the hook. This sentiment, however, does not last. He argues that credibility is important in a campaign and goes on to document other instances where Gore is alleged to have exaggerated. He even mentions earlier warnings Gore received about his exaggerations. Gore is left to say, "I'm going to try to do better."

It is clear that the debates cost Gore. Bush was able to establish a level of credibility with many voters, while Gore was losing credibility. Coming out of the debates, Gore's image was tarnished by charges that he had trouble telling the truth. Bush aides were even referring to Gore as a "serial exaggerator" (Perez-Pena, 2000). Interestingly, the Gore campaign was frustrated by what they saw as a double standard. Their charges of Bush inaccuracies did not resonate as did the Bush claims about Gore. For example, in the second debate, Bush made an error when he claimed that the three men who killed James Byrd would be executed (two of the three received the death penalty). Gore and his staff also attempted to point out other Bush misstatements made during the course of the election (Lawrence & Page, 2000). While it is not clear that the debates cost Gore the election, it is clear that they cost him momentum and may have cost him his small lead in the polls. For example, the

CNN/*USA Today* tracking poll released on October 3, the day of the first presidential debate, gave Vice President Gore a slight lead of two percentage points over George Bush (Holland, 2000b). The first CNN/*USA Today* tracking poll results that included only postdebate interviews was released four days after the final debate. It showed George Bush with an 11 percent lead in the polls (Holland, 2000e).

Summary of Defining Moments

In both 1992 and the 2000, we once again witnessed how defining moments contribute both positively and negatively to a candidate's image. In 1992, George H. Bush's inability to grasp or answer audience member Marisa Hall's question left viewers with an image of a candidate who could not relate to much of the electorate. Early in 2000, the George W. Bush campaign laid the groundwork for what would be the defining moment of the fall debates. By establishing Gore's honesty as a concern early in the campaign, *any* Gore misstatements during the debates were bigger problem for the vice president. Consequently, following the debates, Gore was viewed as less trustworthy than Bush. This would be a problem for any presidential candidate in any year, but it was especially problematic for Gore in the wake of a Clinton administration that always seemed to be struggling with trust.

Conclusion

Presidential debates continue to be an important source of information as voters form candidate images. It also remains clear that debates are most important in a close election (Zakahi & Hacker, 1995). It is apparent that the debates were more important in the Clinton and Bush (1992) campaign and the Bush and Gore (2000) campaign than they were in the Dole and Clinton (1996) campaign. It seemed unlikely, regardless of the debates, that Dole had a chance to beat an incumbent Clinton in 1996. But Clinton and Bush were locked in a tight struggle in 1992, and, as we know, Gore did not become president in 2000 even though he won a majority of the popular vote. These two elections provide continuing evidence of the importance of debates in presidential elections. It would be a mistake to assume, however, that it is only the debates themselves that contribute to candidate images. As my analysis has indicated, even before candidates get together to debate, the regular "debate about debates" and the "expectations game" have the potential for contributing substantially to candidate image formation.

References

Allen, Mike, and Terry M. Neal. 2000. "Bush Revising Campaign Strategy." *Washington Post*, September 7, A1.
Associated Press. 1996a. "Dole Camp Says Consider Nader for Debate." *New York Times*, September 1, A34.
———. 1996b. "Counts on Debates to Better His Prospects." *New York Times*, September 7, A10.
———. 2000. "Bring It On." August 5. www.cbsnews.com/stories/2000/08/05/politics/main222129.shtml.
Ball, Karen. 1996a. "Bob Aims to Tongue-Lash, Bill Goes into Training for Crucial Debates. *Daily News*, September 29, 35.
———. 1996b. "Bob & Bill Debate the Expectations." *Daily News*, October 4, 12.
Balz, Dan. 1992. "Bush Campaign Rejects Proposal for 3 Debates." *New York Times*, September 4, A16.
———. 1996a. "Perot Is Rejected by Debates Panel." *Washington Post*, September 18, A1.
———. 1996b. "Two Clinton-Dole Debates Slated." *Washington Post*, September 22, A19.
———. 2000a. "Gore Endorses Commission's Prime-Time Debate Plan; Bush Still Noncommittal about a Specific Schedule." *Washington Post*, August 30, A8.
———. 2000b. "Gore, Bush Agree to 3 Debates in Prime Time." *Washington Post*, September 15, A1.
———. 2000c. "Debate Changes Little." *Washington Post*, October 5, A1.
Balz, Dan, and Claudia Deane. 2000. "Bush Overtakes Gore in Poll; Small Swing toward Republican Sets Up 2nd High-Stakes Debate." *Washington Post*, October 11, A1.
Bazinet, Kenneth R. 2000. "Cheney Aims & Fires at Gore on Credibility." *Daily News*, September 25, 6.
Benedetto, Richard. 1992. "Little in Poll to Cheer Perot." *USA Today*, October 5, 6A.
———. 1996. "Poll Finds Little Going Dole's Way: Approval Rating for President Reaches a Four-Year High of 60%." *USA Today*, September 3, 4A.
Benoit, William, Mitchell McKinney, and Lance Holbert. 2001. "Beyond Learning and Persona: Extending the Scope of Presidential Debate Effects." *Communication Monographs* 68: 259–273.
Berke, Richard. 1992. "The 1992 Campaign." *New York Times*, October 2, 1.
Broder, David. 1992. "Debate on Debates Underway." *Washington Post*, September 15, A8.
Bruni, Frank. 2000a. "Democrats: Looking Ahead." *New York Times*, August 18, A20.
———. 2000b. "Bush Suggests Willingness to Move on Debates." *New York Times*, September 8, A16.
Bruni, Frank, and Alison Mitchell. 2000. "The 2000 Campaign: The Issues." *New York Times*, September 2, A1.
"Bush and Gore Wrap Up Nominations." 2000. *Houston Chronicle*, March 15, A1.
"Bush No 'Oxford man,' but Promises Debate." 1992. *USA Today*, September 11, 4A.
"Bush Play on Debates Misses the Point." 2000. *USA Today*, September 5, A26.
Cable News Network (CNN). 2000a. "Bush Refocuses Campaign on 'Real People'; Debate Schedule May Be Settled Soon." September 8. www.cnn.com/2000/ALLPOLITICS/stories/09/08/campaign.wrap/index.html.

———. 2000b. "National Results." September 8. www.cnn.com/ELECTION/2000/results/.
———. 2000c. "Bush Attacks Gore's Trustworthiness." September 16. www.cnn.com/2000/ALLPOLITICS/stories/09/16/bush.interview/index.html; www.cnn.com/2000/ALLPOLITICS/stories/09/16/presidential.debates/ index.html.
———. 2000d. "Presidential Candidates Face Crucial Debate Today." October 3. www.cnn.com/2000/ALLPOLITICS/stories/10/02/ campaign.wrap/index.html.
———. 2000e. "Bush, Gore Spin Debate Their Way as Campaigning Resumes." October 4. www.cnn.com/2000/ALLPOLITICS/stories/10/04/presidential.debate/index.html.
———. 2000f. "Gore Pledges to Get Facts Straight, Refrain from Sighing in Second Debate." October 10. www.cnn.com/2000/ALLPOLITICS/stories/10/10/campaign.wrap/index.html.
Clifford, Timothy. 1992. "Bush-Clinton Debate, Debate Goes Nowhere." *Newsday*, September 19, 8.
Commission on Presidential Debates. n.d. "1992 Debates." www.debates.org/pages/his_1992.html (accessed August 1, 2003).
Connolly, Ceci, and Terry M. Neal. 2000. "Nominees Carry Debate Themes Back on Road; Bush Attacks Rival's Veracity as Gore Decries Negative Politics." *Washington Post*, October 5, A18.
"Debate Panel Picks Sites, Limits Field." 2000. *Los Angeles Times*, January 8, A5.
"Dole Gains across the Board." 1996. *USA Today*, August 20, 4A.
Dowd, Maureen. 1992. "The 1992 Campaign: News Analysis." *New York Times*, October 16, A1.
Finnegan, Michael, and Ronald Brownstein. 2000. "Gore Rejects Bush Offer on Three Debates." *Los Angeles Times*, September 4, A1.
"Gallup Gives Reagan-Bush 18-Point Lead." 1984. *Washington Post*, September 28, A6.
Gallup Poll. 2000. *Election 2000*. www.gallup.com/election2000/.
Goldman, Peter, Thomas DeFrank, Mark Miller, Andrew Murr, Tom Mathews, Patrick Rogers, and Mielanie Cooper. 1992. *Quest for the Presidency 1992*. College Station: Texas A&M University Press.
"Gore and Bush Prep for Debates." 2000. *Bulletin's Frontrunner*, October 2, 1.
Harris, John F. 1996. "Perot's Status in Debates Won't Be Easily Resolved." *Washington Post*, September 17, A7.
Hart, Roderick P., and Sharon E. Jarvis. 1997. "Political Debate: Forms, Styles, and Media." *American Behavioral Scientist* 40: 1095–1122.
Heller, Jean. 1996. "Debate over the Debates Growing." *St. Petersburg Times*, August 27, 1A.
Hillman, Robert G. 2000. "GOP Turning Gore's Phrases against Him; Republican Spin Machine Distorts His Exaggerations." *Times-Picayune*, April 7, A11.
Hohenberg, John. 1997. *Reelecting Bill Clinton*. Syracuse, N.Y.: Syracuse University Press.
Holland, Keating. 2000a. "CNN/TIME Poll: Gore, Bush Tied; 1 in 5 Voters Undecided." September 8. www.cnn.com/2000/ALLPOLITICS/stories/09/08/cnn.poll/ index.html.
———. 2000b. "Tracking Poll: Bush, Gore in a Dead Heat Going into First Debate." October 3. www.cnn.com/2000/ALLPOLITICS/stories/10/03/tracking.poll/index.html.
———. 2000c. "Poll: Presidential Race a Dead Heat." October 6. www.cnn.com/2000/ALLPOLITICS/stories/10/06/cnn.poll/index.html.

———. 2000d. "Tracking Poll: Bush Holds Narrow Lead in Tight Contest." October 10. www.cnn.com/2000/ALLPOLITICS/stories/10/10/tracking.poll/ index.html.

———. 2000e. "CNN Poll: Bush Gains Solid Post Debate Lead over Gore." October 21. www.cnn.com/2000/ALLPOLITICS/stories/10/21/tracking.poll/index.html.

Kaid, Lynda Lee. 2002. "Video Style and Political Advertising Effects in the 2000 Presidential Campaign." In *The 2000 Presidential Campaign: A Communication Perspective*, edited by Robert E. Denton, 183–198. Westport, Conn.: Praeger.

Kurtz, Howard. 1992. "Campaign Debates: A Contest of Styles with Just a Few Defining Moments; They May Not Sway Votes, but Often Help Crystallize the Choice. *Washington Post*, October 9, A16.

———. 1996. "The Debaters Argue over Expectations." *Washington Post*, September 28, A1.

Langer, Gary. 2000. "Presidential Race Tied." September 8. www.abcnews.go.com/sections/politics/DailyNews/poll000907.html.

Lawrence, Jill. 2000. "Heat of Campaign Gets to Bush, Gore. Close Presidential Race Leads to Verbal Missteps." *USA Today*, October 9, 6A.

Lawrence, Jill, and Susan Page. 2000. "Candidates Use Debate as a Makeover." *USA Today*, October 12, 5A.

Lee, Jessica, and Richard Wolf. 1996. "GOP, Democrat Leaders Play Point-Counterpoint." *USA Today*, September 30, 11A.

Matalin, Mary, James Carville, and Peter Knobler. 1994. *All's Fair: Love, War and Running for President*. New York: Random House.

Matera, Frances, and Michael Salwen. 1996. "Unwieldy Questions? Circuitous Answers? Journalists as Panelists in Presidential Election Debates." *Journal of Broadcasting and Electronic Media* 40: 309–317.

Merida, Kevin. 1996a. "Debating the Details of the Debates; Clinton, Dole Names Negotiators; Perot's Role Remains Uncertain." *Washington Post*, September 5, A11.

———. 1996b. "Dole Team Proposes More, Shorter, One-on-One Debates. *Washington Post*, September 13, A16.

Miga, Andrew, and Joe Battenfield. 2000. "Campaign 2000; Pressure on Gore." *Boston Herald*, October 11, 6.

Mitchell, Alison. 2000. "The 2000 Campaign: The Debates; Bush Puts Forth Alternative Plan for TV Debates." *New York Times*, September 4, A1.

Nagourney, A. 1992. "Clinton Standing on More Solid Ground." *USA Today*, September 24, 4A.

Nichols, Bill. 2000. "Bush Battles 'the Man,' and Gore's Student Gets a Desk." *USA Today*, October 5, 16A.

"Not Debatable, Presidential Debates Are Mandatory and Should Be Conducted under Commission Rules." 2000. *Newsday*, September 6, A30.

Perez-Pena, Richard. 2000. "The 2000 Campaign: The Credibility Issue." *New York Times*, October 9, A14.

Pfau, Michael, and Jong Geun Kang. 1991. "The Impact of Relational Messages on Candidate Influence in Televised Political Debates." *Communication Studies* 42: 114–128.

Philips, Leslie. 1992. "'Serious Tone' Washes Away the Mud." *USA Today*, October 16, 5A.

Richter, Paul. 1996. "Democrats Reject GOP Plan for Four Clinton-Dole Debates." *Los Angeles Times*, September 13, A19.

Robinson, Walter V., and Anne E. Kornblut. 2000. "Campaign 2000/Fact and Fiction; A Day Later, Gaffes Take Center Stage." *Boston Globe*, October 5, A30.

Rosentiel, Thomas B. 1992. "Deal on Debates Is Near, Officials Say. *Los Angeles Times*, October 2, A26.

Rosentiel, Thomas B., and James Gerstenzang. 1992. "Bush Shifts on Debates." *Los Angeles Times*, September 30, A1.

Rosentiel, Thomas B., and David Lauter. 1992. "Clinton and Bush Settle on Debates." *Los Angeles Times*, October 3, A1.

Roth, Bennett. 1996. "Perot Pins Blame on Dole for Exclusion in Debates." *Houston Chronicle*, September 23, 1.

Sack, Kevin. 2000. "The 2000 Campaign: The Vice President; Gore Admits Being Mistaken but Denies He Exaggerates." *New York Times*, October 8, A26.

Schroeder, Alan. 2000. *Presidential Debates: Forty Years of High-Risk TV*. New York: Columbia University Press.

Schwarts, Maralee, and Charles R. Babcock. 1992. "Presidential Debates Set." *Washington Post*, June 13, A12.

Shepard, Scott. 2000. "CAMPAIGN 2000: When Is a Mistake a Mistake?" *Atlanta Journal Constitution*, October 8, 8A.

Siegel, Ed. 1992. "People's Questions Made for Good TV." *Boston Globe*, October 16, 18.

Simon, Roger. 1998. *Show Time*. New York: Times Books.

Stevens, Stuart. 2001. *The Big Enchilada*. New York: Free Press.

"Sure Loser in the Debate: The Format." 1988. *New York Times*, October 15, 30.

"The War Room Drill—TV, the Full Campaign." 1992. *Newsweek*, special issue, November–December, 78–81.

Toner, Robin. 1992. "The 1992 Campaign: The Overview; Impact of Perot on Race So Far Is Termed Scant." *New York Times*, October 4, A1.

Von Drehle, David. 1992. "Part III of Political Miniseries Short on Drama." *Washington Post*, October 16, A33.

Waldman, Myron S. 1992. "Campaign '92; The Debate before the Debates." *Newsday*, September 13, 19.

Walsh, Edward. 1992a. "Clinton Decries Bush Haggling on Debates." *Washington Post*, September 5, A12.

———. 1992b. "Clinton Presses Bush to Agree on Debates." *Washington Post*, September 22, A10.

———. 1992c. "For Clinton Aides, Fear Could Become Reality." *Washington Post*, October 3, A20.

Walsh, Edward, and Donald P. Baker. 1996. "As Debates Debate Lingers, Dole and Perot Rally." *Washington Post*, September 26, A18.

Woodlief, Wayne. 1996. "Politics Inside Out." *Boston Herald*, September 26, 39.

Zakahi, Walter, and Kenneth Hacker. 1995. "Televised Presidential Debates and Candidate Images." In *Candidate Images in Presidential Elections*, edited by Kenneth Hacker, 99–122. Westport, Conn.: Praeger.

8

Interpersonal Communication Styles of Political Candidates: Predicting Winning and Losing Candidates in Three U.S. Presidential Elections

*Timothy Stephen, Teresa M. Harrison,
William Husson, and David Albert*

THE STUDY OF VOTING, especially in American presidential elections, has a long history. Early research understood voter preference in terms of audience demographics (where voter choice was believed to be a function of factors such as social class, ethnicity, and religion), a perspective that gave way by midcentury to an interactive, information-based model in which the voter is seen as an active agent who forms a preference for a candidate based on available information. In the beginning stages of this new perspective, it was thought that candidate preference was an outcome of rational voter assessments of candidate positions on salient political issues (Glass, 1985). However, by the mid-1960s, researchers turned their attention from rational choice models to consider the idea of candidate "images," a concept that refers generally to a potentially manipulable set of meanings attached by voters to a seeker or holder of a political office. Although the literature attests to considerable variety in approaches to operationalizing image, candidate image has most frequently been operationalized in one of two ways: (1) as the composite of a candidate's perceived political positions on a set of campaign issues or (2) as aspects of a candidate's perceived character or personality. As we described in an earlier article (Husson, Stephen, Harrison, & Fehr, 1988), the latter has been by far the most frequently addressed by researchers, with large numbers of studies relating voter choice and media exposure (e.g., in televised debates and in commercials) to perceived qualities of candidates.

The analyses reported in this chapter are designed to address two weaknesses within this body of literature: (1) lack of long-range longitudinal analyses permitting comparative study of images across multiple candidates and elections and (2) a dearth of research addressing the relationship to candidate preference of candidates' interpersonal communication behavior. This article extends earlier work (Husson et al., 1988; Harrison, Stephen, Husson, & Fehr, 1991) in which we examined hypotheses relating voter choice and gender to perceptions of interpersonal communication behaviors of Ronald Reagan and Walter Mondale in the 1984 U.S. presidential election.

Long-Range Analysis

Researchers have often used semantic differential ratings to assess respondents' views of candidates with respect to personality traits such as "honesty," "anxiety," "reliability," "aggressiveness," or "sincerity" (e.g., Kaid, 1995); with respect to performance-related evaluative properties of candidates reflected in such dimensions as "informed" and "qualified" (e.g., Powell, 1977); and with respect to dimensions of emotional warmth and relationship feelings such as "warm," "friendly," "caring," and "involved" (e.g., Pfau, Diedrich, Larson, & Van Winkle, 1995). Likert-type ratings have also been used to assess image (e.g., Andersen & Kibler, 1978; Kendall & Yum, 1984) as have free-response interviews (cf. Miller, Wattenberg, & Malanchuk, 1984) and Q-sort ratings (e.g., Bass, 1997; Marr, 1973; Nimmo & Savage, 1976). Frequently, factor analysis has been employed to locate underlying image dimensions that cut across the content of a larger number of survey items. Lynda Lee Kaid (1995) notes that there is a history of rough correspondence in studies of the dimensionality of image as measured by semantic differentials (she contends that many studies have found between three and five similar image factors), but there has been little cross-referencing or standardization of scales across studies.

Although there is much to be gained in exploring a wide range of potentially important image dimensions, standardization would permit the longitudinal study of stability and change in operant images in American political process—images that cut across candidates and elections—and in the ways audiences respond to those images at the polls. With over thirty years of image research establishing the boundaries of this area of inquiry, there have been relatively few studies of this type, rendering it difficult to understand image as a cross-contextual phenomenon. Indeed our twelve-year, three-election design is among the first to take this perspective and explore the possibility that a few relatively discrete image dimensions might persist across time and provide significant explanatory power.

Some prior studies have looked at images at more than one point in time but, with few exceptions, these studies have used a before-and-after design to study short-term change in images of a single candidate or of a slate of candidates at various points in a campaign (commonly, before and after a pub debate or primary election) or to study the relative contributions of image and issue information at various stages in a single campaign. This pervasive characteristic of studies in the area would suggest that image is conceptualized as a phenomenon attached to particular people acting in the role of political candidates. However, if we take seriously the notion that image is a set of perceived rather than actual qualities of candidates, we may inquire more abstractly into the typicality of images of winning versus losing candidates, male and female candidates, candidates for local and national office, and so on. The present analysis operates at this level, examining the perceived communication qualities of winners and losers across three U.S. presidential elections. Using the same procedures for assessing image in the 1984, 1988, and 1992 election, our study represents a search for persistent perceptual markers generalizable across candidate and election that are predictive of voter choice.

Research that has been conducted across longer spans of time and more than one candidate suggests that the evaluation process is often stable and consistent. According to Arthur Miller, Martin Wattenberg, and Oksana Malanchuk (1984, p. 200), "The aggregate consistency in the use of particular dimensions hints at the possibility that there are enduring, general categories or criteria that people apply in the judgments of political leaders." An intensive single-case study by Larry Bass (1979, 1997) investigated Harold Lasswell's (1960) psychodynamic theory of political image formation in changes over a fourteen-year span. Bass's studies provide support for the Lasswellian theory that political images are extensional representations of structures of evaluation constructed by individuals to cope with subjective experience in the world of interpersonal and family relationships. Bass found considerable stability in political images over the fourteen-year time interval, but his sample was restricted to a single case. Mansfield and Nimmo (n.d.) studied stability of candidate images during a twelve-year period spanning three U.S. presidential elections (1976, 1980, and 1984) using Q-sort technique and a sample of eleven members of the League of Women Voters who completed measures at all three time periods. Mansfield and Nimmo found that images of the "ideal president" were self-consistent across all three elections.

Michael Pfau, Tracy Diedrich, Karla Larson, and Kim Van Winkle (1995) explored an alternative perspective on the longitudinal dynamics of candidate assessment, arguing that, with unknown candidates, perceptions of relational information (that is, how caring, warm, affectionate, and trustworthy a candidate is) weigh most heavily in the candidate's initial appearance to a national audience. As the campaign progresses, however, the importance of relational information declines as voters differentiate the contestants on the basis of knowledge of their relative competence. Pfau et al.'s (1995) analysis provided support for this dynamic.

ntages of a Q-methodological approach is that, given the f scaling Q stimulus items in a quasi-normal distribution tted to have midscale ratings, fewer to have extreme rating matrices of between-sort correlation (most frequently ..... analysis), raters in effect are provided with a procedure that gives much greater weight to items that raters themselves find particularly salient (Stephen, 1985).

Hence, in Q approaches to image assessment, items of no relevance to raters are relegated to the fatter midregion of the Q distribution and are thereby statistically devalued in subsequent intersort correlation. Though our assessment did not use Q methodology, the items we used were obtained from an assessment procedure expressed originally as a Q sort (Stephen & Harrison, 1986), and in transferring the items to a Likert-type format we contrived a means of allowing respondents to declare scale items irrelevant. We felt it was of significant value to permit respondents to declare which stimulus items were useful in the description of candidates rather than to assume that we knew that information ahead of time. We will return to this point later in our discussion of our approach to measurement.

Interpersonal Communication and Image

In contrast to trait approaches, Kaid (1977) found that interpersonal communication among voters was the single best predictor of candidate choice in pre-election polling and called for studies to be conducted to discover which aspects of interpersonal communication performance influence voter choice. Some studies (e.g., Hacker, 1995; Pfau et al., 1995; Schmitt-Beck, 1994) have targeted interpersonal communication as a mediating channel of influence in much the same way that other researchers have viewed television and other mass media as influential channels that impact the kinds of images voters form of candidates (see Hellweg, Dionisopoulos, & Kugler, 1989).

However, outside of our own studies (Husson et al., 1988; Harrison et al., 1991), virtually no other research has conceptualized candidate image as a set of interpersonal communication behaviors displayed by candidates themselves. We have found this surprising since, as we have argued previously (Husson et al., 1988), there are good theoretical reasons for taking a behaviorally descriptive approach rather than attempting to operate at the level of higher order inference inherent in trait descriptions. Audiences may infer traits from observed behaviors, but rules of correspondence in the process of inference that mediates between behaviors and the traits they are taken to represent are hardly invariant. When an audience member concludes that a political candidate is aggressive (that is, possessed of the trait aggressiveness), it is difficult to be sure of the behavioral phenomena that led to that conclusion. Such an inference may be derived from any of a variety of underlying behaviors or may in fact not be related to behavior at all. An audience member may conclude that a candidate is aggressive based on a wide range of observed behavior; indeed, different audience segments may base their common attribution of aggressiveness on altogether different behaviors. Alternatively, an audience segment may conclude that a candidate is aggressive solely because influential opinion leaders say so.

This not only leaves the conceptual waters murky but also places applied social scientists at a substantial disadvantage when trying to translate decades of research on the relationship between image and voter choice into practical recommendations for seekers of political office. We are not sure of the value of recommending to candidates that they "be sincere" or act in ways that are "trustworthy." Hence our approach has been more foundational, measuring perceptions of particular elements of candidates' interpersonal communication behavior. Our data enable us to relate those perceived behaviors to choices that voters make at the polls. An approach that stresses perceptions of behavior (e.g., "smiles frequently") makes it possible to tease apart the foundations of candidate image than would be the case had we treated characteristics at the level of higher-order abstraction (e.g., "is friendly").

Thus it is important to recognize that while our approach indeed takes a perspective on interpersonal communication and candidate image, it is the interpersonal behavior of candidates, not the interpersonal behavior of voters, with which we have been concerned. This places us outside other streams of research in the candidate image literature that incorporate a focus on interpersonal communication. While other studies might well be related to traditions of research examining gatekeeping, social networks, and communication flows, as we have elaborated elsewhere (Husson et al., 1988), our work is perhaps better viewed in the context of person perception or parasocial interaction research.

In previous work (Husson et al., 1988), we examined the relative importance of perceptions of candidate communication behavior and perceptions of candidate stands on campaign issues. Our data, taken from the 1984 Reagan–Mondale election, indicated that perceptions of communication behavior were by far the stronger predictor. We subsequently used the same data set to inquire about the relative importance of issues versus perceptions of candidate communication behavior in the prediction of voting choices for male and female respondents (Harrison et al., 1991). That study lent support to a conclusion derived from Nancy Chodorow's (1978) object relations theory of gender and interpersonal orientation that while both issues and interpersonal communication behavior would be consequential for both women and men, perceptions of interpersonal communication behavior would play a greater role in the evaluative processes of women than they would for men.

Our focus in this chapter is on the question of consistencies in perceptions of the communication behavior of winning and losing presidential candidates. In order to address this, we repeated during the 1988 and 1992 presidential elections the procedures we employed during the 1984 election. Our analysis addressed the following research questions:

1. How consistent are respondents' perceptions of the communication characteristics of winners and losers?
2. Is it possible to differentiate winners and losers on the basis of perceived communication behavior?
3. What is the dimensional structure of perceptions of winning and losing candidates' perceived communication behavior?
4. Over the course of the three elections, what was the relative importance of perceptions of political issues versus perceptions of candidates' communication behavior in the prediction of voter preference?

In addition, we present a case study of changes in perceptions of George Bush's interpersonal communication behavior since we measured perceptions of Bush as a winning candidate in the 1988 election and as a losing candidate in the 1992 election.

Method

Sample and Procedures

The sample consisted of three groups of respondents recruited at the time of the 1984, 1988, and 1992 U.S. presidential elections. At each election, data were collected from the same three eastern U.S. universities (one additional university was included in 1984). The total sample consisted of 1,215 respondents: 401 for the 1984 election, 563 for the 1988 election, and 251 for the 1992 election. In each case, the sample contained slightly more females than males, though the ratio was consistently proportional across the three samples. For the 1984 election the sample was 52 percent female, for the 1988 election the sample was 54 percent female, and for the 1992 election the sample was 55 percent female.

During the last week of each election, respondents were asked to complete a three-part questionnaire during regularly scheduled classes set aside for this purpose. Part 1 of the questionnaire evaluated perceptions of the interpersonal behavior of the primary presidential candidates (Reagan and Mondale in 1984, Bush and Dukakis in 1988, and Clinton, Bush, and Perot in 1992). Part 2 was a survey assessing perceptions of respondents' attitudes toward election issues, their perceptions of the candidates' stands on these issues, respondents' voting intentions, and respondents' habits of information consumption.

Procedures and measures deviated little at the three points of the study. In each instance, respondents were recruited from the same university populations and completed responses the day of the election. Measures differed only in the specific issues that were represented and of course in the presidential candidates used as targets for the interpersonal perception assessments. The sets of campaign issues, culled from pre-election analysis from major national newspapers and newsmagazines, were in each case the top ten salient content issues for the election. We assessed respondents' perceptions of the candidates' position on each issue as well as the respondents' opinion of the importance of each issue. Five issues were salient across all three elections: abortion, taxes, crime, defense spending, and the environment.

In our earlier work on the 1984 election, we studied image in terms of perceptions of Walter Mondale and Ronald Reagan. For the present study, however, our interest was not in the qualities of particular candidates but rather in perceived qualities of winners and losers. Thus, while we asked respondents in 1988 to rate Bush and Dukakis, and in 1992 to rate Clinton and Bush, these ratings were recoded following each election, and the combined data set consists of a set of ratings of winners (combining ratings of Reagan, Bush, and Clinton) and losers (combining ratings of Mondale, Dukakis, and Bush).

Our studies have used a novel approach to investigate relationships between perceptions of interpersonal communication. Respondents were asked to rate each candidate on a 100-item inventory of verbal and nonverbal behavior typically displayed by individuals in interpersonal settings. Items in the inventory were adapted from an instrument developed to provide detailed descriptions of interpersonal communication style (Stephen & Harrison, 1986). The instrument was chosen because it provided a large and diverse sample of potentially relevant aspects of interpersonal behavior that respondents might use in constructing candidate images. Representative items include "laughs frequently"; "listens intently and carefully"; "explains by using examples, analogies, or stories"; and "controls what gets talked about."

During the last week of each of the three elections, respondents were asked to assess the extent to which each of the 100 communication-style items was characteristic of the behavior of each major candidate. Respondents did this by rating the candidates on a five-point scale ranging from "least characteristic" to "most characteristic." The procedure was designed so that all the presidential contenders could be rated simultaneously on the same item. For example, in the 1984 election, respondents were asked to write the letter "R" (for Reagan) or "M" (for Mondale) in spaces that represented one of the five scale points. Respondents were explicitly instructed that they could fill in the same scale value for multiple candidates if they felt both candidates deserved the equivalent rating on the item. For the 1992 election, in addition to the candidates of the major national parties, respondents rated Ross Perot.

In addition, respondents were given the opportunity to declare any item irrelevant as a behavior in terms of which they could characterize all the candidates they were rating or a particular candidate. It seemed possible that our respondents might differ in the degree to which they felt they could evaluate candidates with respect to the various aspects of communicative interaction reflected in the inventory. This might occur because of differences in exposure to or perception of media representations of the two candidates. Rather than force our respondents to rate Reagan and Mondale on every item, therefore, we felt it would be a more appropriate procedure to permit them to select only those descriptions about which they felt they could make valid judgments. A consequence of this procedure was that the size of our sample of rated items (i.e., items that were not declared irrelevant) varied from item to item. We therefore selected for analysis only those items for which 80 percent of our respondents provided a rating other than "irrelevant."

Candidate preference was measured by asking respondents to indicate whether they had "definitely" made up their minds about their candidate of choice or whether they were as yet undecided. Those who had definitely made up their minds were then asked to identify their preferred candidate (any of the principal candidates in the election or someone else, whom they could write in). In subsequent analyses involving the candidate preference measure, data analysis was performed using only those respondents who had definitely made a choice between the Democratic and Republican Party candidates. Too few subjects ($n = 26$, or 3.1 percent of the total combined sample) were definitely inclined toward Ross Perot in the 1992 election to merit including these cases in our analyses.

Results

The focus of our investigation was first on the question of cross-election consistency in candidate image and subsequently on the question of the substance of images of winners and losers. Clearly the consistency issue was prerequisite—if there was no consistency, there would be little point in speaking of generalized images of winners and losers in American presidential politics. On the other hand, to find evidence of consistency is to begin to address the question of image content. We explored the issue of consistency in two ways. First, we looked for variability across the three elections in the range of interpersonal communication items deemed relevant by subjects. Finding remarkable consistency, we then turned to an exploration of the factor structure of the interpersonal ratings across the three elections. At this point, we revisited an issue we examined in the 1984 election (Husson et al., 1988) on the relative importance of issues and images in the prediction of voter choice. Finally we considered the case of stability and change in perceptions of George Bush, a winning candidate in 1988 and a losing candidate in 1992.

Variability in Item Relevance

In our analysis of the 1984 election (Husson et al., 1988), we reported that after applying the 80 percent valid cases criterion, thirty-six communication-style items remained for analysis. This outcome was consistent across the three elections. Table 8.1 presents the thirty-six communication-style items that were deemed relevant in describing both winners and losers across the three elections by 80 percent of the combined sample. One additional item (5. "Likes to tell stories or anecdotes") was deemed relevant in describing winners but not in describing losers. With only five exceptions, these are the same items that we reported in the earlier study.

It is instructive to note the clear and consistent differentiation with respect to characteristics of winners and losers. Generally, winners appear to respondents to communicate in a more self-contained, secure, relaxed, and interpersonally functional manner. In an interesting contrast to this trend, winners are less likely to be perceived as treating the other as an equal (item 23), somewhat less likely to admit being wrong (item 41), and slightly more likely to be perceived as giving vague answers (item 59). Otherwise, however, they are textbook studies in optimal, nondefensive interpersonal communication behavior. Next to them, losers are perceived in ways that appear to be somewhat overbearing, tense, contentious, histrionic, and serious.

As a group, ratings of these thirty-six loser perceptions and thirty-seven winner perceptions do an impressive job in predicting voting preference. Entering all variables as a block in a multiple regression analysis yields a multiple R of .86, $F(73,115) = 4.49$, $p < .001$, accounting for 74 percent of the variance (adjusted $R = .58$) in the dependent variable. Even accepting the diminished adjusted R value, this is a considerably better prediction than reported typically in the literature relating candidate image to voter choice. Prediction was

TABLE 8.1
Mean Ratings of Winners and Losers on Communication-Style Variables

Item	Winners	Losers
1. Controls what gets talked about	3.16	3.48
2. Dominates others in conversation	3.13	3.43
3. Tells jokes frequently or injects humor into the conversation	3.55	2.76
4. Laughs frequently	3.54	2.80
10. Has a loud voice	2.94	3.29
12. Smiles frequently	4.08	3.39
13. Explains by using examples, analogies, or stories	3.75	3.47
15. Overstates ideas or exaggerates them to emphasize a point	3.68	3.70
18. Gestures dramatically	3.03	3.42
19. Shows attention by directing his/her body towards the listener	3.78	3.59
20. Uses facial expressions and/or meaningful gestures	3.63	3.30
22. Intellectualizes and tries to reason through a topic	3.39	3.54
23. Treats the other person as an equal	2.89	3.05
30. Expresses ideas well, speaks easily and smoothly	3.62	3.40
31. Insists that terms be carefully defined	3.28	3.53
32. Chooses words carefully	3.46	3.68
35. Is quick to challenge or object	3.86	3.99
36. Picks up details in others' conversations	3.70	3.84
37. Brings up topics in the right time and place	3.42	3.20
39. Behaves in a sympathetic or considerate manner	3.42	3.28
41. Is the sort of person who will admit being wrong	2.56	2.72
44. Makes frequent and appropriate eye contact	4.03	3.76
45. Appears confident and sure that he/she is right	4.21	4.06
53. Listens intently and carefully	3.63	3.62
59. Gives vague answers—does not take a stand	3.20	3.17
63. Has social poise and presence; appears socially at ease	4.09	3.44
69. Disagrees frequently	3.46	3.72
72. Takes the initiative; offers suggestions, information, or plans	3.54	3.44
77. Chooses words which fit the subject and are appropriate for the audience	3.53	3.70
78. Behaves assertively	3.85	3.69
79. Behaves in a fast-paced way; acts quickly	3.20	3.12
84. Is likely to blame or accuse	3.47	3.64
87. Is calm and relaxed in manner	3.82	3.47
91. Seems to be aware of the impression he/she makes on others	3.87	3.35
92. Can be judgmental	3.68	3.70
100. Tends to be liked and accepted by others	3.97	3.02

slightly better using winner perceptions alone ($R = .79$, $F [37,171] = 7.42$, $p < .001$) over using loser perceptions alone ($R = .68$, $F [36,172] = 4.24$, $p < .001$), but the best results were obtained by combining both sets of items. There were no significant overall sex effects in the ratings: the results reported applied equally well to males and females.

Dimensionality of Candidate Communication

In the next stage of our analysis, we used factor procedures to probe interdependencies in the set of items that had passed the 80 percent criterion. Factor analyses were computed separately for items describing interpersonal communication behavior of winners and items describing interpersonal communication behavior of losers. We used principal components analysis with orthogonal rotation determining the number of factors to retain based on examination of a scree plot of diminishing variance accounted for among a larger set of potential factors with eigenvalues greater than 1. The solution for winners (see table 8.2) yielded five factors that together accounted for 45 percent of the variance. The solution for perceptions of losing candidates (see table 8.3) yielded five factors together accounting for 44 percent of the variance.

As tables 8.2 and 8.3 attest, there is no consequential difference between the factor solutions for perceptions of winners and perceptions of losers. The same critical dimensions are operative in the evaluation of both types of candidates. The primary dimension (factor 1 for both winners and losers) appears to describe an attentive, thoughtful, considerate, egalitarian interaction style. A separate cluster of items (factor 2 for losers and factor 3 for winners) identifies a good-natured convivial quality in interaction exemplified by laughing and smiling and sharing anecdotes. A third dimension (factor 2 for winners and factor 4 for losers) consists of a set of items that reference self-confidence, social presence, and assertiveness. A fourth dimension (factor 4 for winners and factor 3 for losers) consists of a set of items that suggest aggressive verbal attack. The last dimension (factor 5 for both winners and losers) suggests an ability to speak with great volume and force and compelling gestures so as to dominate interactions with others. All in all, this suggests that a successful presidential candidate requires mastery of a broad interactional range; a healthy, balanced demeanor; and considerable oratorical facility.

Issues Versus Images in Candidate Choice

This analysis was conducted using the same procedures used in our study of the 1984 election. Four sets of variables were created: a set of perceptions of communication behaviors of winners, a set of perceptions of communication behavior of losers, ratings on the five issues common across the three elections (abortion, taxes, defense spending, the environment, and crime), and a set of ratings representing respondents' judgments of the importance of each of the five issues. We wished to assess the relative contributions of each of these sets

TABLE 8.2
Factor Analysis: Perceptions of Winning Candidate's Communication Behavior

Factor 1	Loading
53. Listens intently and carefully	.71
31. Insists that terms be carefully defined	.68
22. Intellectualizes and tries to reason through a topic	.64
72. Takes the initiative; offers suggestions, information, or plans	.59
36. Picks up details in others' conversations	.58
39. Behaves in a sympathetic or considerate manner	.56
41. Is the sort of person who will admit being wrong	.56
37. Brings up topics in the right time and place	.55
32. Chooses words carefully	.53
23. Treats the other person as an equal	.48
59. Gives vague answers—does not take a stand	−.47
77. Chooses words which fit the subject and are appropriate for the audience	.44
15. Overstates ideas or exaggerates them to emphasize a point	−.44

Factor 2	
63. Has social poise and presence; appears socially at ease	.76
87. Is calm and relaxed in manner	.63
45. Appears confident and sure that he/she is right	.60
78. Behaves assertively	.59
100. Tends to be liked and accepted by others	.51
44. Makes frequent and appropriate eye contact	.42
1. Controls what gets talked about	.40

Factor 3	
4. Laughs frequently	.78
5. Likes to tell stories or anecdotes	.76
3. Tells jokes frequently or injects humor into the conversation	.76
13. Explains by using examples, analogies, or stories	.63
12. Smiles frequently	.62

Factor 4	
84. Is likely to blame or accuse	.64
92. Can be judgmental	.62
69. Disagrees frequently	.62
35. Is quick to challenge or object	.51

Factor 5	
18. Gestures dramatically	.70
10. Has a loud voice	.56
19. Shows attention by directing his/her body towards the listener	.53
2. Dominates others in conversation	.42

TABLE 8.3
Factor Analysis: Perceptions of Losing Candidate's Communication Behavior

Factor 1	Loading
32. Chooses words carefully	.65
31. Insists that terms be carefully defined	.65
22. Intellectualizes and tries to reason through a topic	.61
36. Picks up details in others' conversations	.56
53. Listens intently and carefully	.55
37. Brings up topics in the right time and place	.54
30. Expresses ideas well; speaks easily and smoothly	.53
41. Is the sort of person who will admit being wrong	.48
23. Treats the other person as an equal	.48
72. Takes the initiative; offers suggestions, information, or plans	.46

Factor 2	
4. Laughs frequently	.71
12. Smiles frequently	.71
20. Uses facial expressions and/or meaningful gestures	.59
3. Tells jokes frequently or injects humor into the conversation	.55
13. Explains by using examples, analogies, or stories	.47

Factor 3	
84. Is likely to blame or accuse	.73
92. Can be judgmental	.68
69. Disagrees frequently	.62
35. Is quick to challenge or object	.59
15. Overstates ideas or exaggerates them to emphasize a point	.51
59. Gives vague answers—does not take a stand	.41

Factor 4	
63. Has social poise and presence; appears socially at ease	.68
45. Appears confident and sure that he/she is right	.61
87. Is calm and relaxed in manner	.60
91. Seems to be aware of the impression he/she makes on others	.51
77. Chooses words which fit the subject and are appropriate for the audience	.45
100. Tends to be liked and accepted by others	.43

Factor 5	
2. Dominates others in conversation	.72
1. Controls what gets talked about	.59
10. Has a loud voice	.57
18. Gestures dramatically	.52

of variables. Prior to doing so, we reduced the two sets of communication behavior items using multiple regression. Two regression analyses were conducted, one for the set of winner perceptions and one for the set of loser perceptions. In each case, the variables were entered as a group and then the group reduced through backward elimination of variables that did not account for unique portions of the variance in candidate preference, the dependent variable.

The multiple regression analyses reduced the set of winner variables to nine items (numbers 5, 15, 23, 36, 37, 45, 53, 59, and 89—see table 8.1) accounting for 57 percent ($R = .75$, $F[9,199] = 28.7$, $p < .001$) of the variance in voter preference and reduced the set of loser variables to six items (numbers 13, 15, 18, 23, 72, and 84) accounting for 40 percent ($R = .63$, $F[6,202] = 22.54$, $p < .001$) of the variance in voter preference.

When all four sets of variables were thus prepared, our main analysis was conducted using the SPSS TEST procedure, which allows one to estimate which designated subsets of items within the regression equation contribute uniquely to variance in the dependent measure, voter preference. This unique contribution is indicated by the squared semipartial correlation associated with those variable subsets one may wish to evaluate (Cohen & Cohen, 1983). In the source table reported in table 8.4, the semipartial statistic is identified as "RSQ Change."

Reiterating the results of our analysis of the 1984 campaign, political items reflecting perceptions of candidates' stands on the issues made a significant (RSQ change = .02) but barely perceptible contribution in an otherwise powerful prediction equation. Perceptions of issue importance did not contribute

TABLE 8.4
Effects of Communication Style and Political Issue Variables on Candidate Preference

Source	DF	Sum of Squares	RSQ Change	F	Sig F
Style items					
Winners	9	12.10	.15	14.7	.001
Losers	6	9.3	.10	15.8	.001
Issues items					
Issues	5	1.45	.02	2.95	.01
Importance	5	.39	.00	.79	ns
Regression	25	55.33		22.53	.001
Residual	346	33.98			
Total	371	89.31			

Note: Multiple $R = .79$; R square $= .62$; adjusted R square $= .59$.

significantly. Perceptions of candidates' interpersonal communication behaviors (winners' RSQ change = .15; losers' RSQ change = .10) accounted for nearly all the predicted variance in voter preference.

Stability and Change in Perceptions of George Bush

Finally, we turned to a consideration of the unique opportunity afforded to our analysis by the fact that George Bush was a winning candidate in 1988 but a losing candidate in 1992. We explored how perceptions of Bush changed using correlational analysis. To do so, we computed the mean ratings for each of the interpersonal communication items for Bush in 1988 and for Bush in 1992. We also computed combined mean ratings on the items for the other two winners (Reagan and Clinton) and for the other two losers (Mondale and Dukakis). We next computed correlations between these various sets of ratings. The correlation coefficients yield indexes of similarity between the sets of ratings, which can usefully be expressed as the percent of overlap by squaring the coefficients (obviously, the issue of statistical significance is not relevant in this application of correlational analysis). The resulting matrix of coefficients in presented in table 8.5.

The results of the correlation analysis reveal that there is some basic similarity (roughly 17 percent overlap) in the mean ratings of winners and losers exclusive of ratings of George Bush. Mean ratings of Bush's interpersonal communication style in 1988 were quite similar ($r = .84$ or 71 percent overlap) to the ratings of Reagan and Clinton, the other winning candidates. Nevertheless, his 1988 ratings bore a nontrivial resemblance ($r = .64$ or 41 percent overlap) to the ratings of Mondale and Dukakis, the other losing candidates. Already somewhat similar in appearance to the other losing candidates, by 1992 that similarity increased ($r = .72$ or 52 percent overlap). More remarkably, however, George Bush's resemblance to other winning candidates dropped to

TABLE 8.5
Correlations among Mean Ratings of Interpersonal Communication: George Bush and Other Candidates

	Other Losers	Other Winners	Bush 1988	Bush 1992
Other Losers				
Other Winners	.42			
Bush 1988	.64	.84		
Bush 1992	.72	.23	.59	

a minuscule level ($r = .23$ or 5 percent overlap). In 1992, George Bush looked less like a winner than other losing candidates. Overall, the analysis suggests the possibility that George Bush's position in the public eye as a successful presidential figure was precarious at the moment of his election and eroded significantly by the end of the 1992 campaign.

Discussion

A number of good summary sources treating candidate image research have been published since we gathered our first wave of data in 1984 (e.g., Glass, 1985; Hacker, 1995; Hellweg et al., 1989; Miller et al., 1984). These sources document a wealth of research on the role of image in U.S. elections and, with the modest contribution of our own studies, it seems reasonable to conclude that image is indeed a powerful and robust predictor of candidate choice. Further efforts toward extending this line of inquiry might well focus now on learning more about the nature and composition of candidate images.

As indicated earlier in this chapter, researchers have taken diverse approaches to conceptualizing images, focusing on personal traits, ideal qualities, relational information, as well as our own reliance on perceptions of interpersonal communication behavior. It may be time now to begin to compare these alternatives with each other in terms of strengths and weaknesses and to consider as well the possibility that there may be interrelationships between them. For example, perceptions of personal traits might well be founded upon perceptions of communication behaviors and constitute the basis upon which trait judgments might be made. On the basis of such research, it may be possible to introduce and test models that explain how candidate images are constructed, and it may be possible to develop standardized measures of image that might be used to extend our knowledge of long-term and cross-candidate effects.

In our view, it is most unfortunate that there has been but a handful of studies spanning multiple elections. Ironically, one of the staples of the image literature is the idea that image became an important factor in voter choice as a result of the evolution of twentieth-century mass media, particularly television. But tests of this assumption and others like it require long-term cross-election analyses. While the field sustains its focus on single elections and highly divergent image constructs, it may miss opportunities to discover broader processes. Given the reasonably mature state of knowledge in the area of image, it seems prudent now to call for such efforts.

On the other hand, although data from many studies suggest that we know that image matters a great deal in candidate choice, it is also apparent that image is not the only factor involved in candidate decision making. While our data document the powerful effects of image, when one compares the amount of variance accounted for in our model uniquely by images (25 percent) and by issues (2 percent), yielding a subtotal of 27 percent with the total variance of 62 percent accounted for, it is apparent that the difference between the two (35 percent) is attributable to an interaction between images and issues that is quite complicated and, so far, unexplained.

Further, we do not know much about the processes of decision making that guide those for whom image is *not* a factor. Accounting for 60 percent to 75 percent of the variance in voter choice is hardly inconsequential, yet 25 percent to 40 percent of the variance in voter choice remains completely unaccounted for by either images or issues, and we doubt strongly that voter choice is much a random or whimsical affair. Following up on our regression analysis of the relationship of the communication-style items to voter choice, we conducted a postmortem on the leftover residual variance (that is, the variance in voter choice unaccounted for by the communication-style items). The residual variance was correlated at the .50 ($p < .001$) level with the vote variable, on which winning candidates had been coded with lower values and losing candidates had been coded with higher values. This means that the residualized scores were greater for those who voted for losing candidates. We interpret this to mean that the perceptions of communication-style items did a better job of accounting for the voting behavior of those who voted for winning candidates. What, then, goes on in the decision processes of those voting for losing candidates? Do they perceive candidates in different terms than those whose support ultimately elects the winner?

Pfau et al.'s (1995) study suggests that interpersonal information matters more in the early evaluation of unknown candidates, but our results support the overwhelming influence of interpersonal information in the evaluation of candidates with high media exposure during the last week of the election. It remains possible, however, that variations in sampling designs used in the two studies are responsible for this difference. Unlike other research exploring candidate images, our data are collected from a college sample, members of which may be more frequently exposed to televised presentations of candidate behavior, accounting in part for the power of image information suggested by our findings.

It is, of course, also worth bearing in mind that the fact that our study relied completely on a college sample diminishes the extent to which our results might be considered generalizable to the population at large. On the other hand, if we assume that young voters are more likely to rely on mass media such as television than more traditional media such as newspapers for information about candidates, our findings may also be more indicative of future trends in candidate decision making.

Another unique factor of our study that served as both a weakness and a strength was our novel use of relevance ratings in our measure of perceived interpersonal communication. These ratings unquestionably boosted both the content and predictive validity of our measure. Using our procedure to discard items about whose relevance our respondents could not reach consensus stripped away 63 of 100 items, resulting in a pool of content that was extremely powerful in its ability to predict voter choice. In a sense, we allowed our respondents to write their own measure of interpersonal communication. However, since we have now employed this procedure in three elections covering twelve years and since we have found that the items chosen are relatively invariant across time, we would recommend that future applications of the item set adopt the reduced set of items and require all respondents to rate them. Ideally, a smaller auxiliary sample would be recruited and given the entire 100-item set with the usual relevance ratings to serve as a check on the possibility that there may eventually be some shift in the selected content. Assuming that no such shift occurs, eliminating the relevance ratings will greatly reduce the large sample attrition we experienced as a result of the requirement of many multivariate analysis techniques (e.g., multiple regression and factor analysis) that data are present on all measures for all subjects employed in the analysis. Using statistical techniques to handle missing values (e.g., mean substitution) is simply unsatisfactory.

In an earlier analysis (Husson et al., 1988), we grounded our exploration of interpersonal communication styles of candidate images in the emerging theoretical perspective in media studies of parasocial interaction. We argued that interpersonal communication behavior is perceived by audience members and used to construct fantasies of the lives and characters of media figures, especially figures with significant television exposure such as political candidates. Drawing on John Caughey (1984), Erving Goffman (1959), Joshua Meyrowitz (1985), and others, we suggested that perceptions of interpersonal communication behavior of candidates constitute the elemental building materials for the construction of more detailed accounts of candidates held by those viewing the behavior of candidates on television. These perspectives support the idea that television exposure not only foregrounds frontstage performances of candidates (e.g., in debates, press conferences, and other formal occasions) but simultaneously leaks more intimate information that becomes the focus for construction of elaborated visions of the candidates as rounded social actors. These perceptions constitute a primary basis for candidate choice.

In reviewing the literature on candidate image, Dan Nimmo (1995) and others suggest the possibility that voters enter the evaluation process with prefabricated notions of ideal qualities for office holders. Candidates are observed in order to assess the degree to which they correspond to an ideal type. The greater the correspondence, the greater the probability the candidate will obtain an audience member's vote. Miller et al. (1984) take a similar position, arguing that audience members reduce the effort of their decision making by applying enduring structures of evaluation, referred to as schemas, in considering candidates.

The results of this study will not resolve this issue, though they provide strong support for the idea that audiences evaluate the interpersonal behavior of candidates using criteria of enduring relevance. Whether voters bring these criteria with them to the campaign or rediscover them in successive elections we cannot say. However, our data suggest quite strongly that from the standpoint of voter preference there are five principal dimensions of relevance in the interpersonal communication behavior of U.S. presidential candidates. We feel these data represent a potential practical benefit in their specificity relative to prior studies. They suggest the possibility that continuing research in this direction will provide value in helping candidates to prepare more successful presentations of self, and this may be particularly useful for certain candidates, Al Gore for example, for whom self-presentation is an ongoing and perplexing concern.

References

Andersen, Paul A., and Robert J. Kibler. 1978. "Candidate Valence as a Predictor of Voter Preferences." *Human Communication Research* 5: 4–14.

Bass, Larry. 1979. "An Intensive Analysis of the Interpersonal Sources of the Symbolic Meaning of the Constitution." *American Journal of Political Science* 23: 101–120.

———. 1997. "The Interpersonal Sources of the Development of Political Images: An Intensive, Longitudinal Study." *Operant Subjectivity* 20, nos. 3–4 (April–July): 117–142.

Caughey, John L. 1984. *Imaginary Social Worlds*. Lincoln: University of Nebraska Press.

Chodorow, Nancy. 1978. *The Reproduction of Mothering*. Berkeley: University of California Press.

Cohen, J., and P. Cohen. 1983. *Applied Multiple Regression/Correlation Analysis for the Behavioral Sciences*, 2nd ed. Mahwah, N.J.: Lawrence Erlbaum.

Glass, David P. 1985. "Evaluating Presidential Candidates: Who Focuses on Their Personal Attributes?" *Public Opinion Quarterly* 49, no. 4 (Winter): 517–534.

Goffman, Erving. 1959. *The Presentation of Self in Everyday Life*. Garden City, N.Y.: Doubleday Anchor.

Hacker, Kenneth L. 1995. "Interpersonal Communication and the Construction of Candidate Images." In *Candidate Images in Presidential Elections*, edited by Kenneth Hacker, 65–82. Westport, Conn.: Praeger.

Harrison, Teresa, Timothy Stephen, William Husson, and Barbara J. Fehr. 1991. "Images vs. Issues in the 1984 Presidential Election: Differences between Men and Women." *Human Communication Research* 18: 209–227.

Hellweg, Susan A., George N. Dionisopoulos, and Drew E. Kugler. 1989. "Political Candidate Image: A State-of-the-Art Review." *Progress in Communication Sciences* 9: 43–78.

Husson, William, Timothy Stephen, Teresa Harrison, and Barbara J. Fehr. 1988. "An Interpersonal Communication Perspective on Audience Images of Political Candidates." *Human Communication Research* 14: 397–421.

Kaid, Lynda Lee. 1977. "The Neglected Candidate: Interpersonal Communication in Political Campaigns." *Western Journal of Speech Communication* 41, no. 4 (Fall): 245–252.

———. 1995 "Measuring Candidate Images with Semantic Differentials." In *Candidate Images in Presidential Elections*, edited by Kenneth Hacker, 131–134. Westport, Conn.: Praeger.

Kendall, Kathleen, and June Yum. 1984. "Persuading the Blue-Collar Voters: Issues, Images, and Homophily. In *Communication Yearbook 8*, edited by R. N. Bostrom, 707–722. Beverly Hills, Calif.: Sage.

Lasswell, Harold. 1960. *Psychopathology and Politics*. New York: Viking Press.

Mansfield, M., and Dan Nimmo. n.d. "Tracking the League: The Stability of Candidate Images across Time and Presidential Debates, 1976, 1980, and 1984." Unpublished manuscript.

Marr, Theodore J. 1973. "Q and R Analyses of Panel Data on Political Candidate Image and Voter Communication." *Speech Monographs* 40: 56–65.

Meyrowitz, Joshua. *No Sense of Place*. 1985. New York: Oxford University Press.

Miller, Arthur H., Martin P. Wattenberg, Oksana Malanchuk. 1984. "Cognitive Representations of Candidate Assessments." In *Political Communication Yearbook 1984*, edited by Lynda Kaid and Dan Nimmo, 183–210. Carbondale: Southern Illinois University Press.

Nimmo, Dan. 1995. "The Formation of Candidate Images during Election Campaigns. In *Candidate Images in Presidential Elections*, edited by Kenneth Hacker, 131–134. Westport, Conn.: Praeger.

Nimmo, Dan, and Robert L. Savage. 1976. *Candidates and Their Images: Concepts, Methods, and Findings*. Pacific Palisades, Calif.: Goodyear.

Pfau, Michael, Tracy Diedrich, Karla M. Larson, Kim M. Van Winkle. 1995. "Influence of Communication Modalities on Voters' Perceptions of Candidates during Presidential Primary Campaigns." *Journal of Communication* 45, no. 1 (Winter): 122–133.

Powell, L. 1977. "Voting Intention and the Complexity of Political Images: A Pilot Study." *Psychological Reports* 43: 343–347.

Schmitt-Beck, Rudiger. 1994. "Intermediation Environments of West German and East German Voters: Interpersonal Communication and Mass Communication during the First All-German Election Campaign." *European Journal of Communication* 9: 381–419.

Stephen, Timothy. 1985. "Q-Methodology in Communication Science: An Introduction." *Communication Quarterly* 33: 193–208.

Stephen, Timothy, and Teresa Harrison. 1986. "Assessing Communication Style: A New Measure." *American Journal of Family Therapy* 14: 213–234.

9

Meta-Analysis of Presidential Candidate Images

Susan A. Hellweg and Brian H. Spitzberg

META-ANALYSIS INVOLVES THE "STATISTICAL INTEGRATION of empirical studies of a common phenomenon" (Glass, McGaw, & Smith, 1981, p. 93). Meta-analysis may be contrasted with primary analysis and secondary analysis of data, since it is specifically designed to analyze data from original quantitative studies in order to determine the strength of findings cumulatively, utilizing each study, rather than each individual subject, as a data point. Meta-analytic techniques have existed for some time, although the term *meta-analysis* was introduced only recently by Glass (1976; see Cooper, 1990, for a detailed history). Meta-analysis is particularly appropriate for the social sciences, where policy decisions cannot typically be made on the basis of single pieces of research (Hedges & Olkin, 1982, 1985). Any single study is constrained in its generalizability by sampling and measurement error, as well as the unique features of design and measurement. The purpose of this chapter is to describe the functions, strengths, and weaknesses of meta-analysis and its applicability to political candidate image research.

Meta-analysis comprises a family of techniques used for varying purposes (Zhao, 1991). Rosenthal (1983) identifies six basic types of meta-analysis. Meta-analyses vary in terms of the kind of results being summarized, whether *significance tests* or *effect sizes*. Either of these sets of results can be analyzed in any one of three general ways: providing mere *summary* results of combined studies, providing *diffuse* tests of whether studies differ among themselves, or conducting *focused* tests of how studies differ according to certain theoretical or methodological factors. Within and across each of these categories, there are numerous variations on the theme. For example, methods have been developed for assessing the comparability of multivariate factor structures across separate samples resulting in a measure analogous to the correlation coefficient (Bushman, Cooper, & Lemke, 1991; Thompson, 1989). Furthermore, meta-analytic techniques are increasingly being developed to test hypotheses, both those originally intended by the primary studies and questions the original authors never anticipated (Archer, 2000). Thus, meta-analysis actually refers to a family of related techniques for aggregating among those studies, and testing hypotheses germane to the primary data (e.g., see Cooper, 1990; Glass et al., 1981; Rosenthal, 1984; Schneider, 1991; Shapiro, 1985; Strube & Hartmann, 1983; Wolf, 1986).

Advantages of Meta-Analysis

Meta-analysis offers a number of advantages over traditional literature reviews (Beaman, 1991; Green & Hall, 1984). Wolf (1986) pointed to five problems inherent in traditional interpretive reviews of literature, each of which potentially can be resolved through meta-analytic procedures. First, a researcher often applies selective inclusion rules on research incorporated in a literature review on the basis of a quality assessment of the primary studies. Such a practice risks a sample of studies that vary according to quality and reviewer bias. Second, the researcher may apply differential subjective weighting to studies included in the literature review in the process of drawing out interpretations of their findings. Such a practice produces conclusions of a biased nature, even if the sample itself is fair. Third, the researcher may offer misleading interpretations of research results, given that the summary results are less formulaic. Even though traditional data may provide an objective set of results, interpretations may easily misrepresent those findings because there are no objective standards for their aggregation. Fourth, variant results of studies may not get explored in terms of particular study characteristics that may account for these findings. That is, the role that systematic methodological differences play may easily be overlooked. Fifth, and closely related, moderating variables associated with the relationships or variables being studied by the researcher may not get fully dissected. Meta-analysis permits various features of studies (e.g., type of sample, type of induction, and type of measure) to be coded and compared. This is particularly important when literatures have produced inconsistent results, because meta-analysis permits testing the influence of design features that might otherwise seem inconclusive in traditional interpretive reviews.

Meta-analyses offer several additional strengths. First, meta-analyses allow researchers to reach stronger conclusions than they can with traditional literature reviews because meta-analyses incorporate statistical evaluation of the primary analyses rather than impressionistic evaluations (Wolf, 1986). Issues such as sampling error and measurement can be estimated precisely, permitting greater precision of inference. Second, because meta-analysis does not typically screen out studies on the basis of quality, it is likely to be more objective and inclusive than a typical literature review (Wolf, 1986). Third, sample size and the number of observations are aggregated across studies, increasing the proportion of the population upon which inferences are derived and reducing sampling error and often, in effect, measurement error.

In summary, meta-analysis offers a relatively systematic set of procedures for aggregating statistical results across studies and yet provides general findings that are interpretable in much the same metric and rhetorical logic of the original studies. The primary advantages have to do with the relative objectivity, precision, and systematic inclusiveness of the approach.

Criticisms of Meta-Analysis

A number of criticisms have been leveled at meta-analytic techniques (Chow, 1987) and defenses made of approaches to secondary literature review (e.g., Cooper, 1984; Stewart, 1984). For the purposes of this chapter, five are reviewed. The first, referred to in the literature as the "apples and oranges" problem, argues that it is inappropriate to mix together studies utilizing differing measuring techniques, subject pool types, operationalizations, and so on (Glass et al., 1981; Rosenthal, 1984; Wolf, 1986). This heterogeneity problem becomes even a greater source of concern when few studies are involved (Wolf, 1986). The obvious risk is that conclusions will be drawn in general that at best apply only to the particular.

The second problem noted in the literature is the tendency of meta-analyses to include weak studies (Glass et al., 1981; Rosenthal, 1984; Wolf, 1986). How a weak study or a good study is operationally defined compounds this problem. In essence, the strength of meta-analysis turns into a weakness, in that expert judgment is disregarded and the result is a bias toward inclusion of poorly conducted studies.

The third problem with meta-analytic efforts is directed at selection bias in the decision to incorporate published studies, dissertations, and unpublished works in a meta-analysis (Cooper, 1990; Glass et al., 1981; Rogers, 1985; Rosenthal, 1984; Strube & Hartmann, 1983; Wolf, 1986). This "file-drawer" problem results from the generally accepted fact that "the probability of publication is increased by the statistical significance of the results" (Rosenthal, 1984, p. 125). The effect is that "nonsignificant findings are rarely published" (Wolf, 1986,

p. 14). Published works are simply easier for meta-analysis researchers to retrieve than unpublished works (Strube & Hartmann, 1983). If only published studies are included in a meta-analysis, what is reported may not be representative of all the studies dealing with the phenomenon under consideration. In addition, by employing mostly published studies, the researcher is liable to overestimate the significance levels and effect sizes because of the bias toward the publication of significant findings (Strube & Hartmann, 1983). Of course, this problem is not unique to meta-analysis, as most ordinary reviews suffer from a lack of file-drawer studies for the same reason—such studies are simply harder to locate and obtain.

The fourth problem involves the use of multiple results from a given study (nonindependent data), creating the impression that the results are more reliable and generalizable than they are in actuality (Wolf, 1986, p. 14). This may even be a problem with sets of studies conducted by the same researcher(s), which may be more similar than studies involving different researchers and research traditions (Rosenthal, 1984). For example, a meta-analysis might locate ten investigations of candidate image, five of which were conducted by the same researcher or research team. Furthermore, if each of these five investigations consisted of multiple studies (say, each was a two-study investigation), then two-thirds of the data for this meta-analysis are correlated by virtue of similar measurement and methodological approach.

The fifth problem, often ignored by meta-analysts because it is considered largely outside their paradigm of research, is that qualitative and rhetorical analyses are typically excluded as irrelevant data. Because qualitative and interpretive studies do not produce comparable statistical results, they are treated as virtual nonentities in the review of relevant data on a given subject, except in fleshing out rationale and interpretation. The potential importance of this for candidate image research should be apparent, given the extensive rhetorical analyses and criticisms conducted of political discourse and campaign strategy. Specifically, many potential implications of qualitative research cannot be integrated with the conclusions of meta-analytic research because of significantly divergent bases for inference.

Resolving Meta-Analysis Weaknesses

Several scholars have posited ways to overcome the limitations of meta-analysis cited above. For the apples and oranges problem, the various types of studies can be coded and their similarities or dissimilarities empirically compared and tested (Green & Hall, 1984). While such procedures may serve to establish whether or not clusters of studies produce consistent effects, "a bit of uniqueness is lost almost every time individual studies are grouped or classified" (Schneider, 1991, p. 313). In addition, with each grouping contrast of studies, the sample size within each group becomes smaller, and sometimes the number of studies within each contrast group becomes too small to generate confidence in the comparisons.

The second criticism cited about meta-analytic procedures concerned the inclusion of weak studies. The researcher may code the design quality of studies and subsequently determine whether the results varied as a function of this criterion (Wolf, 1986). Alternatively, Rosenthal (1984) suggests differential weighting based on quality, with a zero weighting signaling the dropping of studies. However, O'Keefe (1991) contended that the lower the number of available studies on the phenomenon examined in the meta-analysis, the more important it is that the literature search be exhaustive. In the process of excluding or weighting studies, low-quality primary investigations may be included in a meta-analysis. Regardless, meta-analysis permits the methodological strengths and weakness of all the studies involved to be reported (Rogers, 1985).

The third problem identified with meta-analytic techniques is selection bias, resulting from the tendency of significant findings to appear more often than nonsignificant findings in published works. The first response to counter the selection bias problem is clear articulation and reporting of inclusion and exclusion criteria. Known excluded studies can be coded and compared to those included to examine any systematic biases (O'Keefe, 1991). In response to this file-drawer problem, it is possible to determine "the number of additional studies with nonsignificant results that would be necessary to reverse a conclusion drawn from the meta-analysis ... thus providing some estimate of the robustness and validity of the findings" (Wolf, 1986, p. 15). This "failsafe" estimate can provide reassurance of the stability of results independent of potentially unknown file-drawer studies. By incorporating unpublished studies in the meta-analysis (either actual or hypothetical), a potential bias against nonsignificant findings or contrary conclusions can be corrected (Light & Pillemer, 1984).

The fourth problem cited concerns the use of nonindependent data. When multiple studies are conducted by the same researcher(s) or use similar methods, measures, or samples, data no longer represent independent data points. When observations are not independent, it violates assumptions of most inferential statistics (e.g., D'Alessio & Allen, 2000, pp. 141, 144). Various researchers approach this problem differently, some limiting the analysis to a fixed number of results from each study, others averaging the results from the same study (Wolf, 1986). Similarly, Cooper (1990) indicated that some researchers treat each effect size reported in a study independently, irrespective of the total number reported. Finally, it is possible to code those features that suggest nonindependence, and contrast those groups of studies with those studies that are more heterogeneous to examine the empirical impact of nonindependence.

The fifth problem, ignoring qualitative and interpretive analyses, has only recently been addressed (Noblit & Hare, 1988). Although triangulation continues to be a methodological goal of many researchers (Zhao, 1991), there are few rigorous and objective methods for ascertaining correspondence among differing research paradigms (Schwandt, 1989). At this point, it is still largely up to the reviewer to determine the relevance and interpretive significance of qualitative and rhetorical studies.

In summarizing the status of meta-analysis vis-à-vis traditional literature reviews, Hale and Dillard (1991) offered both caution and solace:

> Meta-analyses, like qualitative reviews, involve subjective judgment, post hoc analyses, and a narrowing of the range of possible theories rather than the definitive pronouncement of one, clear victor. Moreover, meta-analyses will frequently suffer from less than optimal numbers of subjects, estimate, and messages. Despite these similarities, meta-analysis is clearly to be preferred over purely qualitative reviewing because it isolates and makes explicit the points of subjective judgment in the review process. (p. 470)

The essential lesson therefore, is that, like any research endeavor, some meta-analyses are better than others. A variety of criteria have been suggested for the conducting and reporting of meta-analyses (e.g., Hale & Dillard, 1991). Such criteria include admonitions such as the following: use a theoretical model as the basis for testing hypotheses; identify the relevant domain of study, including all available studies; make studies available to readers; make coding decisions explicit and theoretically relevant; use multiple coders or raters; provide reliability estimates; and provide a careful consideration of rival explanations and study limitations (Bullock & Svyantek, 1985). Clearly, in particular applications, meta-analysis offers certain advantages over traditional literature reviews, but only when performed with attention to the possible flaws and limitations of the method.

Meta-Analysis Procedures

Various techniques for performing meta-analysis have been described in the literature (Allen & Preiss, 2002; Schafer, 1999). A few are presented briefly here. There are several in-depth discussions of meta-analytic procedures available (consult Cooper, 1990; Glass et al., 1981; Hedges & Olkin, 1985;

Hunter, Schmidt, & Jackson, 1982; Rosenthal, 1984; Strube & Hartmann, 1983; Wolf, 1986). Cooper (1990) described the following as generic meta-analysis techniques: combining probability levels across studies and failsafe Ns; computing a frequency analysis of positive and negative results, followed by a sign test, in order to establish whether or not positive or negative results are associated with studies to a greater degree than one would expect by chance; estimating average effect sizes with confidence intervals (which typically requires converting various statistical effect estimates into a common effect statistic, such as Cohen's d); and performing a homogeneity analysis to explore components of studies that could moderate outcomes (p. 149)

Rosenthal (1978) offered seven methods for combining inference test results across studies in order to acquire an overall test of the null hypothesis. According to Cooper (1990), the method of adding Zs, the most frequently utilized of the seven measures, requires "(a) converting the (one-tailed) p-level for each inference test to its associated Z-scores . . . (c) dividing the sum by the square root of the number of inference tests, and (d) looking up the p-level associated with the cumulative Z-score" (p. 146). Using the method of adding Zs, Rosenthal provided a formula for differentially weighting inference tests (e.g., determined by the methodological rigor associated with the studies), thus allowing them to contribute unequally to the cumulative test.

The failsafe N allows the meta-analyst to ascertain the number of studies that collectively would be required in the sample to produce a null finding, changing a significant cumulative outcome to a nonsignificant one on the basis of their inclusion (Cooper, 1979; Rosenthal, 1979). Rosenthal (1983) illustrated the value of this technique with a meta-analysis of ninety-four experiments on interpersonal self-fulfilling prophecies. He asked how many file-drawer (i.e., new, filed, or otherwise unretrievable) studies with null results it would take to bring the meta-analytic effect size down to a null result. The results indicated that "3,263 studies averaging null results ($z = .00$) must be crammed into file drawers before one would conclude that the overall results were due to sampling bias in the studies summarized by the reviewers" (p. 85). Such an outcome seems so highly unreasonable that substantial confidence can be placed in the meta-analytic effect-size estimate.

Estimating effect sizes provides an indicator of the magnitude of the impact of the independent variable upon the dependent variable. According to Cooper (1990), "Because the parameter estimates contained in meta-analyses are often based on an extremely large number of research participants, the likelihood of not rejecting the exact null hypothesis becomes exceedingly small, while estimates of effect size become highly reliable" (Cooper, 1990, p. 147). Two measures of effect size are the d-index, which "involves dividing the difference between the two group means by either their average standard deviation or the standard deviation of the control group" (Cooper, 1990, p. 147), and the *r*-index, which "measures the degree of linear relation between two variables" (p.148; see also McGraw & Wong, 1992).

Homogeneity analysis, according to Cooper (1990), is one of the three methods available for examining variance in effect sizes. Specifically, the technique first "applies significance tests to determine whether sets of effect sizes exhibit more variance than expected by sampling error" (p. 149), and then allows the researcher to determine whether or not study components offer an explanation for effect size variation (i.e., whether or not they moderate or mediate findings across studies).

Application of Meta-Analysis to the Study of Candidate Image

Meta-analysis has been applied to studies of various phenomena in the social sciences, associated with the psychology and communication literature as well as with the clinical and educational contexts. Despite over 4,912 titles in *PsycInfo* periodical search engines referring to meta-analysis in their titles or abstracts (as of August 9, 2004), 82 titles or abstracts in *Communication Abstracts* (as of August 9, 2004), and a variety of other data-based engines, no applications of the method could be located explicitly regarding candidate image. However, there are several investigations that clearly reveal analogous or relevant inquiries that help illustrate the potential value of meta-analytic approaches to presidential candidate image literature. These are studies that have reviewed effects of political perceptions assessed across studies to estimate their magnitude. Candidate variables, such as attitude homophily, candidate attractiveness, and amount or objectivity of political knowledge, are all relevant to candidate image.

Zhu, Milavsky, and Biswas (1994) conducted a study in an attempt to separate the effects of presidential debates on candidate image and voter (i.e., perceiver) issue knowledge: "Four possible outcomes could be expected: the debate affects both images and issues, neither images nor issues, only images but not issues, and only issues but not images" (p. 303). They located thirty-six studies relevant to these outcomes, but did not pursue an actual meta-analysis of the research, and instead interpreted "overall trends in debate effects." They concluded that, among other things, "data show clearly that most of what is now known about debate effects came from studies of the first televised presidential debates in the 1960 election and from the debates in the 1976 election" (Zhu et al., 1994, p. 306). Their tabular review revealed that effects on issue knowledge and image perception were quite mixed, with three issue and five image studies showing "substantial/consistent" effects, four issue and ten image studies showing "moderate/mixed" effects, and one issue study and nine image studies showing no effects. The relevance of this study is that the data would have been much more precisely estimated through meta-analytic procedures, which could report an actual effect size and determine if there were factors that account for why some studies find one type of (or no) effect rather than another.

D'Alessio and Allen (2000) conducted a meta-analysis of media bias in presidential elections. They located fifty-nine studies relevant to gatekeeping (selecting stories from one party relative to another), coverage bias (amounts of time, lines, and so on, devoted to one party over another), and statement bias (representation of content favorable to one party relative to another). They found that type of medium made some difference, in that there were few biases in newspaper or newsmagazine coverage, but there were small but measurable biases in television coverage. Given these results, a rather secure conclusion was derived that "there is no evidence whatsoever of a monolithic liberal bias in the newspaper industry" (D'Alessio & Allen, 2000, p. 148), and only "a very small, and not completely consistent, liberal (or at least pro-Democratic) bias" (p. 149) in coverage and statement favorability in TV network coverage of elections. The confidence of such conclusions is bolstered by the recognition that in this study, "A total of 1,149 newspapers (albeit with a number of repeats) in 12 different presidential campaigns—a total of over 60,000 articles—... are represented" (D'Alessio & Allen, 2000, p. 150).

In a somewhat novel application of meta-analytic procedures, Emmers-Sommer and Allen (1999) summarized all studies published in *Human Communication Research* over its twenty-five years of publication that investigated media effects. Their meta-analysis produced a wide variety of summary statistics. For example, most relevant to candidate image, they found evidence that "as children get older, they understand the media better" (Emmers-Sommer & Allen, 1999, p. 488); "as IQ increases, television viewing decreases" (p. 488); "television consumption does distract and does indeed interfere with an individual's ability to complete tasks" (p. 488); "the mass media do indeed increase knowledge about political issues" (p. 489); "findings indicate support for cultivation theory" (p. 489); and, in general, "effects for experimental research are stronger than that for survey research" (p. 489). The latter finding, in particular, illustrates a rather practical conclusion by which the literature on media effects can be more accurately interpreted on the basis of design features.

There are certainly possibilities for the application of meta-analysis in the study of candidate image. First, the effect sizes of various variables of interest could be summarized across studies. The effects of voter or perceiver variables, such as gender (see Harrison, Stephen, Husson, & Fehr, 1991), ethnicity, party affiliation, and the like, could be assessed across studies to estimate their magnitude. Candidate variables, such as attitude homophily, candidate attractiveness, candidate rank or incumbency, type of message (e.g., Pfau & Burgoon, 1988), and televised debate effects, could be estimated. Second, a number of factor-analytic studies have attempted to define the structure of candidate image (see Hellweg, Dionisopoulos, & Kugler, 1989; Hellweg, Walker, King, & Spitzberg, 1990; Husson, Stephen, Harrison, & Fehr, 1988). To the extent that the same credibility or image scales are used across studies, meta-analytic comparison of obtained factor solutions could ascertain the cross-sample stability in the structure of candidate image. Third, it is conceivable that moderator variables can be identified in such research.

As an analogue, Stiff (1986) hypothesized that attitude change is curvilinear to involvement. Although not predicted by the authors of the original investigations, the studies were coded in terms of low, moderate, and high levels of involvement, and, as predicted, the most attitude change occurred at moderate levels of involvement. Candidate image, as an attitude construct, could be similarly investigated across studies with varying methodological factors (e.g., experimental, quasi-experimental, and naturalistic) or measured variables (e.g., involvement and issue awareness) that moderate the effects observed. This latter application of meta-analysis reveals the approach to be much more than a mere synthesizer of results. Meta-analysis actually permits the testing of post hoc hypotheses generated on the basis of evidence of heterogeneity in the primary data and of a priori hypotheses not even envisioned in the primary studies (Hale & Dillard, 1991).

Conclusion

Meta-analysis, as an "analysis of analyses" (Glass, 1976), provides a statistical means by which to evaluate empirical data across separate studies of a particular concept in order to ascertain the strength of those combined results. As such, it would seem appropriate to apply the technique in the study of political candidate image. Because of the rapidly increasing volume of literature that exists in connection with the study of candidate image in the context of political advertising and political candidate debates, for example, meta-analytic efforts in these areas might be particularly appropriate. Through such pursuit, the meta-analytic researcher might be able to derive conclusions about those studies that have been directed at understanding how candidate image functions in these contexts beyond what an impressionistic literature review might be able to achieve.

References

Allen, M., and R. W. Preiss. 2002. "Meta-Analysis and Interpersonal Communication: Function and Applicability." In *Interpersonal Communication Research: Advances through Meta-Analysis*, edited by M. Allen, R. W. Preiss, B. M. Gayle, and N. A. Burrell, 3–12. Mahwah, N.J.: Lawrence Erlbaum.

Archer, J. 2000. "Sex Differences in Aggression between Heterosexual Partners: A Meta-Analytic Review." *Psychological Bulletin* 126: 651–680.

Beaman, A. L. 1991. "An Empirical Comparison of Meta-Analytic and Traditional Reviews." *Personality and Social Psychology Bulletin* 17: 252–257.

Bullock, R. J., and D. J. Svyantek. 1985. "Analyzing Meta-Analysis: Potential Problems, an Unsuccessful Replication, and Evaluation Criteria." *Journal of Applied Psychology* 70: 108–115.

Bushman, B. J., H. M. Cooper, and K. M. Lemke. 1991. "Meta-Analysis of Factor Analyses: An Illustration Using the Buss-Durkee Hostility Inventory." *Personality and Social Psychology Bulletin* 17: 344–349.

Chow, S. L. 1987. "Meta-Analysis of Pragmatic and Theoretical Research: A Critique." *Journal of Psychology* 121: 259–271.

Cooper, H. M. 1979. "Statistically Combining Independent Studies: A Meta-Analysis of Sex Differences in Conformity Research." *Journal of Personality and Social Psychology* 37: 131–146.

———. 1984. *The Integrative Research Review: A Systematic Approach*. Beverly Hills, Calif.: Sage.

———. 1990. "Meta-Analysis and the Integrative Research Review." In *Research Methods in Personality and Social Psychology*, edited by C. Hendrick and M. S. Clark, 142–163. Newbury Park, Calif.: Sage.

D'Alessio, D., and M. Allen. 2000. "Media Bias in Presidential Elections: A Meta-Analysis." *Journal of Communication* 50: 133–156.

Emmers-Sommer, T. M., and M. Allen. 1999. "Surveying the Effect of Media Effects: A Meta-Analytic Summary of the Media Effects Research in *Human Communication Research*." *Human Communication Research* 25: 478–497.

Glass, G. V. 1976. "Primary, Secondary, and Meta-Analysis of Research." *Educational Researcher* 5: 3–8.

Glass, G. V., B. McGaw, and M. L. Smith. 1981. *Meta-Analysis in Social Research*. Beverly Hills, Calif.: Sage.

Green, B. F., and J. A. Hall. 1984. "Quantitative Methods for Literature Reviews." *Annual Review of Psychology* 35: 37–53.

Hale, J. L., and J. P. Dillard. 1991. "The Uses of Meta-Analysis: Making Knowledge Claims and Setting Research Agendas." *Communication Monographs* 58: 463–471.

Harrison, T. M., T. D. Stephen, W. Husson, and B. J. Fehr. 1991. "Images versus Issues in the 1984 Presidential Election: Differences between Men and Women." *Human Communication Research* 18: 209–227.

Hedges, L. V., and I. Olkin. 1982. "Analyses, Reanalyses, and Meta-Analysis." *Contemporary Education Review* 1157–1165.

———. 1985. *Statistical Methods for Meta-Analysis*. Orlando, Fla.: Academic Press.

Hellweg, S. A., G. N. Dionisopoulos, and D. B. Kugler. 1989. "Political Candidate Image: A State of the Art Review. In *Progress in Communication Sciences*, vol. 9, edited by B. Dervin and M. J. Voigt, 43–78. Norwood, N.J.: Ablex.

Hellweg, S. A., W. A. Walker, S. W. King, and B. H. Spitzberg. 1990. "Comparative Candidate Evaluation: Voter Intention as a Function of the Grounding of Image Criteria and Image Agenda Setting by Candidates." Paper presented at the International Communication Association conference, Dublin, Ireland, June.

Hunter, J. E., F. L. Schmidt, and G. B. Jackson. 1982. *Meta-Analysis: Cumulating Research Findings across Studies*. Beverly Hills, Calif.: Sage.

Husson, W., T. Stephen, T. M. Harrison, and B. J. Fehr. 1988. "An Interpersonal Communication Perspective on Images of Political Candidates." *Human Communication Research* 14: 397–421.

Light, R. J., and D. B. Pillemer. 1984. *Summing Up: The Science of Reviewing Research*. Cambridge, Mass.: Harvard University Press.

McGraw, K. O., and S. P. Wong. 1992. "A Common Language Effect Size Statistic." *Psychological Bulletin* 111: 361–365.

Noblit, G. W., and R. D. Hare. 1988. *Meta-Ethnography: Synthesizing Qualitative Studies*. Newbury Park, Calif.: Sage.

O'Keefe, D. J. 1991. "Extracting Dependable Generalizations from the Persuasion Effects Literature: Some Issues in Meta-Analytic Reviews." *Communication Monographs* 58: 472–481.

Pfau, M., and M. Burgoon. 1988. "Inoculation in Political Campaign Communication." *Human Communication Research* 15: 91–111.

Rogers, E. M. 1985. "Methodologies for Meta-Research." In *Organizational Communication: Abstracts, Analysis, and Overview*, vol. 10, edited by H. H. Greenbaum, S. A. Hellweg, and J. W. Walter, 13–33. Beverly Hills, Calif.: Sage.

Rosenthal, R. 1978. "Combining the Results of Independent Studies." *Psychological Bulletin* 85: 185–193.

———. 1979. "The 'File-Drawer Problem' and Tolerance for Null Results." *Psychological Bulletin* 86: 638–641.

———. 1983. "Meta-Analysis: Toward a More Cumulative Social Science." In *Applied Social Psychology Annual*, vol. 4, edited by L. Bickman, 65–93. Beverly Hills, Calif.: Sage.

———. 1984. *Meta-Analytic Procedures for Social Research*. Newbury Park, Calif.: Sage.

Schafer, W. D. 1999. "Methods, Plainly Speaking: An Overview of Meta-Analysis." *Measurement and Evaluation in Counseling and Development* 32: 43–61.

Schneider, W. 1991. "Reviewing Previous Research by Meta-Analysis." In *Studying Interpersonal Interaction*, edited by B. M. Montgomery and S. Duck, 303–320. New York: Guilford.

Schwandt, T. A. 1989. "Solutions to the Paradigm Conflict: Coping with Uncertainty." *Journal of Contemporary Ethnography* 17: 379–407.

Shapiro, D. A. 1985. "Recent Applications of Meta-Analysis in Clinical Research." *Clinical Psychology Review* 5: 13–34.

Stewart, D. W. 1984. *Secondary Research: Information Sources and Methods*. Newbury Park, Calif.: Sage.

Stiff, J. B. 1986. "Cognitive Processing of Persuasive Message Cues: A Meta-Analytic Review of the Effects of Supporting Information on Attitudes." *Communication Monographs* 53: 75–89.

Strube, M. J., and D. P. Hartmann. 1983. "Meta-Analysis: Techniques, Applications, and Functions." *Journal of Consulting and Clinical Psychology* 51: 14–27.

Thompson, B. 1989. "Meta-Analysis of Factor Structure Studies: A Case Study Example with Bem's Androgyny Measure." *Journal of Experimental Education* 57: 187–197.

Wolf, F. M. 1986. *Meta-Analysis: Quantitative Methods for Research Synthesis.* Newbury Park, Calif.: Sage.

Zhao, S. 1991. "Metatheory, Metamethod, Meta-Data-Analysis: What, Why, and How?" *Sociological Perspectives* 34: 377–390.

Zhu, J.-H., J. R. Milavsky, and R. Biswas. 1994. "Do Televised Debates Affect Image Perception More than Issue Knowledge? A Study of the First 1992 Presidential Debate." *Human Communication Research* 20: 302–333.

10

Using Cognitive Measurement for Analysis of Candidate Images

Kenneth L. Hacker

THIS CHAPTER DESCRIBES SEVERAL RESEARCH METHODS that may be employed for the examination of cognitive aspects of political candidate images. As evident in the literature, there are numerous variations in how candidate images are operationalized. The procedures described here fit the assumption that candidate images are best conceptualized as cognitive representations of presidential candidates in which image content is determined by receivers or voters more than by researchers.

From a cognitive perspective of candidate images, these research methods should be useful in studying both the content and formation of the images.[1] The content of the images is dependent on the theoretical definition of images being used and the formation of images is a construction process that occurs over time. Three methods of cognitive measurement will be described in this chapter: cognitive response analysis, content analysis, and political discourse analysis.

Human communication research has increasingly been examining cognitive aspects of social interaction. Scholars who study the cognitive side of communication tend to assume that how receivers represent message to themselves determines how they respond to those messages and add parts of the messages to their memory. A strong assumption held by many communication scientists is that cognitions mediate the effects of messages on memory and behavior. Persuasion studies indicate that cognitive responses generally correlate significantly with attitudes.[2] The notion of cognitive response is not a reference to retention but rather to active thought in direct relationship to received messages.

As with communication research in general, there is an increasing focus on the relationship between cognition and communication in the study of political communication. Regardless of how the presidential candidate image is defined by the researcher, there is likely to be the assumption that the beliefs and impressions that constitute the candidate image are formed to some extent by cognitive processes and are stored in memory as cognitive structures. It should not be uncommon, therefore, for political communication researchers to assume that candidate images are related to cognitive structures and processes. An elementary conceptual model of this assumption is shown in figure 10.1. The figure illustrates the following assumptions. The most generalized memory structure for candidate memory is the candidate schema. A schema is a knowledge structure for any subject that contains all of the knowledge about that subject and also has connections to other relevant schemata. For example, a schema of G. W. Bush may be linked to a schema of Republicans.

A candidate schema is likely to be associated with schemata for other candidates, political parties, ideologies, and so on. Cognitive processing refers to the ways in which incoming messages and information are evaluated and related to previously stored knowledge, attitudes, and images. Attitudes toward candidates, like any other attitudes, are affective orientations toward the candidates and have the two key characteristics of valence (positive or negative) and intensity (how positive or negative). While there is much work to do in testing the hypothesized relationships in such a model, scholars of political communication generally assume that cognitions about candidates affect the images that are formed regarding those candidates.

There are two basic means in which perceptions or impressions of message stimuli register effects on attitudes, images, or schemata. These are cognitive

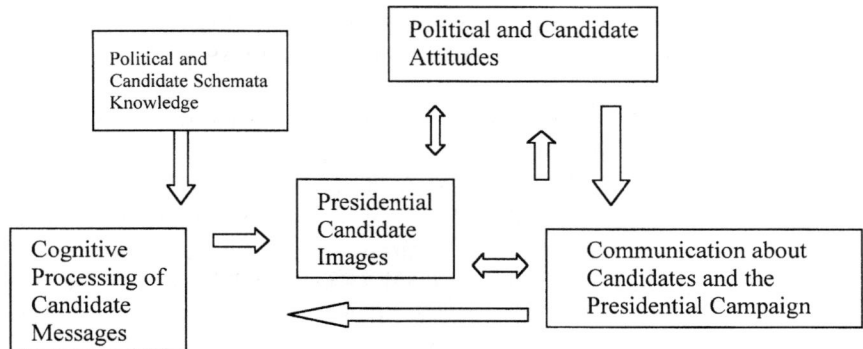

FIGURE 10.1
Cognition and Presidential Candidate Images

(belief) messages and affect (emotion) messages. While this chapter focuses mainly on the cognitive, it will also note and attempt to accommodate the possibility that emotional effects can be measured or observed in ways similar to the cognitive measurement described here. Message responses are likely to include both cognitive responses and emotional responses (see Hacker, chapter 5, this volume). At this point in time, however, most studies of candidate images gather information about emotional reactions as what people "feel" in cognitive terms about candidates.

One advantage of measuring cognitions in studying images is that the researchers are no longer limited to impressions of candidate issue position and impressions of personal traits of the candidates. It has long been known in history, political science, and communication science that presidents are evaluated in relationship to economic conditions, foreign policy situations, ideologies, political parties, and other factors that are not the usual image factors of issue and character impressions.

Michael Pfau (2002, p. 253) notes that the candidate communication effects on images are "co-mingled," meaning that the effects of one form of candidate messages are mixed with the effects of other forms. As with all human communication, what the candidate says is important but the way in which the messages are stated is also important to voter evaluations (Pfau, 2002). This suggests that relational messages from candidates to voters, both verbal and nonverbal, may create content accumulated into voters' presidential candidate images. Pfau notes how Bill Clinton created very effective relational messages in his 1992 presidential debating by generating impressions of affection, enthusiasm, warmth, caring, willingness to listen, receptivity, and interesting interaction with voters. In contrast, Al Gore in his 2000 debates created relational impressions of being overly aggressive, irritating, and impolite to his opponent (Pfau, 2002). While many of these impressions are created nonverbally by the candidates, and they can overpower what they do with substantive comments about issues, it is possible to examine how voters process these relational messages by asking them to recall the events.

The most common means of doing research in voting studies and political communication research have been survey research, secondary data analysis of existing survey data, experiments, and quantitative content analysis of media or political figure communication messages. There is another body of research and methods that explores what is commonly known as political psychology and the study of political cognition.

Questionnaires and surveys are useful to gain data about beliefs, attitudes, perceptions, and how important variables related to these are related to each other and to voting behaviors. While some questions and responses are closed-ended, others are open-ended. In the latter case, the responses have to be coded by some form of content analysis.

Whether open-ended or closed-ended, there are always issues of validity. Substantial error has been found in questions such as asking people who they voted for in a past presidential election. For example, in 1960, 49 percent of respondents said they voted for Kennedy, while in 1962, 56 percent said they did, and in 1964, 64 percent said they voted for him (Flanigan & Zingale, 1998).

The earliest approaches to candidate images relied on source credibility scales, and the construct of candidate image was conceptually equated with perceptions of candidate persona. This approach, while once dominant, has attracted increased challenges over the past few years (Hacker, Zakahi, Giles, & McQuitty, 2000). Candidate source credibility is important but is not likely to represent all that is important to voters' images of candidates.

Most of the existing literature on candidate image to date has failed to adequately distinguish the concept of attitude from that of candidate image. In fact, some operational definitions of candidate image mirror those of attitudes about candidates.

The view presented here is a pre-attitudinal view of candidate image. In other words, consistent with research in psychology on attitudes, it is assumed that voters have attitudes about the referents for their images. However, the presidential candidate image is more of a cognitive representation albeit one than can include emotional impressions (see Hacker, chapter 5, on dual processing of image content).

This view of candidate images makes them more like schemata than attitudes. To some extent it can be argued that a candidate image is a schema about a political candidate. Thus, a presidential candidate schema and a presidential candidate from a cognitive view may have no substantial or important differences as constructs. However, one could argue that a candidate image is more of a mental model and has less stability and permanence than a schema. It is likely that a candidate image is something in between a schema and a mental model. This is because of the evidence that images of candidates fluctuate by candidates and campaigns and can be modified through various processes of communication while still being somewhat stable over time.

There are two main types of cognitive measurement strategies for candidate image research: one is static (structure focus), and the other is dynamic (process focus). Static measures of PCI include questionnaires, surveys, experiments, and content analysis of political discourse. Static measures provide data about single points in time. Studies like longitudinal or panel studies move closer to dynamic studies but still are generated by a succession of static studies. The key point about static measures is that structures or relationships between variables are studied rather than processes of how those structures or variables are generated and modified. Most candidate image research has been static.

Dynamic or process measurement of PCIs involves methods that seek to track formation of the images over time. Such methods may include discourse analysis, cognitive response testing over time, lag sequential analysis, and protocol analysis.[3] With dynamic measurement, one seeks to measure not only structures but also how structures are constituted in time and perhaps how one process affects another process in the generation and modification of these structures.

Structures and Communication

Structures exist in all areas of human experience—physics, music, language, social systems, organizations, planning, cognition, and communication. Along with all structures are processes. Pure structural views might ignore important processes. Within any study of structures, therefore, there is always the possibility of studying processes, and with the study of any processes, there is always the potential to study structures that result from those processes. As there are cognitive structures and social structures, there are also communication structures. Recent communication theories like adaptive structuration theory have pointed out the communication structures (roles, rules, patterns, constraints, and so on) that are both affecting and affected by social interaction. Studies that relate cognition to communication have observed the communication structures such as social representations.

The study of candidate images has traditionally noted how the image structures affect voting and how the images are changed by communication processes such as viewing TV news, watching a presidential debate, or talking with friends.[4] We have sufficient documentation today that images change in response to various message environments, but we lack theoretical formulations regarding how the images originate, change, and are predictably modified by numerous and varying forms of communication, particularly in a relative sense.

Research that relates image changes to communication changes has the potential to provide useful knowledge regarding the processing of messages into information, the organizing of stored information and knowledge, the integration of newly accepted information into previously stored knowledge, and the monitoring of campaign communication in terms of existing images and schemata.

There is a two-way process of images affecting communication and communication affecting images that needs far more explanation than we have today. Communication can provide inputs into thinking and the cognitive processes that activate various schemata. Communication can also stimulate political reasoning. Additionally, it can facilitate cognitive organization and related personal meanings to social meanings, thus providing a coherence of personal impressions with cultural ones.

Cognitive Systems and Cognitive Structures

Within the mind are cognitive systems made up of various cognitive structures, connections of structures, processes, and operations. The minimal view of cognitive systems is that of the black box in which input is processed by unknown mental processes and output that is different from input is produced. A step beyond the black-box version of the mind is that of linear information processing, which basically treats the mind like a computer. There are five steps that are assumed as endemic to human information processing: information input, central processing, information storage, retrieval, and utilization of the processed information (Griffin, 2000). The use of an information processing approach is intended to identify aspects of the cognitive system that link inputs to outputs (Greene, 1988). For images, the goal is therefore to ascertain how candidate images link messages about candidates to output behaviors like expression of candidate evaluation and actual voting choices.

Persuasion research and cognitive studies generally indicate that beliefs are the building blocks of cognitive systems (van Dijk, 1998). Clusters of beliefs form "belief systems" or attitudes in most accounts. Both can be related to values, which are ideals and sometimes thought of as core beliefs. Generally attitudes have both cognitive and emotional dimensions, while beliefs are thought to be only cognitive. Knowledge structures contain beliefs and attitudes and may be related to values as when evaluations and judgements are being made. Emotions are also important parts of cognitive systems, especially since affect is an essential part of attitudes. When one feels strongly about a political situation, there are beliefs that make the emotions salient and perhaps justify them subjectively. A major part of what the mind does beyond thinking and processing messages is the building of knowledge structures and the building of various forms of memory.

There are networks of connections in the mind that may parallel the neural networking of the brain, albeit in differing forms. There are levels of abstraction in the cognitive system. At the lower levels are more concrete and more local beliefs and impressions. At the higher levels are cognitions, which summarize and move upward to more abstract models or representations. For candidate images, this might work something like this:

Highest level: candidate image—Candidate A is better than B.
Mid-levels: Candidate B has better plans for the government.
Lowest level: impressions—Candidate A is inexperienced and B has good ideas about social programs.

The notion of hierarchical organization is common in linguistics and has become more current in communication studies as hierarchies have been argued for coordinated management of meaning theory, action assembly theory, cognitive planning theory, and other theories of communication.

To some extent, the cognitive system organization just described can be seen in social discourse in forms of framing and discourse structural systems. There are two directions in which information can be processed in the cognitive system hierarchies. First, there is inductive control moving from concrete to general in which higher-order cognitions are limited to the patterns of lower-order ones. Then there is the downward consistency or monitoring of local communication behavior by higher-order cognitive generalizations and representations.

One fascinating aspect of cognitive systems is that lower-level cognitions may be lost as they are subsumed by higher-level cognitions, which act to summarize lower-level beliefs or propositions (van Dijk, 1998). This is consistent with research indicating that voters participate in real-time or continuous ("online") processing of candidate characteristics, always abstracting as they form more and more summary cognitive representations of the candidates.

Specific Structures

Dismissing sweeping generalities about political cognition as overly speculative allows us to study the structures and functions of political cognitive structures on their own and in systemic relations to each other. We know that cognitive structures are constructed with experiences and various processes of thinking, adapting, and communicating. Candidate images need to be distinguished from candidate attitudes and candidate schemata.[5] Attitudes are not the same as schemata. Schemata are general knowledge structures with lots of cognitions in various hierarchies of signification. They look like linguistic trees when drawn out on paper. Attitudes are clusters of beliefs with emotional elements added, which add up to behavioral dispositions that are either positive or negative with some degree of intensity.

As shown in persuasion theory, attitudes are close to behavioral intentions. The theory of reasoned action (TRA), however, shows that attitudes toward objects are not as useful for predicting behaviors, as attitudes toward actions become more explanatory in conjunction with measures of influence by significant others (*subjective norms*). Since the TRA does not explain what the interaction of attitudes toward behavior and subjective norms constitutes as cognitive structures, we might assume that it is an important cognitive structure since it is directly predictive of intention, which is highly correlated to behavior. It might be that presidential candidate images are composed of beliefs, candidate attitudes, and action attitudes. The image is not held to either a type of attitude or a type of schema. The candidate image is more generalized than the candidate attitude and set of candidate beliefs.

After identifying this tentative structure, it is necessary to explain process and contents. The problems with cognitive approaches to political communication are the ones attached to any cognitive studies including political psychology, political cognition, and studies of candidate images or political schemata. Much of the time, the concepts and constructs are loosely defined and operationalizations vary by researcher or research tradition. Another problem is that constructs are defined but not differentiated from other constructs that may have similar conceptual and operational definitions.

Cognitive Response Theory and Presidential Candidate Images

According to the research supporting cognitive response theory, messages evoke reactions in the minds of message receivers, and there are three possible directions for these reactions—positive, negative, and neutral (Perloff, 1993). This approach to communication assumes that receivers are active participants in the message-reception process (Perloff, 1993). It also assumes that cognitive responses mediate the effects that messages have on attitudes (Perloff, 1993). Attitude change is believed to occur in the desired direction only to the extent that cognitive responses are moving in the desired direction. Studies indicate that attitudes toward messages are predictable by the number of arguments an individual generates in response to those messages (Perloff, 1993). Many decades ago, cognitive response research discovered that self-persuasion is the strongest type of persuasion (Perloff, 1993).

Online cognitive processing cannot be tested or measured with survey or questionnaire methods. This is because these methods test affective responses to stored and recalled beliefs rather than cognitive responses to message stimuli outside of the questions being asked (Way & Masters, 1996).

Summative models of attitudes assume that beliefs are cognitively integrated into the structures (cognitive structures) we call attitudes. For any attitude object (the subject being considered), there can be a large number of beliefs, but at the point of measurement (however done), there are likely to be a limited number of most salient beliefs (O'Keefe, 2002). This is one reason why it is important to measure attitudes and images across time instead of only at single moments. Candidate images may be seen as clusters of beliefs, which are evaluated and combined with emotions that generate the dispositions that we know as attitudes.[6]

As candidate images are clusters of beliefs (cognitions about anything relevant to perceptions of the candidates), we can see that messages have strongest effects when they alter the images. Sociocognitive theory assumes that an attitude is an evaluation of a knowledge structure (something stored in memory). This approach to attitudes does not have a specific means of calculating beliefs to get figures about attitude strength (intensity) and direction (valence).

Cognitive Research Methods

There are no direct observation methods for studying cognition. Still, cognitive processes can be observed in their behavioral and communicative manifestations. You can test what a person has as knowledge by asking them what they know. You can test memory by asking that input be displayed as output.

An adequate analysis of a cognitive system will account for structures, contents, processes, and relationships among these. In political communication, as with general communication research, this is rarely done.

Discourse analysis is a method used to locate ideology (van Dijk, 1998). Unlike content analysis, which seeks to find variable relationships only at surface levels of content, discourse analysis seeks to find underlying principles and rules. It will look for how surface structures like claims or propositions are linked to each other and guided by a small set of principles that remain unarticulated but that seem inviolable by the surface structure productions.

Thus, discourse analysis connects the explicit to the implicit. There is a description of manifest content along with likely strategies for presentation and interpretation. Political beliefs, attitudes, images, schemata, and so on can be organized from simple to complex levels. Such organization and reorganization can be accomplished in social interaction (van Dijk, 1998). A sociocognitive view assumes that there are personal cognitive representations but also social representations that are influenced by social interaction while housed in minds. A social representation is a cluster of social beliefs related to social memory (van Dijk, 1998). Studies show that candidate images can be affected by interpersonal conversations (Hacker, 1995).

Cognitive Views of Ideology

Political scientists privilege parties and minimize ideologies as determinants of election voting. When controlling for party issues, ideology has a small role in determining vote. This is due to the fact perhaps that ideology is defined as external systems of thought—the kind of dogmas we talk about with the political spectrum.

William Flanigan and Nancy Zingale (1998) argue that ideology can have varying levels of influence in elections and that there does not appear to be a direct effect of ideology and voting as there is with party. On the other hand, they also note that what political scientists call "issue constraint" suggests that ideologies are useful to keep issues positions consistent. We also know that partisanship and ideologies are positively related. As a person perceives political messages, there will be some goal for doing so. Activated in this process are certain types of stored knowledge as well as ideology.

Along with facts in political communication, the receiver is exposed to levels of inference that accompany the facts. Themes are presented and perceived in political communication. Propositions are not simply taken from the presentation, but the receiver creates his or her own as the process of interpretation proceeds. Some of the structures formed by the receiver will control the rest of the process.

Cognitive Response Testing and Measurement

Cognitive response theory preceded the elaboration likelihood model (ELM) of persuasion but provided key propositions that ground the ELM and the heuristic-systematic model (HSM).

Experts in marketing moved from thinking about message effects as only creating retention to thinking instead of marketing as getting agreement and then retention. With both CRT and the ELM, what counts the most in message reception is how the receivers respond and what thoughts and feelings they generate in their minds as they respond to messages given to them.

A message may serve as an argument or as a cue depending on its relevance to the topic at hand as well as on the degree of relevance of the topic to the receiver. This is important because cognitive responses may reveal what aspects of candidates' presentations are cues and which are arguments under these two sets of conditions.

Voters, following the logic of the ELM, can form reasonable responses to political messages through a variety of means of processing the messages. There is a probabilistic nature to this way of describing political perception. At one extreme of the ELM continuum of elaboration is processing done with no thinking of information about issues, and the other end involves processing with complete thought about issues. While the message types may not be determinable a priori due to the fact that receivers respond as they will, increasing voter relevance and decreasing distraction are likely to increase the focus on issues rather than on cues. If the attitude-image parallel suggested here is valid, the variance in candidate image change, like the variance in attitude change, should be related to the amount of elaboration and cognitive responses to issues. The higher the responses to issues, the more likely the images will be issue dominant, and the lower the elaboration, the more likely the candidate images will be personality and other-cue dominant.

As with attitude change, changes in candidate images may be short-term or long-term since both are constructs that are built from beliefs that are affected by changes in the message environment. Clearly, the processes related to candidate image formation are related to what we know about human information processing and cognitive systems. This is why cognitive response testing can provide data on what voters are thinking about in relation to messages and the images they both form and utilize.

One important contribution of the ELM is its findings about what factors, if increased, can increase elaboration or the scrutiny of the quality of arguments. As with cognitive response theory before it, the ELM postulates that when a receiver argues along with the persuader in a positive direction, attitudes are being changed positively, and the same thing occurs in the negative direction when the receiver counterargues in response to the persuader's messages. Research and theoretical work with the ELM have shown that previous theories of persuasion such as cognitive dissonance theory are likely to apply with high elaboration more than low elaboration and that the processes explained by theories such as classical conditioning theory are likely to occur more with low elaboration.

One point made by the ELM researchers is that it is important to note the differences between types of independent variables, particularly moderating and mediating variables. Moderating variables influence the strength or direction of the relationship between an independent and dependent variable. In contrast, a mediating variable is a necessary link between an independent variable and dependent variable. Visually, this might apply to images in a way shown in figure 10.2.

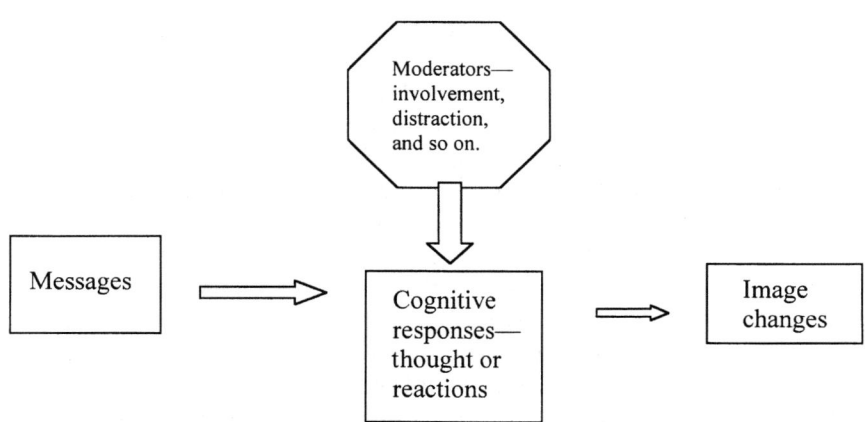

FIGURE 10.2
Cognitive Response Model of Candidate Image Formation

The role of the moderating variables is crucial because the links between independent variables, mediating variables, and dependent variables can be changed by the states of these moderators.

It is possible to measure cognitions through verbalization in two basic ways, reactive and nonreactive. In reactive measurement, receivers cognitively respond to messages presented to them. In nonreactive measurement, subjects simply talk or interact freely with each other. We now look at cognitive response testing.

Thought Listing and Cognitive Response Measurement

Cognitive response analysis is used in persuasion research to observe subjects' attitudes (Ostrom, Bond, Krosnick, & Sedikides, 1994). Ostrom et al. (1994) note that what subjects write down in this procedure is similar to what is found with Likert-type scales but that subjects also describe persuader credibility and the quality of the arguments made.

In a cognitive response measurement situation, subjects have written down their positive and negative reactions to messages they have been shown. The next task for the researcher is to code those responses in ways consistent with the aims of cognitive response theory and the ELM.

Petty and Cacioppo (1981) describe a method they use that was developed by Brock (1967) and Greenwald (1968). In this "thought-listing" procedure, subjects are given a few minutes to list the thoughts they had during exposure to some messages. They are given sheets of paper with blank lines and asked to write down one thought per line. The thoughts are then coded as either favorable or unfavorable to the position advocated in the message exposure.

A cognitive-response approach to communication helps us gain insights into reactions that are receiver directed (Perloff, 2003). It can also show how those reactions influence evaluation of the persuader's messages. Cognitive response theory, the ELM, and the HSM all assume that receivers are active processors of messages.

Favorable cognitive responses are important for measuring changes in attitudes in the direction being advocated by the persuader (Perloff, 2003). One unresolved issue with the ELM is how receivers simultaneously process through the central and peripheral routes (Perloff, 2003). Cognitive responses can only be observed indirectly. Coding schemes can obviously vary by researcher and research project.

Thought listing is a technique used to assess variation in elaboration (O'Keefe, 2002). Immediately following a set of messages, receivers are asked to list their thoughts that occurred during message exposure. O'Keefe (2002) argues that the number of issue-related messages is the measure of elaboration (issue-relevant thinking). Another means of classifying or coding the responses is by favorability. It is also possible to code substantive content in the responses.

ELM researchers have generally pretested messages for argument strength by measuring which messages are responded to with predominantly positive responses and which arguments are responded to mostly with negative reactions. All of this applies to those subjects who have been instructed to think or elaborate about the topic (O'Keefe, 2002).

A unique aspect of the thought-listing procedure is that subjects rather than researchers code the listed thoughts for valence. In other words, subjects code their own data. An index of positive cognitive responses can be created with the following formula (Fleming and Petty, 2000):

# of positive thoughts – # of negative thoughts/total # of thoughts

While ELM research generally looks at only positive, negative, and neutral cognitive responses, many researchers are interested in other reactions such as emotional responses (Wansink, Ray, & Batra, 1994). The more general the elicitation instructions, the more probable it is to receive irrelevant responses (Wansink et al., 1994). Therefore, the researchers have to identify what is relevant as cognitive content before doing the cognitive response testing. Sometimes subjects will replay content of exposed messages; this can detract from what researchers are most interested in—their cognitive reactions (Wansink et al., 1994). Pre-exposure elicitation can direct subjects' processing of message content so that cognitive response measures are more directed toward specific image dimensions. Subjects can also be given postcontent instructions to provide responses about certain aspects of what they were exposed to. In both cases, researchers must be careful not to direct the subjects too much in order to avoid having them edit out important responses or add in thoughts that might not have been relevant during exposure (Wansink et al., 1994).

Protocol Analysis

Subsequent verbalization like thought-listing techniques and concurrent verbalization are both types of protocol analysis. For the study of candidate images, these can be useful in numerous ways. First, they can serve as dependent variables when the researcher wishes to see what effects there are for incoming campaign messages. Second, they can serve as independent variables when the researchers want to test image effects on voting or other cognitive structures such as attitudes. Third, they can serve as moderating variables or intervening variables in various models linking messages to behaviors such as voting choices.

In open-ended cognitive response measurement, all thoughts are encouraged as long as they are relevant to the research being done because the researcher seeks to minimize biased reporting by subjects.

Response Latency

Response latency measures show how long it takes for a subject to produce a response to a stimulus (Greene, 1988). If one takes a longer time to produce such a response, the researcher may infer that there is less salience to the memory structure because it takes longer to access. While it may not be immediately apparent how this could be applied to image research, it should be possible for testing relative strengths or salience of image components.

One use of response latency testing is to measure attitude accessibility. By measuring how long it takes for a person to respond to questions about how they like or dislike a subject, it is assumed that this reflects how accessible the attitude is from memory (Fazio & Roskos-Ewoldsen, 1994). Because images are also cognitive structures within the cognitive system, there may some utility to test how salient or how accessible certain aspects of image content are with the same method. However, the utility of this possible image test has yet to be attempted and assessed.

Concurrent Verbalizing

Rather than having subjects write down responses after message presentations, it is possible to have them speak aloud while they view or hear messages. Having subjects verbalize thoughts while they engage in a particular activity is a method known as protocol analysis (Frey, Botan, & Kreps, 2000).

With all of the methods just described, it is possible to also use content analysis and discourse analysis to code the data. We now turn to content analysis.

Content Analysis

One way to analyze open-ended responses is with content analysis (CA). Themes can be coded, as can various traits or impressions. Computerized coding programs can do coding, or coding can be done manually by two or three human coders. It is important for the researcher in the latter case to calculate and describe the intercoder reliability using appropriate formulae for doing so.

Content analysis is defined as systematic, quantitative analysis of communication or message content. It is also the analysis of manifest visible communication content, not motives or reasons behind content. Content analysis involves systematic procedures for analyzing recorded content and consists of procedures for categorizing communication content for the purpose of measuring variables and testing the significance of relationships among variables.

Content analysis tabulates countable data in the form of words, images, phrases, speech acts, meaning units, sentences, or whatever other kind of unit of enumeration the researchers consider most important. Units of enumeration are the numerical count used for coding the units of analysis. For example, one might code words (units of analysis) within a sample of paragraphs (units of analysis). The units of enumeration are surface-structure units of discourse. Content analysis generally does not analyze deep-structure units of communication.

Political Discourse Analysis

Discourse analysis (DA) is concerned with discourse processing and sociocognitive phenomena in communication. It should not be confused with either rhetorical or literary criticism. Language-in-use, that is, discourse, is the primary subject matter of DA, but because there is a sociocognitive concern to DA, three components must be accounted for: sender, receiver, and receivers. Whatever is considered content/messages in communication can be examined as discourse.

A discourse analysis (DA) strives to reveal structures of meaning and the function of those structures and meanings with a global as well as a local context. Both production and comprehension/interpretation are accounted for in a DA, even if one side is of more concern than the other.

Teune van Dijk (1998) argues that cognitive concepts can be discovered in how they explain language use. Discourse features reflect underlying mental and cognitive structures. A theoretical view does what has been neglected—explain the specific structures and operations of an ideology.

A DA looks, therefore, not only for surface structures and deeper structures explaining the surface structures, but also for principles and rules that guide the production and comprehension of discourse. Discourse production and discourse comprehension are not simple matters of either direct representation or direct interpretation. Instead, both processes involve aspects of cognition and memory, which add aspects of reconstruction to both sides.

Comprehension: Messages perceived —— messages reconstructed —— memory
Production: Memory —— messages reconstructed —— messages presented

All human communication involves discourse processing if the message exchange is at all symbolic.

From a DA methodology, political perception works as follows. Within the mind, we have a control system that regulates the flow of information between short-term memory and long-term memory. This control system has goals for any given episode of communication or perception (e.g., "I will watch TV news to get polling data"). Stored knowledge and ideologies are related to control. Episodic memory (part of long-term memory used for all incoming experiences) reminds us of events that occurred in the past few days. Schemata that are relevant to the structure of the received discourse are activated. This activation is accompanied by the activation of scripts and frames.

Connotations of words illustrate how some of this works. If you hear that someone is a "sympathizer," a macrostructure that is negatively associated with this term may exert more influence that the word itself, which lexically is neutral. Lexicalization is both a surface-structure and deep-structure phenomenon. The deeper aspects involve semantics. Political discourse involves descriptions, alleged facts, propositions, ways of organizing the discourse (such as moving inductively or deductively), facts or claims, contrasts, denials, generalizations, and so on, and so on. All of these are of interest to those doing DA. It is important that a DA be structured itself into levels of analysis, however.

Applying DA to candidate images may involve tracking how communication, whether in media or interpersonal forms, generates ways of thinking and speaking about candidates and elections. This approach assumes that voters shape their images in relation to discourse, that images are malleable up to a certain point in a presidential campaign, and that language and thought are closely related.

Possible Problems with Cognitive Measurement

With cognitive response measurement, there are possible problems in rates of speaking, thinking, and verbalizing. Speaking is faster than writing, and the brain processes messages faster than the rate of speech and the rate of writing. If one stops the message presentation to let people write or speak their responses, there may be a distraction effect. While concurrent verbalization has the advantage of real-time thoughts in relation to real-time messages being presented, there is a problem of thoughts interacting with presented message content. Still, these measures are useful, and many researchers consider them as reliable and valid as traditional quantitative scales like Likert-type items and semantic differential items.

Another possible problem with cognitive measurement is how to best gather voter data that involve little thought but may be producing important components of candidate images.

It is common to hear criticisms of cognitive measurement, in part because cognitions can only be measured indirectly. Some critics also argue that verbal reports are problematic because subjects do not have access to their higher-order cognitive processes (Benoit & Benoit, 1986). Despite these limitations, however, researchers note that the usefulness of verbal reports depends on how the reports are elicited (Benoit & Benoit, 1986). Verbal reports of attitudes have been found to be highly correlated with behaviors (Benoit & Benoit, 1986).

Conclusion

Cognitive measures of candidate images can provide valid and reliable means to discover image components and ways in which images change in relation to specific sets of messages. Research is needed to find out what kinds of cognitive response are most likely to affect image formation.

Cognitive responding is not just about valenced reactions to messages but also about symbolic manipulation and integration of impressions into existing schemata. One advantage of the various methods described in this chapter is the capturing of image components that are more voter-determined than researcher-determined. Additionally, the frequency-count nature of some of these methods allows a kind of weighting for which image components are relatively most important to voters who hold these images.

Notes

1. A cognitive approach to images differs from source credibility, attitude, and personality approaches in that the cognitive approach is more inclusive of any impressions that voters store about candidates and use in evaluating the candidates.

2. Perhaps one answer to the still-unanswered question about the difference between attitude and image might lie in the fact that the formation of cognitive responses changes valence and/or intensity of attitudes. This suggests that images are most likely more like schemata for candidates than merely candidate attitudes.

3. Lag sequential analysis involves predictions of certain types of content from other types at various times. Protocol analysis involves gathering verbalization during an event or task.

4. The study of images in relationship to messages is what distinguishes political communication research on images from studies on this topic in political psychology.

5. Such conceptual clarification may help to build the vocabulary of political image research by refining differences in concepts and their assumed differences in structural components and functions.

6. If this is true, there should be higher correlations between attitudes and vote than between image items and vote.

References

Benoit, Pamela, and William Benoit. 1986. "Consciousness: The Mindlessness/Mindfulness and Verbal Report Controversies." *Western Journal of Speech Communication* 50: 41–63.

Brock, T. C. 1967. "Communication Discrepancy and Intent to Persuade as Determinants of Counterargument Production." *Journal of Experimental Social Psychology* 3: 296–309.

Fazio, Russell, and David Roskos-Ewoldsen. 1994. "Acting as We Feel." In *Persuasion: Psychological Insights and Perspectives*, edited by Sharon Shavitt and Timothy Brock, 71–93. Boston: Allyn & Bacon.

Flanigan, William. H., and Nancy Zingale. 1998. *Political Behavior of the American Electorate*. Washington, D.C.: Congressional Quarterly Press.

Fleming, Monique, and Richard Petty. 2000. "Identity and Persuasion: An Elaboration Likelihood Approach." In *Attitudes, Behavior, and Social Context: The Role of Norms and Group Membership*, edited by Deborah J. Terry and Michael A. Hogg, 171–199. Mahwah, N.J.: Lawrence Erlbaum.

Frey, Lawrence, Carl Botan, and Gary Kreps. 2000. *Investigating Communication: An Introduction to Research Methods*. Boston: Allyn & Bacon.

Greene, John. 1988. "Cognitive Processes: Methods for Probing the Black Box." In *A Handbook for the Study of Human Communication*, edited by Charles Tardy, 37–66. Norwood, N.J.: Ablex Publishing.

Greenwald, A. G. 1968. "Cognitive Learning, Cognitive Response to Persuasion, and Attitude Change." In *Psychological Foundations of Attitudes*, edited by A. G. Greenwald, T. C. Brock, and T. M. Ostrom, 147–170. New York: Academic Press.

Griffin, Em. 2000. *A First Look at Communication Theory*. Boston: McGraw-Hill.

Hacker, Kenneth. 1995. "Interpersonal Communication and the Formation of Candidate Images." In *Candidate Images in Presidential Elections*, edited by Kenneth Hacker, 65–82. New York: Praeger.

Hacker, Kenneth L., Walter R. Zakahi, Maury J. Giles, and Shaun McQuitty. 2000. "Components of Candidate Images: Statistical Analysis of the Issue-Persona Dichotomy in the Presidential Campaign of 1996." *Communication Monographs* 67: 227–238.

O'Keefe, Daniel. 2002. *Persuasion: Theory and Research*. Thousand Oaks, Calif.: Sage.

Ostrom, T. M., C. Bond, J. A. Krosnick, and C. Sedikides. 1994. "Attitude Scales: How We Measure the Unmeasurable." In *Persuasion, Psychological Insights and Perspectives*, edited by S. Shavitt and T. C. Brock. Boston: Allyn & Bacon.

Perloff, Richard. 1993. *Political Communication*. Mahwah, N.J.: Lawrence Erlbaum.

———. 2003. *The Dynamics of Persuasion*. Mahwah, N.J.: Lawrence Erlbaum.

Petty, Richard E., and John T. Cacioppo. 1981. *Attitudes and Persuasion: Classic and Contemporary Approaches*. Dubuque, Iowa: Wm. C. Brown.

Pfau, Michael. 2002. "The Subtle Nature of Presidential Debate Influence." *Argumentation and Debate* 38: 251–261.

van Dijk, Teune. 1998. *Ideology*. London: Sage.

Wansink, Brian, Michael Ray, and Rajeev Batra. 1994. "Increasing Cognitive Response Sensitivity." *Journal of Advertising* 23: 62–74.

Way, B. M., and R. D. Masters. 1996. "Emotion and Cognition in Political Information-Processing." *Journal of Communication* 46: 48–65.

11

Measuring Candidate Images with Semantic Differentials

Lynda Lee Kaid

UNLIKE POLITICAL OBSERVERS who have popularized the term political "image" as a nebulous and vague concept, scholars have generally agreed that candidate image is actually a complex construct that reflects both what a candidate projects and a voter perceives. The complexity of the concept and the need to consider this multiplicity of image construction have led researchers to many ways of measuring political candidate images. Of the many approaches developed over the past five decades of empirical political image research, the semantic differential scale has become one of the most well-accepted measuring devices.

Development of the Semantic Differential

Charles Osgood, George Suci, and Percy Tannenbaum (1957) are generally credited with the development of semantic differential scales "to measure meaning." They argued that a series of bipolar adjectives could be used to define semantic space and represent the dimensions of meaning in regard to a concept. Applying their system to political "person" and "issue" concepts, they successfully used semantic differential scales in the 1952 presidential election, eliciting dimensions of semantic differentiation that conformed to their general dimensions of evaluation, potency, and activity. Although they used ten bipolar adjective scales (wise-foolish, dirty-clean, fair-unfair, safe-dangerous, strong-weak, deep-shallow, active-passive, cool-warm, relaxed-tense, and idealistic-realistic), they found that three items could be used to represent the overall scale: fair-unfair for evaluation, strong-weak for potency, and active-passive for activity (Osgood et al., 1957, p. 107).

After the pioneering work of Osgood et al. (1957), a host of researchers began using semantic differentials as a technique for measuring candidate image. Some early users such as Joseph and Marion McGrath (1962) developed their own list of bipolar adjectives (in this case, a fifty-item set of scales). Others (Anderson & Bass, 1967; Rosenbaum & McGinnies, 1969; Stricker, 1963) based their scale choices on the original work of Osgood et al. (1957), sometimes adapting and reconfiguring particular items to represent broader conceptualizations of image factors.

In closely related work, communication researchers developed semantic differential scales to measure the concept called *ethos* or *source credibility* (Andersen & Clevenger, 1963). Many early empirical researchers used the semantic differential technique to uncover dimensions of source credibility for public figures in much the same way that political communication researchers used the scales to measure "candidate image." Early pioneers in this work, such as James McCroskey (1966) and David Berlo, James Lemert, and Robert Mertz (1969–1970), used a variety of scales and factor analysis to investigate image structures.

Uses of Semantic Differential Scales

In political image research, semantic differential scales have been used in two basic ways. First, sets of items (usually bipolar adjectives rated on six- or seven-point scales) have been summed to provide a kind of overall evaluation of candidate image. These sums are interpreted as representing positive or negative evaluations, or perhaps increases or decreases in the favorableness of a candidate's image (Anderson & Bass, 1967). Sometimes these sum scores are used to test differences in pretest/post-test images resulting from exposure to a particular communication stimulus (Garramone, 1986; Kaid & Hirsch, 1973; Kaid & Sanders, 1978; Kaid, Singleton, & Davis, 1977; Sanders & Pace, 1977; Thorson, Christ, & Caywood, 1991). In other cases, the scores are used to look at changes in image structures over longer periods of time. Samuel Mudd and Alan Pohlman (1976) used a series of semantic differential scales to measure changes in images of 1972 presidential candidates and concluded that such scales can be used "to detect change in profile level and clarity [of candidate image] across time" (p. 228).

The use of the semantic differential approach to measure changes in candidate images across time also acknowledges the notion that candidate images are not static concepts. Rather, "The 'image' of the source is dynamic in that it both influences and is influenced by the communication event" (Berlo et al., 1969–1970, p. 576).

In their summary form, as gestalt measures of candidate images, semantic differential scales can also be used to correlate with other important measures of voter decision-making processes. For instance, Susan Hellweg and Stephen King (1983) have shown that the comparative evaluation of candidate images on semantic differential scales can predict voting behavior choices. Other researchers have used such image scales to test for the ability to discriminate among candidate qualities and to relate these discriminations to media effects and voting behavior (Choi & Becker, 1987).

Second, semantic differential scale items have been factor-analyzed to suggest dimensions of candidate image. As researchers came to accept semantic differentials to measure image, more attention was focused on the development of factor structures, and attempts were made to suggest interrelationships between sets of items or adjectives and representations of differential aspects of candidate images. For instance, Jack Douglas (1972) developed a much more diverse set of image factors that did not fall into the three basic dimensions of evaluation, potency, and activity outlined by Osgood et al. (1957). Bill Kjeldahl, Carl Carmichael, and Robert Mertz (1971) also used factor analysis on a set of thirty-nine bipolar adjectives measuring candidate image and concluded that the items fell into five different factors. Other researchers developed additional factor structures (Roberts, 1973), while yet other researchers argued for the use of semantic differentials with Q-analytic techniques as a way of grouping individuals with similar image evaluations of candidates (Marr, 1973).

When semantic differentials have been used to look at factors or dimensions of candidate image, many researchers have concluded that most candidate images are made up of three to five factors. Generally, an evaluative factor (sometimes called performance, experience, or credibility) is dominant and accounts for the largest amount of variance in the candidate's image. Such factors are similar to the "authoritativeness" or "competence" factors of source credibility–measurement devices. The second most common factor may be a style or demeanor or appearance factor. Sometimes researchers have distinguished between scales that seem to represent a personal image and those that represent a political image. While there is no absolute agreement on what scales make up these factors, there is a general trend toward a reduction in the number of items and the number of factors needed in a semantic differential in order to adequately represent a candidate's image. Few researchers now use more than ten to twelve individual items in a scale.

Suggestions for Future Research

Although semantic differential scales, both as summary measures of evaluation and to suggest factorial dimensions, have become an accepted way of measuring candidate image, a major problem has been the failure of researchers to settle on one or more standard semantic differential scale sets that can be used repeatedly and replicably, permitting comparison across studies. Most semantic differentials measuring candidate image are "born anew" with each new candidate image study.

One solution to this unsystematic generation of scales would be for researchers to adopt a uniform scale that might generate comparable data over time. The scale suggested here has been used, with some variations and adaptations, for nearly three decades. The result of extensive testing since 1968, this scale was derived from tests and factor analysis of an initial set of forty-five scales at Southern Illinois University and subsequently tested in real political campaigns (Kaid & Hirsch, 1973; Kaid et al., 1977; Sanders & Pace, 1977).

This scale (see figure 11.1) and its versions have been used by researchers to measure candidate image with great success in numerous situations. The twelve-item scale generally achieves high levels of reliability with Cronbach's alpha levels ranging from .83 (Kaid, Downs, & Ragan, 1990) to as high as .92 (Kaid, Leland, & Whitney, 1992). The scale has also been successfully transferred across cultures and used in studies of candidate image in other countries, although reliability levels have sometimes been lower (Kaid, 1991; Kaid & Holtz-Bacha, 1993).

The adoption of this or some other accepted scale for measuring candidate image across studies would help researchers to establish more reliable and dependable measures of this complex concept. Researchers could then concen-

	1 2 3 4 5 6 7	
UNQUALIFIED:	___:___:___:___:___:___:___:	QUALIFIED
UNSOPHISTICATED:	___:___:___:___:___:___:___:	SOPHISTICATED
DISHONEST:	___:___:___:___:___:___:___:	HONEST
BELIEVABLE:	___:___:___:___:___:___:___:	UNBELIEVABLE
UNSUCCESSFUL:	___:___:___:___:___:___:___:	SUCCESSFUL
ATTRACTIVE:	___:___:___:___:___:___:___:	UNATTRACTIVE
UNFRIENDLY:	___:___:___:___:___:___:___:	FRIENDLY
INSINCERE:	___:___:___:___:___:___:___:	SINCERE
CALM:	___:___:___:___:___:___:___:	EXCITABLE
AGGRESSIVE:	___:___:___:___:___:___:___:	UNAGGRESSIVE
STRONG:	___:___:___:___:___:___:___:	WEAK
INACTIVE:	___:___:___:___:___:___:___:	ACTIVE

FIGURE 11.1
Semantic Differential Scale to Measure Candidate Image

Note: In earlier studies, the scales "serious-not serious," "spender-saver," "modern-old-fashioned," and "conservative-liberal" were sometimes substituted for "aggressive-unaggressive," "active-inactive," "strong-weak," and "believable-unbelievable." Earlier versions also sometimes used "handsome-ugly" in place of "attractive-unattractive."

trate on developing factoral structures and testing replicably the effects of various communication stimuli on candidate image formation.

References

Andersen, K., and T. Clevenger. 1963. "A Summary of Experimental Research in Ethos." *Speech Monographs* 30 (June): 59–78.

Anderson, L. R., and A. R. Bass. 1967. "Some Effects of Victory or Defeat upon Perception of Political Candidates." *Journal of Social Psychology* 73: 227–240.

Berlo, D. K., J. B. Lemert, and R. J. Mertz. 1969–1970. "Dimensions for Evaluating the Acceptability of Message Sources." *Public Opinion Quarterly* 33: 563–576.

Choi, H. C., and S. L. Becker. 1987. "Media Use, Issue/Image Discriminations, and Voting." *Communication Research* 14: 267–291.

Douglas, J. 1972. "The Verbal Image: Student Perceptions of Political Figures." *Speech Monographs* 39: 1–15.

Garramone, G. 1986. "Candidate Image Formation: The Role of Information Processing. In *New Perspectives on Political Advertising*, edited by L. L. Kaid, D. Nimmo, and K. R. Sanders, 235–247. Carbondale: Southern Illinois University Press.

Hellweg, S. A., and S. W. King. 1983. "Comparative Evaluation of Political Candidates: Implications for the Voter Decision-Making Process." *Central States Speech Journal* 34: 134–138.

Kaid, L. L. 1991. "The Effects of Television Broadcasts on Perceptions of Political Candidates in the United States and France." In *Mediated Politics in Two Cultures: Presidential Campaigning in the United States and France*, edited by L. L. Kaid, J. Gerstlé, and K. R. Sanders, 247–260. New York: Praeger.

Kaid, L. L., V. C. Downs, and R. Ragan. 1990. "Political Argumentation and Violations of Audience Expectations: An Analysis of the Bush-Rather Encounter." *Journal of Broadcasting and Electronic Media* 34: 1–15.

Kaid, L. L., and R. O. Hirsch. 1973. "Selective Exposure and Candidate Image: A Field Study over Time." *Central States Speech Journal* 24: 48–51.

Kaid, L. L., and C. Holtz-Bacha. 1993. "Audience Reactions to Televised Political Programs: An Experimental Study of the 1990 German National Election." *European Journal of Communication* 8: 77–99.

Kaid, L. L., C. M. Leland, and S. Whitney. 1992. "The Impact of Televised Political Ads: Evoking Viewer Responses in the 1988 Presidential Campaign." *Southern Communication Journal* 57: 285–295.

Kaid, L. L., and K. R. Sanders. 1978. "Political Television Commercials: An Experimental Study of Type and Length." *Communication Research* 5: 57–70.

Kaid, L. L., D. L. Singleton, and D. Davis. 1977. "Instant Analysis of Televised Political Addresses: The Speaker versus the Commentator." In *Communication Yearbook I*, edited by B. Ruben, 453–464. New Brunswick, N.J.: Transaction.

Kjeldahl, B. O., C. W. Carmichael, and R. J. Mertz. 1971. "Factors in a Presidential Candidate's Image." *Speech Monographs* 38: 129–181.

Marr, T. J. 1973. "Q and R Analysis of Panel Data on Political Candidate Image and Voter Communication." *Speech Monographs* 40: 56–65.

McCroskey, James C. 1966. "Scales for the Measurement of Ethos." *Speech Monographs* 33 (March): 65–72.

McGrath, J. E., and M. F. McGrath. 1962. "Effects of Partisanship on Perceptions of Political Figures." *Public Opinion Quarterly* 26: 236–248.

Mudd, S., and A. Pohlman. 1976. "Sensitivity of Image Profile and Image Clarity Measures to Change: Nixon through Watergate." *Journal of Applied Psychology* 61: 223–228.

Osgood, C. E., G. J. Suci, and P. H. Tannenbaum. 1957. *The Measurement of Meaning*. Urbana: University of Illinois Press.

Roberts, C. 1973. "Voting Intentions and Attitude Change in a Congressional Election." *Speech Monographs* 40: 49–55.

Rosenbaum, L. L., and E. McGinnies. 1969. "A Semantic Differential Analysis of Concept Associated with the 1964 Presidential Election." *Journal of Social Psychology* 78: 227–235.

Sanders, K. R., and T. J. Pace. 1977. "The Influence of Speech Communication on the Image of a Political Candidate: 'Limited Effects' Revisited." In *Communication Yearbook I*, edited by B. Ruben, 465–472. New Brunswick, N.J.: Transaction.

Stricker, G. 1963. "The Use of the Semantic Differential to Predict Voting Behavior." *Journal of Social Psychology* 59: 159–167.

Thorson, E., W. G. Christ, and C. Caywood. 1991. "Selling Candidates like Tubes of Toothpaste: Is the Comparison Apt?" In *Television and Political Advertising*, vol. 1, edited by F. Biocca, 145–172. Hillsdale, N.J.: Lawrence Erlbaum.

Conclusion: Present and Future Directions for Presidential Candidate Image Research

Kenneth L. Hacker

IN THE 1995 VOLUME ON CANDIDATE IMAGES, we learned many interesting structural facts about presidential candidate images (PCI). Today, we have more information about candidate image structure and contents and also about image-formation processeses. Concurrently, we have seen that the recent arguments made claiming that campaigns and short-term voting determinants are not important have been usurped by empirical generalizations that show the contrary. Evidence today supports long-standing views that there are essential contributions of communication and image formation to voting decisions. Presidential candidate images are repeatedly found to be important constructs in voting and political communication research by scholars in both communication science and political science.

Jay P. Greene (1993) takes some of the shine off of the infamous vote forecasting models by noting that they are based on multiple regression equations that include important predictor variables but that are often wrong. With his model, for example, Ray Fair projected that George Bush Sr. would badly beat Bill Clinton in 1992 (Greene, 1993). The trouble with these models is their assumption that campaigning does not matter. This is somewhat ironic since they include such "fundamentals" as presidential popularity or presidential job approval. Voter perceptions of liking or disliking a president as a person (popularity) or approving or disapproving of a president's record in office (job approval) cannot possibly be independent of communication and messages encountered in mass media news, political advertising, and interpersonal conversations.

As many scholars have observed, even small changes in voter preferences can have large effects on elections. While factors like partisan identification are undeniably forceful for most voters, there is always that block of voters entailing undecided, independent, or swing voters who can move the election victory toward one candidate and away from the others. Fine-grained analysis of elections shows that presidential campaigns are won largely on the basis of partisanship and ideological fundamentals but that these factors are made more or less salient through campaign communication, and many of the independent or swing voters are likely to be more influenced by the processes of campaign persuasion than by simple party identification. These latter voters are the ones who commonly say that they vote for the person, not the party. As witnessed historically with Reagan Democrats and Clinton Republicans, campaigns certainly do matter.

There are many types of impressions that impinge on candidate images and contribute to their formation. Arguably, any type of impression, once stored, is a possible component of a presidential candidate image or at least affects other components in the image. Yet we have seen that researchers are looking for patterns in what inputs are most important as determinants of voting. This has led to the fairly common assumption today that voting results from one major long-term factor (party identification) and two major short-term factors (candidate issue positions and candidate character).

The study of presidential candidate images goes back to at least the 1970s (Hellweg, this volume). During the decades of candidate image research, there have been at least three major areas of divergence in how images are defined and measured. For example, some scholars believe that voters compare candidates against an ideal presidential candidate image, while others argue that each candidate is evaluated against candidate-specific criteria (Hellweg, this volume).

A second area of contention concerns the degree of importance of issues in how voters evaluate candidates and form images of them. Many experts believe that issues are simply not important in candidate evaluations and images. Others say they are critical. Some argue that candidate positions on issues generate candidate persona or character impressions (Hellweg, this volume). Another area of divergence concerns the assumption that images do not include candidate issue positions. This assumption has been widely challenged with empirical testing (Hellweg, this volume). Future studies need to ascertain why some scholars still believe that issues do not affect images or function as components of images when many studies show that issue positions and persona impressions are highly correlated. Many scholars in both communication science and political science today view issues and persona as both significantly influencing voting decisions. There is a common assertion in today's candidate image literature about issues that consist of essential character traits such as honesty, strong leadership abilities, and so on being used by candidate and voters to construct the candidate images. A different view is that issue positions taken by candidates may indeed have this effect, but they still have significant associations with traits that partially make up the candidates' images.

Researchers have found that sincerity is one of the most important attributes of presidential candidate images (Benoit & McHale, this volume). This is an important finding for many reasons including the need we have to sort out which kinds of candidate traits appear to be most important for voters when making their choices among presidential candidates. More research is needed to see how candidate traits change in salience in relationship to political environment and historical circumstances. While persona and issue positions are not orthogonal, it appears in the results of many studies that issue positions are used by candidates to generate general character perceptions (Funk, this volume). Some candidates are likely to benefit from positions on issues themselves and then from persona impressions that are attributed to their stands on the issues (Funk, this volume). Carolyn Funk has shown the importance of image changes in relation to scandals that plague a presidential administration.

While honesty and sincerity are key attributes in candidate images, there is an argument that voters also prefer candidates who appear the most genuine or authentic (Louden & McCauliff, this volume). The degree of perceived authenticity of voters may be assessed during debates, speeches, and other opportunities for observation of how true to themselves candidates appear to be (Louden & McCauliff, this volume). The concept of authenticity argued by Louden and McCauliff (this volume) opens up doors to testing new dimensions of candidate evaluation that go beyond the traditional measured traits of honesty, sincerity, and so on. Empirical testing can determine how important this trait is in relation to previously discovered traits that voters consider important in presidential candidates.

For decades, there have been studies about candidate images from preferred conceptual and operational views, and these studies have provided useful knowledge about the nature of images. However, there is still little effort in most candidate image work to formulate theories of candidate image formation or to clarify how the image construct differs from other information processing or constructs. One reason that there has been little progress in formulating theories and models of candidate image formation is that extant theories from the social sciences have been rarely employed in candidate image research. There is some movement in this direction, however, as evidenced in the work of Benoit and associates on functional theory (Benoit & McHale, this volume), models in political science that attempt to indicate how voters reach decisions about presidential candidates, and Hacker's (this volume) attempt to bring the elaboration likelihood model (ELM) from persuasion theory into discussions about image formation. Hacker (this volume) seeks to map out some possible theoretical directions for linking dual processes into single explanations of candidate image formation or change. The arguments remain at the level of informed speculation and need testing with various forms of research to create models of image formation and change. There may be nothing wrong with scratching the surface when you are at the surface.

Kaid and Chanslor (this volume) make the strong argument that Nimmo and Savage (1976) were correct in asserting that candidate images result from an interaction of existing voter knowledge and messages presented by the candidates. While this is a convincing argument, most candidate images are not measuring this kind of interaction but are relying more on source credibility scales or measures that are voter determined. Because of the fact that it is now known that campaigns generate learning effects more than direct behavioral effects, we are gaining more specific knowledge today about how particular types of campaign messages are affecting voters' images. It is clear that TV spots have causal effects on images and that those images are correlated with voting decisions (Kaid & Chanslor, this volume).

Walter Zakahi shows how presidential TV debates contribute to the presidential candidate image-formation process. This includes the effects of negotiations from communication about whether debates will occur and then about their actual formats. Other interesting influences on the images of the presidential candidates is what are known as "defining moments" in the debates. Then, of course, there are substantial impressions that are created when the actual candidate debates occur (Zakahi, this volume).

Timothy Stephen, Teresa Harrison, William Husson, and David Albert (this volume) observe how interpersonal communication behaviors of the candidates can affect images and how these effects can overpower candidates' positions on issues. This seems consistent with Zakahi's observations about the power of defining moments.

In their discussion of meta-analysis procedures, Susan Hellweg and Brian Spitzberg (this volume) argue that this statistical method can help candidate image researchers to aggregate findings across numerous candidate image studies. This application allows a summarizing of effects sizes across studies. Hacker (this volume) suggests that cognitive response measures from persuasion, content analysis, and discourse analytic procedures can all be used for gathering data about candidate images in an open-ended manner. Kaid once again demonstrates how useful the semantic differential is for tracking image changes related to changes in message stimuli.

No matter how much we look at the candidate evaluation process or candidate evaluation constructs like schemata, attitudes, and images, we find important points of divergence and convergence. Across various studies, including those in this book, we see the following points of agreement regarding presidential candidate images. Messages in presidential campaigns have indirect effects on voting through changes they cause in the candidate images and related cognitive constructs and psychological factors. Winners of presidential election campaigns are most likely the candidates who were best able to generate the most positive candidate images in relation to their competitors. All of the message sources during a presidential campaign, whether advertising, candidate speeches, debates, or the like, affect or modify the presidential candidate images. The points of divergence are especially interesting because they make clear where new lines of research are needed. While some researchers continue to split candidate issue impressions from candidate persona impressions and equate candidate images with the latter, others see candidate images as composite structures including both candidate issue impressions and candidate persona impressions.

Needed Research

There is a great need to clarify the specific nature of presidential candidate images (PCIs) in relation to other cognitive constructs. This remains a neglected area for serious study in political communication research. Despite the rigorous research conducted in PCI studies, there is still a neglect of how PCIs are related to other elements in cognitive systems and how the components of PCIs are relatively weighted by voters if they are. There are statements that recognize these issues, but little data analysis that addresses them.

There are some reports that relate voting decisions to candidate schemata while ignoring candidate images. These studies are just as flawed as the image studies that ignore candidate schemata and suffer from the simple problem of overly narrow focus on single constructs. This is a sharp criticism intended to open up the lens used by voting researchers.

In the introduction of this book, I noted that all of the chapter authors had been asked to address certain PCI issues. These issues were (1) how candidate image can be more precisely defined as a construct; (2) how candidate images originate and change over time (again, authors were asked to account for this); (3) why candidate image is a useful construct as opposed to other constructs such as candidate schemata, political attitudes, or simply candidate evaluations; (4) why there has been so much discrepancy in the conceptual and operational definitions of candidate images; (5) what specific processes of communication during campaigns appear to be most related to the formation of candidate images; (6) how, as candidate images form, they differ in structure and content; and (7) how candidate images relate to the long-term factors, such as ideologies and partisanship, that influence voter decision making.

There remains little progress in differentiating candidate images from other constructs such as schemata and attitudes. Measurement issues are still a thorny issue in candidate image research, and there is still conflict among definitions, both conceptual and operational. Still, there is increased recognition that components of images once thought to be independent are now recognized as interrelated. This is most obvious for candidate issue positions and candidate persona impressions. The competition among definitions may be less of a problem than it was in the past, since measures are more refined today and competition within the social sciences for any given construct is a constant. This does not suggest, however, that we should not expect more convergence among definitions as research goes forward.

The time has arrived to refine the conceptual and operational descriptions of the elements making up candidate images beyond simplistic categories of either candidate issue impressions (CII) or candidate persona impressions (CPI). Even with dual-process or multiple-process models of PCI formation, there are most likely multiple sets of voter impressions making up both categories and having specific importance in themselves. Two examples of this are retrospective voting and prospective voting.

In presidential campaigns, voters choose between two competitors or between one challenger and one incumbent. One type of issues position processing (CII) is known as retrospective voting and consists of evaluating the record of the incumbent during the past four years (Abrahamson, Aldrich, & Rohde, 2001). As Bush runs for reelection in 2004, he will be evaluated somewhat differently by voters than he was in 2000 if personality was far more important than issues in 2000. Every running incumbent has to face this fact. For competitors, challengers, and incumbents, voters also engage in another CII process that is known as prospective voting. Prospective voting involves an assessment of issues and promises made by both (or all) the candidates about those issues (Abrahamson et al., 2001).

More study is needed regarding image-formation processes, stages of image formation in relation to stages of presidential campaigns, and how images are changed in relation to circumstances and competition.

All presidential campaigns must involve what is known as response shaping. It is also known as image building. Those who are uninformed do not have much resistance, but this does not mean that they have motivation. Both are challenges for the presidential candidate. Image building can be seen as close to the tasks of most persuasion whether the persuasion is political, social action, or commercial. The common activities are shown in table C.1.

Practitioners know that they must direct the image-formation process in order to win a presidential election. This includes building cognitions, shap-

TABLE C.1
Three Stages of Presidential Candidate Image Formation

Attitude Formation Objective	Attitude Intensification Objective	Attitude Conversion Objective
Response Shaping	*Response Reinforcing*	*Response Changing*
Informing/persuading	Arguments	Cognitive dissonance
Image building	Image reinforcement	Image alteration
Impressions	Incentives	Motivation
Beliefs and knowledge	Social norms and interpersonal communication	Interpersonal and mass support system
Noncommitment	Acceptance latitude	Rejection latitude
Beliefs/cognitions	Attitudes/images	Values

ing images, using beliefs to accumulate into attitudes toward the candidates, targeting messages toward problematic beliefs, and associating one's candidate to key values held by voters.

Ethics and PCI Formation

Ethics issues are seldom raised in discussions about candidate images. Yet such discussions are needed since political consultants are continuously using communication strategies and tactics to shape images. Wayne (1992) notes that those voters who can be most easily persuaded are those with the least knowledge about the election. Political efficacy in the United States has declined and is still very low.

Presidential candidate images should not be reduced to simple lists of traits, issue positions, or combinations of both despite the fact that this has been the nature of most image research thus far. We have indications that such approaches are simply insufficient to capture the multidimensional aspects of candidate images.

The Kennedy–Nixon debates, which were the first of the modern televised presidential debates, were more substantive than subsequent presidential debates, yet most of the journalistic and academic coverage of those debates was about stylistic issues such as lighting, makeup, and Richard Nixon's five o'clock shadow (Waterman, Wright, & St. Clair, 1999). Issues can be generated from polling data and focus groups, and these may not be the strongest concerns for the voters. Such issues can be used by political consultants directing candidate communication to differentiate candidates enough to create shifts in support.

One large ethical problem is that public opinion dominates the formulation of policies. This creates what are called wet-finger politicians. Voters think less about platforms and more about thin issues and large personalities. However, as we learn more about how images are formed and how they are manipulated, scholars can offer more knowledge to voters about how they are shaping their voting choices, how they can gain more control over the inputs that end up as components of their presidential candidate images, and how the next president enters the White House as the result of how voters process messages in the campaign.

References

Abrahamson, Paul, John Aldrich, and David Rohde. 2001. *Change and Continuity.* Washington, D.C.: Congressional Quarterly Press.

Greene, Jay. 1993. "Forecasting Follies." *American Prospect* 4. http://www.prospect.org/print/V4/15/greene-j.html.

Nimmo, Dan, and Robert L. Savage. 1976. *Candidates and Their Images: Concepts, Methods, and Findings.* Pacific Palisades, Calif.: Goodyear.

Waterman, Richard, Robert Wright, and Gilbert St. Clair. 1999. *The Image-Is-Everything Presidency: Dilemmas in American Leadership.* Boulder, Colo.: Westview Press.

Wayne, Stephen W. 1992. *The Road to the White House.* New York: St. Martin's Press.

Index

agenda setting, 14, 35, 96
attitudes, 2, 4, 108, 120, 121, 126, 127, 206, 211, 212,214, 217, 218, 219, 221, 240
attitude accessibility, 108
attitude homophily, 23, 26, 30, 87

Biden, Joe, 77
Bush, George, H. W., 11, 12, 16, 27, 33, 34, 39, 57, 60, 135, 138, 140, 142, 152, 153, 154, 155, 159, 160, 161, 162, 163, 164, 165, 166, 167, 171, 182, 183, 185, 191, 237
Bush, G. W., 5, 6, 7, 8, 9, 13, 16, 68, 73, 77, 85, 93, 97, 99, 105, 106, 107, 120, 127, 128, 142, 143, 151, 152, 156, 157, 158, 162, 164, 167, 169, 170, 171

calculated authenticity, 91
campaign promises, 51
Carter, Jimmy, 24, 27, 33, 39, 57, 105, 151, 15
characterological coherence, 94, 95
charisma, 31, 52, 134
Clinton, Bill, 7, 9, 11, 12, 15, 16, 39, 40, 50, 57, 60, 65, 68, 69, 70, 72, 73, 74, 76, 77, 85, 96, 98, 135, 136, 138, 140, 142, 152, 153, 154, 155, 159, 160, 161, 162, 164, 165, 166, 167, 171, 183, 191, 213, 237
cognitive heuristics, 119
communication behaviors of candidates, 16, 29, 87, 205, 178, 180, 181, 182, 185, 187, 190, 193, 194, 195
concordance, 55
Condit, Gary, 75
content analysis, 14
"cult of personality," 105
cybernetics, 110

defining moments, 16, 151, 249
Dole, Robert, 16, 40, 69, 98, 136, 138, 142, 154, 155, 161, 162
dual consolidation principle, 126
Dukakis, Michael, 12, 33, 140, 164, 183, 191

elite politics, 76
entertainment media, 70
ethics, 17, 243
expectations game, 160

Ford, Gerald, 159, 164
forecasting models, 12
framing, 96
functional theory, 49, 239

Gore, Al, 5, 6, 7, 8, 9, 12, 13, 67, 85, 90, 92, 93, 97, 98, 105, 106, 107, 156, 157, 158, 162, 163, 167, 169, 170, 171, 213

Hart, Gary, 15, 65, 77
heuristic mapping, 94

ideal president image, 3, 29, 31, 32, 33, 52, 194, 212, 238
ideology, 2, 7, 12, 13, 29, 121, 122, 220, 239
interpersonal communication, 180, 220
issue-image dichotomy, 27, 38, 88, 111, 134

Kennedy, John, 31, 69, 151, 159, 243
Kerry, John, 99, 100, 128

longitudinal studies, 39, 54, 56, 58, 127, 178, 179, 192

McCain, John, 8, 91, 100, 163
McGovern, George, 31, 32, 33, 35
mental models, 122, 123
Mondale, Walter, 30, 70, 159, 183, 184, 191

news media, 3, 14, 67, 70, 215
Nixon, Richard, 11, 31, 32, 33, 35, 39, 57, 69, 151, 159, 243
negativity effect, 67
nonverbal behavior of candidates, 30

partisanship, 2, 4, 7, 10, 12, 17, 75, 107, 116, 238
party images, 4

perception, 3, 11, 14, 15, 27, 35, 36, 37, 40, 49, 60, 106, 108, 129, 185, 187, 212, 226
Perot, Ross, 16, 153, 160, 183, 184
person perception, 117
persuasion, 15, 23, 106, 113, 118, 218
political efficacy, 4
political socialization, 3
prospective voting, 5

Q-methodology, 22, 32, 178, 179, 180, 233

rational campaign model, 25
rational choice models, 177
Reagan, Ronald, 24, 27, 30, 33, 34, 39, 58, 68, 85, 105, 159, 183, 184, 191
response shaping, 242
retrospective voting, 5, 242
Roosevelt, Franklin, 11

schemata, 3, 108, 120, 121, 123, 195, 214, 217, 218, 219, 226, 240, 241
single-factor models, 109
source credibility, 2, 11, 22, 30, 34, 111, 114, 116, 232
structure of candidate images, 69, 112, 120, 133, 140, 179, 187, 195, 212, 214, 215, 216, 217, 219, 220, 224, 226, 232, 237, 241
symbolic interactionism, 3

transactional process, 145

unitary decision making, 11
unitary models, 21, 24, 38

videostyle, 136
voting decisions, 2, 10, 12, 13, 15, 16, 22, 23, 25, 27, 108, 109, 115, 193, 233, 239, 244

About the Contributors

David Albert has seventeen years of professional communications and public policy experience. He holds an M.S. from Rensselaer Polytechnic Institute, an M.A. from the State University of New York at Albany, and a B.A. from Siena College.

William L. Benoit (Ph.D., Wayne State University, 1979) is professor of communication at the University of Missouri. He has published eight books (five on political communication) and over 125 articles and book chapters, many on political communication. He has published in such journals as *Communication Monographs*, *Journal of Communication*, *Quarterly Journal of Speech*, *Political Communication*, *Critical Studies in Media Communication*, *Philosophy & Rhetoric*, and *Communication Education*. He has served as the chair of the Political Communication Division of NCA and is currently editor of *Journal of Communication*.

Mike Chanslor is assistant professor of mass communication at Northeastern State University. His research specialties include political advertising content and effects, and he is the author of numerous journal articles, book chapters, and convention papers on those subjects.

Carolyn L. Funk is associate professor in the School of Government and Public Affairs and director of the Commonwealth Poll at Virginia Commonwealth University. She received her Ph.D. in social psychology from the University of California, Los Angeles. She has written extensively on candidate images and candidate evaluations; her research interests include public opinion toward candidates, policy issues, and government.

Kenneth L. Hacker (Ph.D., University of Oregon, 1986) is professor of communication studies at New Mexico State University, Las Cruces. He has two main lines of research. The first concerns political communication and presidential candidate images. The second concerns computer-mediated communication and participation in democratic political systems. He is the editor of the 1995 volume *Candidate Images in Presidential Elections* and the coeditor (with Jan van Dijk) of *Digital Democracy: Issues of Theory and Practice* (2000). He is presently doing additional research on ethical issues concerning communication about genetic variation research and the use of strategic political messages to diffuse political polarization in situations of international or intercultural conflict.

Teresa M. Harrison is professor and chair of the Department of Communication at the University at Albany. In addition to her interest in presidential candidate images, her research has focused on computer-mediated communication, democratic practices and processes, democratic organizations, and, most recently, how World Wide Web technologies can be used to promote local community development. She is managing editor of the *Electronic Journal of Communication* (www.cios.org/www/ejcrec2.htm).

Susan A. Hellweg is professor and the associate director in the School of Communication at San Diego State University. She has published more than forty articles, chapters, and monographs. With Michael Pfau and Steven Brydon, she coauthored *Televised Presidential Debates: Advocacy in Contemporary America* (1992). Dr. Hellweg has served on the editorial boards of the *Journal of Applied Communication Research*, the *Journal of Communication*, *Management Communication Quarterly*, and *Western Journal of Communication*.

William Husson is visiting assistant professor in the Department of Communication at the State University of New York at Albany. His research interests include media and politics, new communication technologies, and visual communication.

Lynda Lee Kaid is professor of telecommunication and senior associate dean of the College of Journalism and Communications at the University of Florida. She previously served as the director of the Political Communication Center and supervised the Political Commercial Archive at the University of Oklahoma. Her research specialties include political advertising and news coverage of political events. A Fulbright scholar, she has also done work on political television in several Western European countries. She is the author or editor of fourteen books, including *Videostyle in Presidential Campaigns, The Electronic Election, Civic Dialogue in the 1996 Campaign, New Perspectives on Political Advertising, Mediated Politics in Two Cultures, Political Advertising in Western Democracies,* and *Political Campaign Communication: A Bibliography and Guide to the Literature.* She has also written over 100 journal articles and book chapters and over 100 convention papers on various aspects of political communication.

Allan Louden (Ph.D., University of Southern California, 1990) is associate professor of communication at Wake Forest University. He has published in such journals as *Communication Monographs, Communication Research, Argumentation and Advocacy, Politics and Policy, Journal of Language and Social Psychology,* and *Communication Education.* He is director of debate at Wake Forest and is involved with debate program development in Eastern Europe. He also has consulted with senate and governor campaigns.

Kristen McCauliff is completing her master's degree at Wake Forest University. She graduated from Central Michigan University. She has presented several papers at the NCA conference and has pursued her interest in politics. At Wake Forest, she has served as an assistant debate coach after a distinguished competitive career at CMU.

John P. McHale (Ph.D., University of Missouri, 2002) is assistant professor of communication at Illinois State University

Brian H. Spitzberg (Ph.D., University of Southern California, 1981) is professor in the School of Communication at San Diego State University. He studies communication skills and assessment, as well as relational communication and forms of intimate aggression, stalking, and violence.

Timothy Stephen (Ph.D., Bowling Green State University, 1980) is professor of interpersonal communication at the University of Albany.

Walter R. Zakahi is professor of communication studies and head of that department at New Mexico State University. In addition to his work in political communication with Kenneth Hacker, he has conducted extensive research in the area of interpersonal communication. In 2000, their manuscript "Components of Candidate Images: Statistical Analysis of the Issue-Persona Dichotomy in the Presidential Campaign of 1996" appeared as the lead article in *Communication Monographs.* Professor Zakahi is serving as the editor of *Communication Reports* for the years 2004–2006.

CLINTON PUBLIC LIBRARY

Krochmal   745.51
                                    K
745356·

The art of wood burning

Clinton Public Library
Clinton, Iowa

DISCARD